JOURNAL FOR THE STUDY OF THE OLD TESTAMENT
SUPPLEMENT SERIES
399

To Rhonda

Woman Wise

Wife of My Youth

Wise King – Royal Fool

Semiotics, Satire and Proverbs 1–9

Johnny E. Miles

T & T CLARK INTERNATIONAL
A Continuum imprint
LONDON • NEW YORK

Copyright © 2004 T&T Clark International
A Continuum imprint

Published by T&T Clark International
The Tower Building, 11 York Road, London SE1 7NX
15 East 26th Street, Suite 1703, New York, NY 10010

www.tandtclark.com

British Library Cataloguing-in-Publication Data
A catalogue record for this book is available from the British Library

Library of Congress Cataloging-in-Publication Data
A catalogue record for this book is available from the Library of Congress

Typeset by ISB Typesetting, Sheffield
Printed on acid-free paper in Great Britain by The Bath Press, Bath

ISBN 0-567-08093-5

CONTENTS

ACKNOWLEDGMENTS

Every project, however appraised, that comes to completion does so with the aid and support of many. But I would be remiss if I did not convey my warmest appreciation to three individuals in particular, who deserve much recognition. First, I want to express my deepest gratitude to James Kennedy whose shared vision for and cooperative guidance of this project from its inception has proved invaluable in its completion. Throughout my doctoral studies, he proved to be the ideal mentor and a true friend, qualities that I hope I can emulate, and for that I shall always be greatly indebted. I shall forever cherish our discussions, much of which we had during my four years as his graduate assistant. As a mentor, he inspired the necessity of a spirit of creativity in scholarship, which he himself expertly modeled, to explore texts anew from alternative perspectives. As a friend, he encouraged critical engagement while never withdrawing his support even in the midst of disagreement.

Second, I have the profoundest admiration for William Bellinger who, undoubtedly, must be the scholar's scholar. His impeccable knowledge of the Hebrew Scriptures, Old Testament scholarship and his amiable demeanor has garnered his high esteem among colleagues and students. But above all else, his caring encouragement and sensitivity to my needs during his stint as the Graduate Studies Director at Baylor University, Texas, fueled my persistence throughout the doctoral studies program. Words alone inadequately express the great respect I have for him.

Third, I want to extend a heartfelt thanks to Andy Moore. His acuity in English grammar and style made his keen eye for details a welcome and necessary contribution to a formal writing project that would have certainly lacked its professionalism otherwise.

I also want to offer a special thanks to friends who, like iron sharpening iron, have sharpened and unknowingly prepared me for this project. How I miss the frequent banter about things sacred and profane with friends who have long since gone on their respective life-journeys!

Finally, but certainly not least of all, I owe a debt of gratitude and love to my family, who have constantly been supportive throughout my educational journey. My parents, James and Paulette Miles, and my sister Teresa have always believed in me more than words by them may have ever expressed. My heart goes to the love of my life, my wife Rhonda. Her undying love saw in me that which I could not, and her unwavering support kept me going when I felt I could no longer go on. My children, Caleb, Hannah and Leah, have demonstrated remarkable patience in the face of time often stolen, and undeservedly so, from them for this study, a fact not lost on me as I have tried to make up for it.

ABBREVIATIONS

AB	Anchor Bible
ABRL	Anchor Bible Reference Library
ANET	James B. Pritchard (ed.), *Ancient Near Eastern Texts Relating to the Old Testament* (Princeton: Princeton University Press, 1950)
AS	Advances in Semiotics
BerO	Berit Olam
Bib	*Biblica*
BibInt	Biblical Interpretation Series
BibLit	Bible and Literature Series
BSac	*Bibliotheca Sacra*
BTB	*Biblical Theology Bulletin*
BZAW	Beihefte zur *ZAW*
CBQ	*Catholic Biblical Quarterly*
CBQMS	*Catholic Biblical Quarterly*, Monograph Series
CJF	*The Chicago Jewish Forum*
FCB	Feminist Companion to the Bible
GCT	Gender, Culture, Theory
HBInt	History of Biblical Interpretation Series
HeyJ	*Heythrop Journal*
HUCA	*Hebrew Union College Annual*
ICC	International Critical Commentary
Int	*Interpretation*
JANESCU	*Journal of the Ancient Near Eastern Society of Columbia University*
JBL	*Journal of Biblical Literature*
JQR	*Jewish Quarterly Review*
JSOT	*Journal for the Study of the Old Testament*
JSOTSup	*Journal for the Study of the Old Testament*, Supplement Series
JSS	*Journal of Semitic Studies*
LBS	Library of Biblical Studies
LCBI	Literary Currents in Biblical Interpretation
MT	Masoretic Text
NCB	New Century Bible
OTG	Old Testament Guides
OTL	Old Testament Library
OTM	Oxford Theological Monographs
Presb	*Presbyterion*
RB	*Revue biblique*
SBLDS	Society of Biblical Literature Dissertation Series
SBS	Stuttgarter Bibelstudien
SBT	Studies in Biblical Theology
SEÅ	*Svensk Exegetisk Årsbok*
Sem	*Semitica*
SemeiaSt	Semeia Studies

SJ	Studia Judaica
SJOT	*Scandinavian Journal of the Old Testament*
StudHier	*Studia Hierosolymitana*
TJOJT	*Tradition: A Journal of Orthodox Jewish Thought*
TynBul	*Tyndale Bulletin*
VT	*Vetus Testamentum*
VTSup	*Vetus Testamentum*, Supplements
WBC	Word Biblical Commentary
WMANT	Wissenschaftliche Monographien zum Alten und Neuen Testament
ZAW	*Zeitschrift für die alttestamentliche Wissenschaft*
ZBK	Zürcher Bibelkommentare

Introduction

Modern, Western culture has long labored under the (de)(il)lusion that a perfect, unambiguous and universal language once existed. But that language, as the Tower of Babel narrative insinuates, disappeared with the curse of differentiated languages. Numerous dreams to 'restore' the language of Adam have propelled the search for the perfect language, which intends to heal from the wound of a multiplicity of tongues.

Concurrent with this search, a 'modernist' approach to semiotics, the study of signs, has dominated the view of language, what it is and what it does, in the modern Western world by emphasizing that the fundamental goal of language is to convey meaning. From this perspective, the consequence of such a goal for biblical studies is to uncover the message contained in the Bible. Signs, an indispensable element in the sending and receiving of messages, comprise every message. In fact, no sign ever appears that is not all or part of some message. Modernist semiotics assumes that 'there is a message and it is "in" the biblical text(s)…and the purpose of semiotics is to assist in the exegetical extraction of that message'.[1] But some texts, such as poetry, because of their derivative linguistic forms of metaphor and connotation, modify the correct linguistic form so that meaning becomes distorted and ambiguous at best. In a modernist semiotics, poetry, regarded as a linguistic aberration, becomes marginalized as secondary (and inferior) to the primary non-fiction.

By contrast, a 'postmodernist' approach to semiotics assumes that language inherently conceals and privatizes. There is no universal, much less perfect, language, only the modernist (de)(il)lusion of universality. And while the message may be a coded secret, meaning is not 'in' the biblical text. The Bible does not contain a message, or many messages, that are in the text waiting to be excavated by correct exegesis. All exegesis, deeply ideological contra its feigned disinterest or objectivity, is eisegesis. Meaning depends on the reader who 'plays' the text just as playing a game depends on the player.[2] Derivative linguistic forms, such as metaphor and

---

1. For a more thorough comparison between 'modernist' and 'postmodernist' semiotics, their ideologies and their different assumptions about language, see George Aichele, *Sign, Text, Scripture: Semiotics and the Bible* (Interventions, 1; Sheffield: Sheffield Academic Press, 1997), pp. 9–49.

2. By the use of 'play' is certainly not meant anything trivial. Both sender and receiver play with the message as one might play a musical instrument. No two performers play a musical score in the same way. 'Play' is for postmodernism a (metaphorical) play of metaphors, an endless shifting and fragmentation of multiple and possible meanings. The play of signifiers and the play of intertextuality contribute to the creation of meaning. Meaning is the play between the moving parts (e.g. reader and signs) of the semiotic machine. Aichele, *Sign, Text, Scripture*, pp. 39–40.

connotation, become primary in a postmodern semiotics, which focuses on these elements of language that distort or obscure meaning as crucial in the collaborative production of meaning.

Given the inferior status relegated to poetry by the modernist view of language dominant in biblical scholarship, I deliberately chose the rather unorthodox perspective of postmodern semiotics in this book to demarginalize (the) poetry (of Proverbs 1–9) in biblical studies. By reveling in the play of language, the postmodernist semiotic approach of this book proposes the poetic function of Proverbs 1–9 as a satire on Solomon. Chapter 1 sets the stage by surveying the landscape of biblical scholarship on Proverbs 1–9 with the intention of carving out space in the landscape for a reading strategy that assumes the poetic qualities of this text as its focal concern. Chapter 2 erects the framework for a postmodern semiotic theory, including the foundation of poetics, whereby to navigate the strange, new world of Proverbs 1–9. Chapter 3 briefly introduces the subject of satire prior to engaging the prologue, a poetic cue to what follows, to intuit *what is not said* at the surface level of expression. Chapter 4 picks up on the first point of critique against Solomon in the prologue's subjacency with the aim of determining the true nature of the 'wisdom' of Solomon. Chapter 5 takes up the second point of critique against Solomon in the prologue's subjacency to analyze an erotic conte(x)(s)t in which the father advises the 'son' (understood semiotically as Solomon) against sexual relations with the Other Woman (אשה זרה). Chapter 6 examines the contrastive banquet-scenes of Woman Wisdom and Woman Folly to reveal several metaphorical dimensions, all of which underscore a decision of life or death for the 'son', in this allegory. Finally, Chapter 7 summarizes the observations of previous chapters as the ending returns us to the beginning of Proverbs 1–9.

We may liken the poetry of Proverbs 1–9 to a net, a type of labyrinth, in which every point connects with every other point. As this study maneuvers through the various significations establishing each connection, the journey through such a labyrinth attends to the minutia of its every detail. Although tedious, if not tortu(r)ous at times, the close 'play' (of)(with) this poetry with all its complexities, ambiguities, metaphors and connotations will not likely appeal to some, especially those whose logical positivist penchant for fixed denotation(s) will surely only meet with frustration. But for others who have acclimated to a postmodern culture, the experience of such a journey in this well-known corner of the world of Wisdom literature refreshes and becomes its own 'play'ful enjoyment.

Chapter 1

PROLEGOMENON

James Crenshaw once described Wisdom literature as an 'orphan' because of its virtual neglect by scholars at the turn of the twentieth century.[1] During the twentieth century, scholars have sought to rectify this problem with extensive investigations into Wisdom literature especially within the last forty to fifty years. Yet, the book of Proverbs particularly remains an 'orphan', in essence, because the attention given it has been peripheral at best. Concerns other than the poetic character of this 'orphan' have overshadowed its identity. By engaging these concerns via a survey of various historical- and literary-critical approaches to Proverbs 1–9, I intend to carve out a space for a reading strategy that values the poetic character of this 'orphan' as its focal concern.

A Survey of Modern Scholarship of Proverbs 1–9

By the second half of the nineteenth century, mainline biblical scholarship had dispensed with the traditional view that King Solomon composed the book of Proverbs.[2] Historical criticism rendered such blind adherence to this traditional position as naiveté. The work of Franz Delitzsch and Crawford Toy during this

---

1. Two principal factors for this neglect were: (1) the difficulty of integrating wisdom tradition (which lacked the concept of salvation history) with traditional attempts at Old Testament theology and (2) the absence within the Hebrew canon of two wisdom texts (Sirach and the Wisdom of Solomon) that were relegated in the Jewish and Protestant traditions to the lesser deutero-canonical status. 'Prolegomenon', in Crenshaw (ed.), *Studies in Ancient Israelite Wisdom* (LBS; New York: Ktav, 1976), pp. 1–60 (1–3); also see R.B.Y. Scott, 'The Study of the Wisdom Literature', *Int* 24 (1970), pp. 20–45 (20–23).

2. Scholars appealed to the superscriptions within Proverbs and to Jewish tradition, which held Solomon as the ideal of wisdom and 'a writer of idealizing non-liturgical poetry', in support of Solomonic authorship (Crawford H. Toy, *A Critical and Exegetical Commentary on the Book of Proverbs* [ICC; Edinburgh: T. & T. Clark, 1899], pp. xix–xx). Yet even prior to 1850, dissenting voices such as Nicholas of Lyra (fourteenth century), Philip Melancthon (sixteenth century), Thomas Hobbes and Baruch Spinoza (seventeenth century), and Johannes Clericus (eighteenth century) questioned Solomonic authorship on the basis of the various collections within Proverbs. But it was the position of J. Eichhorn (1783) (i.e. that Proverbs comprises various collections and bears the name of Solomon solely because he was a famous man) that eventually gained consensus among critics of the second epoch (1850–1900). As a result, scholars soon divided into two camps over the question of dating – pre-exilic or postexilic. See the brief summary of these two epochs by Bernhard Lang in *Die Weisheitliche Lehrrede. Eine Untersuchung von Sprüche 1-7* (SBS, 54; Stuttgart: KBW Verlag, 1972), pp. 11–26.

time period helped to pave the way for historical-critical interests in sources, genre, social background and redactional stages.

Historical-Critical Approaches

Although acknowledging the traditional view, Delitzsch argued that Proverbs presents itself as a composition of various parts, each differing from the other in character and in the period to which they belong.[3] Toy observed that by their differences of tone and content the divisions in Proverbs suggest that it had been formed by the combination of collections of various dates and origins. He parted company with Delitzsch, however, by positing a postexilic date for Proverbs sometime between Job (c. 400 BCE) and Ben Sira (c. 190 BCE) with 1.1–9.18 dating to the middle of the third century BCE.[4]

Sources. Following the lead of Hermann Gunkel's comparative analyses between Egyptian and Israelite wisdom literature, later scholars pursued source-critical interests in an effort to determine literary dependence. Sir E.A. Wallis Budge's publication of *The Teaching of Amenomope* (1923) brought the vague supposition of Egyptian influence upon Israelite wisdom literature into sharper focus.[5] But R. Norman Whybray was the first to scrutinize the relationship between Proverbs

---

3.   Prov. 1.7–9.18 assume the form of the Mashal song (though Delitzsch later qualified this claim, remarking that this material contains little of the technical form of the Mashal) and comprises fifteen Mashal strains: (1) 1.7–19, (2) 1.20–33, (3) 2.1–22, (4) 3.1–18, (5) 3.19–26, (6) 3.27–35, (7) 4.1–5.6, (8) 5.7–23, (9) 6.1–5, (10) 6.6–11, (11) 6.12–19, (12) 6.20–35, (13) 7.1–27, (14) 8.1–36 and (15) 9.1–18. Prov. 1.1–6 forms the title to the book while 1.7–9.18 most likely functions as an introduction to the larger Solomonic Book of Proverbs (10.1–22.16), to which it was prefixed sometime between Solomon and Hezekiah, probably during the reign of Jehoshaphat (*Biblical Commentary on the Proverbs of Solomon* [Grand Rapids: Eerdmans, 1950], I, pp. 12, 22–23, 30).

4.   The departure by Toy from a preexilic to a postexilic date for Proverbs, which became the consensual position, reflects the compelling pressure within scholarship in his day (Cullen I.K. Story, 'The Book of Proverbs and Northwest Semitic Literature', *JBL* 64 [1945], pp. 319–37 [319]). Toy bases his postexilic date on the following arguments: (1) the tacit assumption of monotheism can hardly belong to an earlier time; (2) the absence of characteristic national traits; (3) the social milieu depicted does not bear the marks of old Israel; (4) the philosophical conceptions belong to a time when the Jews came into close intellectual contact with the non-Semitic world (Toy admits the lack of Greek words in Proverbs though hinting at the influence of Greek philosophy); and (5) the use of the terms 'wisdom' and 'wise' bear no philosophical sense in the non-Wisdom books of the Old Testament. *Proverbs*, pp. xx–xxvi.

5.   Scholars immediately hailed a direct relationship between Amenomope and Proverbs 22.17–24.22. The question of priority naturally arose in the debate over Semitic and Egyptian dependence. For further discussion, see R. Norman Whybray, *The Book of Proverbs: A Survey of Modern Study* (HBInt, 1; Leiden: E.J. Brill, 1995), pp. 6–14, and Glendon Bryce, *A Legacy of Wisdom: The Egyptian Contribution to the Wisdom of Israel* (Lewisburg, PA: Bucknell University Press, 1979), pp. 16–58. John Ruffle characterized this scholarly obsession with literary dependence as 'a kind of academic parlor game of "Spot the Parallel" ', which, ironically, Ruffle could not avoid playing. 'The Teaching of Amenomope and Its Connection with the Book of Proverbs', *TynBul* 28 (1977), pp. 29–68 (30).

1–9 and the Egyptian Instructions.[6] He identified ten lessons or instructions within the collection of Proverbs 1–9,[7] which, he concluded, were deeply influenced by the Egyptian Instructions.[8] The quest for Egyptian sources behind Proverbs 1–9, however, neither sufficiently explained the presence of particular themes or features in Proverbs nor conclusively proved Semitic literary dependence.

As ancient Near Eastern sources such as the Aramaic *Ahiqar*, Assyro-Mesopotamian wisdom texts and Ugaritic material became accessible to scholars, they cautiously referred to an 'international' backdrop to Israelite wisdom.[9] But the lack of significantly documented affinities between Proverbs 1–9 and these sources suggests little, if any, Semitic dependence.[10] Even though William F. Albright argued for Canaanite-Phoenician influence by claiming that 'Proverbs teems with isolated Canaanitisms',[11] non-extant Canaanite wisdom literature renders his hypothesis as purely speculative.

Source analysis neglects the possibility of coincidence of similar thoughts and sayings, which may have originated quite independently in different times and places, as well as the possibility of authorial and/or editorial creativity.[12] Therefore,

---

6. For example, *The Instruction of Ptahhotep*, *The Instruction of King Merikare*, *The Instruction of King Amenemhet*, *The Instruction of Cheti the son of Duauf*, *The Wisdom of Anii*, *The Instruction of Amen-em-opet*, *Papyrus Insinger*, and *The Instruction of 'Onchsheshonqy*.

7. I: 1.8–19; II: 2.1, 9, 16–19; III: 3.1–10; IV: 3.21–24, 27–31; V: 4.1–5; VI: 4.10–12, 14–19; VII: 4.20–26; VIII: 5.1–8, 21; IX: 6.20–25, 32; X: 7.1–3, 5, 25–27. R. Norman Whybray, *Wisdom in Proverbs: The Concept of Wisdom in Proverbs 1–9* (SBT; Naperville, IL: Alec R. Allenson, 1965), pp. 37–51. See also R.B.Y. Scott's designations (I: 1.8–19; II: 2.1–22; III: 3.1–12; IV: 3.21–26, 31–35; V: 4.1–9; VI: 4.10–19; VII: 4.20–27, 5.21–23; VIII: 5.1–14; IX: 6.20–21, 23–35; X: 7.1–27) in *Proverbs. Ecclesiastes* (AB, 18; Garden City, NY: Doubleday, 1965), pp. 14–17, and Lang's *Lehrrede* (I: 1.8–19; II: 2.1–22; III: 3.1–12; IV: 3.21–35; V: 4.1–9; VI: 4.10–19; VII: 4.20–27; VIII: 5.1–23; IX: 6.20–35; X: 7.1–27) in *Die Weisheitliche Lehrrede*, p. 29.

8. Crenshaw ('Prolegomenon', p. 7) observes the following concepts as indicators of such deep influence: the metaphor of the righteous man as a flourishing tree, God as a reliable guide who judges human conduct, and order in life. Whybray also notes significant parallels between Proverbs 1–9 and *The Instruction of Amen–em–opet* – e.g. the injunctions (3.1; 4.1–2; 5.1; 7.1–3), the pupil as 'my son' and the prologues – which bespeak Egyptian influence. Aside from the rare address of 'my son' in Egyptian texts (only once, but common in Mesopotamian literature), considerable differences between the prologues (e.g. no social or professional background in Proverbs) mitigate against Israelite dependence upon Egyptian sources, thus persuading Whybray later to conclude a direct connection between the two as improbable. See R. Norman Whybray, *The Composition of the Book of Proverbs* (JSOTSup, 168; Sheffield: JSOT Press, 1994), pp. 51–52 n. 40.

9. William McKane assumes as much by prefacing his commentary with an International Wisdom section spanning more than 150 pages. *Proverbs* (OTL; Philadelphia: Westminster Press, 1970).

10. Chiefly stylistic differences between *Ahiqar* and Proverbs 1–9 far outweigh their comparisons (e.g. the form of paternal address). And the only documented affinities between Proverbs 1–9 and the Mesopotamian wisdom literature are the paternal address 'my son' and the Instruction genre. See Story, 'Book of Proverbs', pp. 329–32.

11. Albright claimed that Canaanite influence went much deeper than matters of metre, style and language to include the figure of Wisdom, derived from Canaanite mythology. William F. Albright, 'Some Canaanite-Phoenician Sources of Hebrew Wisdom', in Martin Noth and D. Winton Thomas (eds.), *Wisdom in Israel and in the Ancient Near East* (VTSup, 3; Leiden: E.J. Brill, 1955), p. 9.

12. Stuart Weeks comments that this wholesale approach decontextualizes Egyptian and

any conclusions about the extent and direction of literary dependence remain problematic.

Genre. The basic constitutive form of the book of Proverbs is the $m^e shalim$ expressed primarily in the 'sentence sayings' (10.1–22.16; 25–29) or *Aussagespruch*. Nevertheless, the book does contain material (1–9; 22.17–24.22; 31.1-9) that belongs to the instruction and admonition genre or *Mahnspruch*.[13] Both the Sentence and Instruction genres differ considerably from one another with regard to their form, length and tone.[14]

Convinced that Proverbs 1–9 mirrors the Instruction genre, Whybray proffered the original ten instructions as a distinct literary type because their introductory verses (1.8–9; 2.1, 9; 3.1–4; 3.21–22; 4.1–2; 4.10–12; 4.20–22; 5.1–2; 6.20–22; 7.1–3) bear the following common characteristics:

1. They are all addressed to 'my son' ('sons' in 4.1) as the first or second word.
2. They all command the pupil to 'hear', 'receive', 'not forget', and so on, the instruction which follows (a conditional form is used in 2.1).
3. They all assert the personal authority of the speaker: the 'father' or teacher.
4. They all assert or imply the great value and utility of the father's words.
5. There is no reference to any authority beyond that of the father himself ('God and man' in 3.4 is merely a set phrase indicating universality).
6. The word 'wisdom', which occurs only twice (5.1; 4.11), here means ordinary human wisdom and is not treated – in contrast to its use elsewhere in these chapters – as a word of special significance.[15]

The 'ten' discourses, of similar form and length, spoken by the teacher had their own introduction, an invitation to the pupil to hear and obey the teaching, a main body of precise instructions and often a clear conclusion. While they were both in

---

Mesopotamian texts, which arose within their own cultures to respond to its own particular needs and conditions. *Early Israelite Wisdom* (OTM; Oxford: Oxford University Press, 1994), pp. 8–18.

13. Regarding the Sentence and Instruction genres as the only two genres in the book, McKane (*Proverbs*, pp. 1–22) rejects the Instruction genre as a classification of the $m^e shalim$ contra Crenshaw ('Prolegomenon', p. 15) who deems both as expressions of the basic form of the proverb.

14. The former tends to be short, occurs in the indicative mood, and is given to alliteration and assonance whereas the latter tends to be long, occurs in the imperative mood, and is given to didacticism. Instructions typically employ subordinate motive ('ב) clauses to enhance their persuasive power via direct address. McKane, *Proverbs*, p. 3.

The assumption of developmental stages of Israelite wisdom established the dating criterion of a form's simplicity as early and complexity as late. Thus scholars posited a postexilic date for Prov. 1–9 due to its long, complex units. But the discovery of *The Instruction of Onchsheshonqy*, which contains the simplest literary form, proves such an assumption as tenuous. Crenshaw, 'Prolegomenon', p. 13.

15. But Whybray's ability to discern any single basic form hinges on considerable textual emendation (*Composition*, p. 13), for which Weeks (*Early Israelite Wisdom*, pp. 11–12) strongly criticizes him. Also, McKane (*Proverbs*, p. 280) questions the possibility of discerning the 'original text' of Prov. 1–9 to the degree of exactness Whybray claims given the formal impreciseness of the Instruction genre in Egypt.

form, and to a large extent in content, based on the Instruction genre, they did, nonetheless, possess a specific Israelite character.[16]

Independently of Whybray, Christa Kayatz undertook a thorough form-critical analysis of the Egyptian Instructions. Kayatz identified two large groups of Egyptian teachings (i.e. casuistic and imperative introductions)[17] found within Proverbs 1–9 while also noting both differences and similarities between Proverbs 1–9 and the Egyptian Instructions. The strongest of similarities between these two collections occurs in their prologues.[18] Despite the major differences between the two collections,[19] however, Kayatz reinforced Whybray's earlier thesis.

Bernhard Lang understood Proverbs 1–9 to comprise ten *Lehrreden*, wisdom poems (*Lehrgedichte*) and individual sayings. Though lacking uniformity, the commonality of the *Lehrrede* rests in a teacher's speech directed toward the wisdom student.[20] Moreover, Lang assumed the Instruction genre for Proverbs 1–9 while strongly maintaining its specifically Israelite character.

Social Background. The aforementioned theories of foreign influence naturally precipitated interest in the social background of Proverbs. Scholars proposed a variety of historical settings, all of which essentially nuance three fundamental theories.

The first theory posits a royal court setting, especially during the time of Solomon, primarily on the bases of biblical evidence (1 Kgs 5.9–14; 10.1–10, 13, 23–24; Prov. 1.1; 10.1; 25.1) and Egyptian parallels. But such a theory is not

---

16. According to Whybray (*Wisdom in Proverbs*, p. 70), the Israelite author 'neither modified nor was modified by his religious beliefs as an Israelite'. In a later monograph, Whybray revised this thesis no longer arguing for *direct* Egyptian influence on these instructions. Instead, he preferred to speak of parallel developments within an international wisdom tradition (*Composition*, p. 13 n. 4).

17. Those teachings with casuistic introductions focus on the development of officials and predominate in the older Egyptian Instructions whereas those with imperative introductions begin directly with an imperative and predominate in the later Egyptian Instructions, especially *The Instruction of Amen-em-opet. Studien zu Proverbien 1-9. Eine Form- und Motivgeschichtliche Untersuchung unter Einbeziehung ägyptischen Vergleichmaterials* (WMANT, 22; Neukirchen–Vluyn: Neukirchener Verlag, 1966), pp. 15–16.

18. Both prologues contain statements about its author, its occasion of teaching and its purpose statement expressed in an extensive succession of infinitives. But the special ending of Prov. 1–9 (1.7) has no corresponding Egyptian parallel. Kayatz, *Studien zu Proverbien 1-9*, pp. 24–26, 74–75.

19. For example, note the absence in the Egyptian Instructions of the concept of personified Wisdom, the address 'my son' and the speech of Wisdom in the 'I'-form. Nevertheless, Kayatz finds the similarities strong enough to date the *Lehrrede* to the preexilic period of the Solomonic monarchy. She esteems as questionable the general assumption by scholars of a linear development to form (i.e. from short, individual sayings to long units) and content (i.e. from mundane, secular wisdom to 'theological wisdom') as criteria for the postexilic dating of Prov. 1–9. *Studien zu Proverbien 1-9*, pp. 4–5, 12–14. See also Lang, *Die Weisheitliche Lehrrede*, pp. 35–36.

20. Lang also cited the following typical features of commonality in the *Lehrrede*: (1) they begin with addresses to the son, the invitation to hear, the instruction in the imperative and the admonition in the vetitive (the imperfect with אל); (2) the main section (generally in the imperative and vetitive); and (3) the conclusion. *Die Weisheitliche Lehrrede*, pp. 31–33.

without its problems. First, most scholars dismiss the biblical evidence as legendary in nature, as late additions and as indeterminate in meaning.[21] Second, the evidence of Egyptian parallels hinges on assumed analogies between the social realities of Egypt, Mesopotamia and Israel. Gerhard von Rad hypothesized that Solomon imitated the Egyptian court school with scribes,[22] assumed as the חכמים, who produced the Israelite wisdom literature and taught pupils with collections of proverbs as 'a method of generalized mundane instruction and thereafter a way of inculcating Yahwistic piety'.[23] The improbability of extensive relations between Solomon and Egypt as well as the lack of attestation for the חכמים as a professional class of scribes repudiate such suppositions and demonstrate this theory as untenable.[24]

A second theory proposes a scribal school unassociated with the royal court primarily on the bases of biblical evidence (Isa. 28.8-13; 50.4-9; Prov. 22.17-21), schools in Egypt, Mesopotamia and Ugarit, and Palestinian inscriptions. First, a closer examination of the biblical evidence does not substantiate such a theory. At best, the Hebrew Bible points to the existence of literate persons, not schools.[25] Second, the argument for Israelite schools assumes analogies with Egypt, Mesopotamia and Ugarit. But the analogy with Egypt fails in that it was a far more advanced culture than Israel. Moreover, Egyptian wisdom literature showed no signs of having been composed within and for the scribal school. Rather, education was made widely available beyond the confines of the court or temple.[26] Third, Andrè Lemaire and Bernhard Lang adduced archaeological evidence for schools.[27]

---

21. Ironically, Scott rejects the Solomonic superscriptions in Proverbs as historical only to appeal to the superscription 'Men of Hezekiah' (Prov. 25.1) as historical to buttress his theory of a Hezekian court setting for the compilation of Proverbs. 'Solomon and the Beginnings of Wisdom in Israel', in Martin Noth and D. Winton Thomas (eds.), *Wisdom in Israel and in the Ancient Near East* (VTSup, 3; Leiden: E.J. Brill, 1955), pp. 264–66, 272. Against Scott, see Ruffle, 'The Teaching of Amenemope', pp. 34–35. Cf. Crenshaw, *Old Testament Wisdom: An Introduction* (Louisville, KY: Westminster/John Knox Press, rev. edn, 1998), pp. 41–44.

22. Gerhard von Rad, *Wisdom in Israel* (London: SCM Press, 1972), p. 15. William McKane viewed the wise men as statesmen, the royal counsellors of the court. *Prophets and Wise Men* (SBT, 44; Naperville, IL: Alec R. Allenson, 1965), p. 44.

23. McKane, *Proverbs*, pp. 9–10.

24. Concerning the first supposition, only one of Solomon's wives was Egyptian, the gods to whom Solomon turned his heart in his old age were Sidonian not Egyptian and Solomon's relations with King Hiram of Tyre dominate the narrative account of Kings. Scott, 'Solomon and the Beginnings', pp. 265–66. Whybray challenged the second supposition by demonstrating a lack of attestation for the terms חכמה and חכם as designations for a particular professional class. While there were Israelites who had likely acquired a reputation for wisdom in the sense of superior intelligence, there was no evidence for a professional class of royal scribes. Thus Whybray preferred the designation intellectual tradition to that of wisdom tradition. See his *The Intellectual Tradition in the Old Testament* (BZAW, 135; Berlin: Walter de Gruyter, 1974), pp. 55–61.

25. James L. Crenshaw, 'Education in Ancient Israel', *JBL* 104 (1985), pp. 601–15 (602–604).

26. Michael V. Fox, 'The Social Location of the Book of Proverbs', in Michael V. Fox *et al.* (eds.), *Texts, Temples, and Traditions: A Tribute to Menahem Haran* (Winona Lake, IN: Eisenbrauns, 1996), pp. 227–39 (229–30).

27. Lang provides an imaginative picture of an ancient Israelite school with reconstructed syllabi derived from epigraphic evidence such as abecedaries, fragments of alphabets and symbols

Lang unequivocally claimed that Proverbs, specifically the *Lehrrede*, didactic in form, originated in the school and functioned as a textbook for school students.[28] Although impressive, the archaeological evidence admits of alternative explanations and certainly does not support an integrated school system. But if one cannot prove the existence of schools in ancient Israel, then one cannot disprove them either.[29] This theory remains, at best, purely conjectural.

A third theory proffers a family/clan setting primarily on the bases of various maxims in the Egyptian Instructions (which speak of passing down wisdom to one's children, not one's pupils) and the family education alluded to in Proverbs 4.3.[30] Tribal heads and patriarchal fathers promulgated oral instruction comprising both wisdom and law.[31] In such a popular ethos, careful observation of the immediate world resulted in the form of proverbs. Such folk sayings reflected a concern over life by the peasants and landowners.[32] No one contests the fact that parents instructed children in their homes and most likely did so using maxims. Some of the maxims of Proverbs 1–9 may have indeed had the family/clan as their setting.[33] But our ignorance about education in ancient Israel renders the extension of such a prospect to Proverbs 1–9 as speculative.

As convincing as these theories sound, queries into the social background of Proverbs 1–9 have only yielded incertitude. That some material in Proverbs 1–9 may have originated from either of these settings seems possible, but the compilation and redaction of Proverbs 1–9 would certainly exclude the probability of the family/clan setting.

Redactional Stages. The redaction of Proverbs 1–9 assumes developmental stages of composition wherein one can also detect a linear development to Israelite religion.[34] Both Fox and Whybray trace these developments in their reconstruction of three redactional stages of Proverbs 1–9.

and drawings on walls, all of which he interpreted as writing exercises for students. *Wisdom and the Book of Proverbs: A Hebrew Goddess Redefined* (New York: Pilgrim Press, 1986), pp. 29ff.

28. Lang regards the *Lehrrede* as Israelite school literature and sets its *terminus a quo* and *terminus ante quem* as the tenth and third centuries BCE, respectively. Nonetheless, he prefers a preexilic date at the time of Solomon for the *Lehrrede* (*Die Weisheitliche Lehrrede*, pp. 48–60, 100–102, and *Wisdom and the Book of Proverbs*, p. 10).

29. Weeks offers a word of caution against presuming schools as a setting for Proverbs 1–9 given our profound ignorance of educational methods in Israel. *Early Israelite Wisdom*, pp. 153–56.

30. The Egyptian Instructions never use 'father' as an epithet for 'teacher' whereas in the Sumerian schools members of the *edubba* ('tablet house') designated themselves as 'sons' to outsiders and the master teacher as 'father' (Fox, 'Social Location', pp. 230–31, and Crenshaw, 'Education', p. 608).

31. Erhard Gerstenberger claimed the ancient clan- and family-ethos as the origin of efforts to uphold justice since both wisdom and law were concerned with maintaining social order ('The Woe-Oracles of the Prophets', *JBL* 81 [1962], pp. 249–63 [256–58]).

32. Von Rad, *Wisdom in Israel*, p. 17.

33. Scott identifies the following maxims in Prov. 1–9: 3.27–30; 5.15–19; 5.20; 6.1–19; 6.22; 9.7–9 (*Proverbs. Ecclesiastes*, p. 14).

34. Rather than assuming a movement from pure secularism to theological reflection, Crenshaw distinguishes between three fundamental manifestations of Israelite wisdom: family/clan, court and

In the Egyptian stage the Israelites adopted the Instruction genre to develop the ten instructions of Proverbs 1–9.[35] The wisdom of this stage, distinctly anthropocentric, depicted God as a vague, remote sovereign who put certain inflexible rules into operation. This view came into sharp conflict with that of the dynamic God of the eighth to sixth century prophetic tradition, thus precipitating the reinterpretation of secular wisdom.[36]

In the Yahwistic stage, marked by attempts to reinterpret secular wisdom, four distinct features emerged: (1) Yahweh now became the source of wisdom; (2) redactors identified the 'fear of Yahweh' with wisdom (Prov. 1.7, 29; 2.5; 9.10); (3) Yahweh is now independent of the world order and in control of man's fate; and (4) following upon this independence, redactors called for trust in God (3.5, 7).[37] The *Lehrrede* underwent subsequent expansion with the wisdom (2.2–4, 10–15; 4.5–9, 13; 7.4) and Yahweh additions (2.5–8; 3.26; 5.21), both of which represent attempts to reinterpret the instructions in specific ways.[38] The Wisdom poems (1.20–33; 3.13–20; 8) were appended to the instructions to interpret the father's teaching in terms both of wisdom and the 'fear of Yahweh'.[39] Chapter 9 forms a dramatic climax to chapters 1–9 and provides an explanation of their symbolism.[40] Verses 5 and 6 of the prologue (perhaps an introduction to the instructions at an early compositional stage) were later interpolated to give it a wider application to material added later.[41] 'Finally, 1.7 and 9.10 were inserted to create a

---

theological/scribal. Family wisdom aimed at the single goal of the mastering of life, demonstrated a hortatory stance and used the proverbial style. Royal court wisdom aimed at the education of a limited clientele of potential rulers and advisers to persons in power, demonstrated a secular stance and used the didactic method. Theological wisdom aimed at the education of all, demonstrated a dogmatico-religious stance and used the dialogico-admonitory method. See Crenshaw, 'Prolegomenon', p. 3, and *Old Testament Wisdom*, pp. 77–79.

35. Fox comments that Egyptian wisdom only influenced the metaphysical, theological, ethical and social presuppositions and concepts of Israelite wisdom. 'Aspects of the Religion of the Book of Proverbs', *HUCA* 39 (1968), pp. 55–69 (57, 59).

36. McKane assumed the fundamentally secular nature of early wisdom in Israel. This secular character of wisdom tradition brought it into bitter clashes with the prophetic tradition even though no evidence exists to support such a conflict (*Prophets and Wise Men*, pp. 61–62).

37. Fox, 'Aspects', pp. 57, 64–65.

38. The wisdom additions are closely associated with and even virtually identified with the father's teaching while the Yahweh additions affirm the subjection of the teacher's authority to Yahweh. See Whybray, *Composition*, pp. 29–32, 59.

39. The juxtaposition of ch. 8 with ch. 7 reveals many verbal and topical links between the two – e.g. both Wisdom and the adulteress stand in the public places (8.1–3; 7.12) and call to the simple (8.5; 7.7); both offer 'love' (8.17; 7.18); and Wisdom offers 'life' (8.35a) while the adulteress's house leads to Sheol (7.27) (Whybray, *Composition*, pp. 35–43, 59).

40. The twin vignettes of 9.1-6 and 9.13–18 portraying personified Wisdom and Folly are probably based on references to Wisdom and the adulterous woman in the instructions. No consensus exists, however, on vv. 7–12 (Whybray, *Composition*, pp. 43–48, 60).

41. Fred Renfroe's understanding of the prologue differs considerably. He argues that the original arrangement of lines were severely disorganized. Verse 6b, the original title, preceded vv. 4ab, 2ab, 3a and 6a. The later additions of vv. 3b and 5 respectively sought to correct the secular and non-ethical tone of the preceding lines and to broaden the spectrum of the audience. Verse 7

framework embracing the whole of chapters 1–9...'[42]

Unlike Whybray, Fox proffers a third stage. The 'theological' stage elaborates upon the relation between Yahweh and wisdom discussed only generally in the Yahwistic stage. Wisdom becomes a divine principle personified, created by Yahweh in the beginning to serve as mediator of his will to men. The Wisdom poem 1.20–33 and 9.1–18 belong to stage two or later, while 3.19 perhaps represents a bridge between stage two and the personification Wisdom poems.[43]

Redactional investigations of Proverbs 1–9 do not assume said text as a unified whole, but rather demonstrates its disunity via the *modus operandi* of disassembling a text only to reassemble it. This painstaking activity of textual atomization garners only conclusions of a possible nature.[44] Any concern about the literary integrity of Proverbs 1–9, however, must focus on its final form rather than engage in cut-and-paste activity.

Clearly, the conclusions of historical critics reflect an interpretative strategy unconcerned with the poetic quality and function of Proverbs 1–9. Instead, the text simply becomes a mirror that one looks *behind* in order to speak about its sources, its literary dependence, its social setting and its developmental stages.

Literary-Critical Approaches

The advent of literary theory (a term used rather broadly here) in biblical studies fostered a wide array of interests, including feminist. With a fresh agenda and strategy, literary-critical readings of Proverbs 1–9 cut against the grain of traditional, historical criticism. But the poetic quality of Proverbs 1–9 does not always remain the focus as the feminist-ideological slant of certain approaches attest. This section will briefly summarize the principal literary-critical approaches of several feminist critics to Proverbs 1–9.

Rhetorical. Of the literary-critical approaches to Proverbs 1–9, perhaps only Phyllis Trible's article 'Wisdom Builds a Poem: The Architecture of Proverbs 1.20-33' comes closest to a concern with poetry *qua* poetry. Using the language of rhetorical criticism, she articulates the literary patterns and rhetorical features whereby to understand the poem itself. In this specific poem Wisdom offers her invitation to the many, but only the one who hears 'will dwell secure and will be at ease from dread of evil'.[45] But even though she recognizes the need to focus on the poetic

---

was absent from the prologue ('The Effect of Redaction on the Structure of Proverbs 1.1-6', *ZAW* 101 [1989], pp. 290–93).

42. While these insertions may have served to mark Prov. 1–9 as an extended introduction to the whole book, nothing would preclude their secondary function of establishing a prologue and epilogue to Prov. 1–9 contra Whybray (*Composition*, pp. 60–61).

43. Fox, 'Aspects', pp. 57, 67–68.

44. Contrary to Whybray (*Composition*, pp. 58, 61), who upholds the possibility of deliberate arrangement, Lang argues Prov. 1–9 as an 'unsystematically compiled piece of school literature without any planned construction, without intellectual unity, and without development of content' (Lang, *Die Weisheitliche Lehrrede*, p. 28).

45. Phyllis Trible, 'Wisdom Builds a Poem: The Architecture of Proverbs 1.20-33', *JBL* 94 (1975), pp. 509–18 (518).

mode, her rhetorical language overpowers the poem by talking over it almost to the point of drowning out its voice.

Literary-historical. Claudia Camp's *Wisdom and the Feminine in the Book of Proverbs* integrates literary and social-historical concerns. From her observations of the female imagery and roles in Proverbs 1–9, she concluded that the female literary configurations indicate the substitution of the family, as symbolized by a centrality of the female, for kingship as the basic institution of postexilic Israel.[46] Personified Wisdom and the Strange Woman present an ideological response to any form of community-disrupting sexual relationships of that period.[47] As a poetic figure, the Strange Woman functions as a multivalent symbol: she is a stranger in the sense of being an adulteress and in the sense of being a foreign national who introduces the dangers of foreign worship.[48] Personified Wisdom embodies the concrete (female qualities) and the abstract (human wisdom tradition), hence her appeal and effectiveness. But the acceptance of the truth-value of her religious claims, argued Camp, hinges on her acknowledgment as an authoritative religious symbol within the system of Yahwism.

Discourse/Feminist Analyses. Carol Newsom explored the ideological function of the discourse that both embodies and generates the symbolic world of Proverbs 1–9. The ideology of Proverbs 1–9 becomes explicit with the textual pattern of interpellation and continual reinterpellation of its readers to take up the subject position of son in relation to an authoritative father. By interpellation occurring within a family context, Proverbs 1–9 endorses the patriarchal family as a continuing social norm. Despite appearances to the contrary, families (more so than discourse) are

---

46. See *Wisdom and the Feminine in the Book of Proverbs* (BibLit, 11; Sheffield: Almond Press, 1985), pp. 239–54. In a later essay, Camp acknowledged the problem of dating this material to the postexilic period, which, she confessed, calls her previous work into question. 'What's So Strange about the Strange Woman?', in David Jobling, Peggy L. Day and Gerald T. Sheppard (eds.), *The Bible and the Politics of Exegesis: Essays in Honor of Norman K. Gottwald on his Sixty-Fifth Birthday* (Cleveland, OH: Pilgrim Press, 1991), pp. 17–31 (19).

47. Two main issues were at stake during the postexilic period: (1) the need for family stability and (2) the need to promulgate pure and proper worship of Yahweh unadulterated by foreign cultic practice (Camp, *Wisdom and the Feminine*, pp. 256–82). The language of deviant sexual behavior ascribed to the Strange Woman symbolizes those forces deemed destructive of patriarchal control of family, property and society. As the metaphor became reified, gender distinction assimilated and labeled ethnic distinction. Woman became the embodiment of defilement. Cf. Camp, 'What's So Strange about the Strange Woman?', pp. 24–29.

48. The connotation of the Strange Woman as adulteress dominates other connotations. Unlike the harlot, the liminal status of the adulteress was intolerable because of her threat to the social structure (Camp, *Wisdom and the Feminine*, pp. 116, 120). More recently, Camp interpreted the Strange Woman in terms of the trickster genre and assumed an underlying unity of personified Wisdom and the Strange Woman. In contrast to this historically dubious assumption, a strict literary analysis might propose the similarities between the two as functioning to stress the son's necessity for wisdom in order to discern between Wisdom and the Strange Woman. Claudia Camp, 'Wise and Strange: An Interpretation of the Female Imagery in Proverbs in Light of Trickster Mythology', *Semeia* 42 (1988), pp. 14–36 (15–33).

not ideologically neutral.[49] Although the mother's authority is invoked as well (1.8; 4.3; 6.20), she does not constitute an independent voice, but rather 'serves as a confirmer of what is presented as essentially patriarchal authority'. 'In the social fabric of patriarchy woman is the essential thread that joins the pieces', but she also 'indicates the seams where the fabric is subject to tears'.[50] Only by resisting the text's explicit interpellative strategies can readers discern the patriarchal assumptions inherent in the problematic discourse of Proverbs 1–9.

Discontented with the perception of voices in Proverbs 1–9 as M (masculine) voices by non-feminist and feminist commentators alike, Athalya Brenner advanced an ambitious, if not tenuous, reading of Proverbs 1–9 as F (feminine) discourse (not just a repository of quoted F voices).[51] The perception of M discourse results from the assumption by commentators of the 'father's instruction to son' genre. The identity of the textual 'sons' need not imply the same gender for the teacher. Only 4.1-4 refers to a father's instruction. Even this ambiguous reference to a father's instruction, claims Brenner, reveals instead an instance of women's 'double voice': the F voice masquerades as an M voice and hides behind an M convention while simultaneously deconstructing that very authority she upholds.[52] Brenner's hypothesis of Proverbs 1–9 as F discourse, however, remains open to critique. First, her otherwise unobjectionable hypothesis lacks sufficient textual corroboration; she appeals only to 4.1-4 and certain passages concerning the Strange Woman and Woman Wisdom.[53] Second, the union of paternal and maternal authority in select passages bespeaks the presence of both M and F voices. Third, Joseph Blenkinsopp posed this question in discussions with Brenner: if an F voice did internalize the culturally and socially dominant M voice, how could one distinguish between the two?[54] The process of an F voice appropriating an M voice would have erased such

49. Carol A. Newsom, 'Woman and the Discourse of Patriarchal Wisdom: A Study of Proverbs 1–9', in Peggy L. Day (ed.), *Gender and Difference in Ancient Israel* (Minneapolis: Fortress Press, 1989), pp. 142–60 (144).

50. Together, personified Wisdom and Folly define and secure the boundaries of the symbolic order of patriarchal wisdom. Their final pairing confirms in Newsom's mind the Strange Woman as an allegory of folly (Newsom, 'Woman and the Discourse of Patriarchal Wisdom', pp. 159 n. 5, 155 and 157, respectively).

51. Brenner claims that by assuming an M discourse, the preponderance of space (and power) of F voices in the text would possibly render such M discourse as self-subversive. Thus Brenner's reading intends to upset an inference that has gained in ascendancy. 'Proverbs 1–9: An F Voice?', in Athalya Brenner and Fokkelien van Dijk-Hemmes (eds.), *On Gendering Texts: Female and Male Voices in the Hebrew Bible* (BibInt, 1; Leiden: E.J. Brill, 1993), pp. 113–30 (114, 116 and 118–19).

52. The dialectics of class relations informs Brenner's argument. Just as weaker subordinates tend to adopt the ethos of their social superiors, so the F voice in Prov. 1–9 identifies with M interests at the risk of self-inflicted depreciation and gender disparagement (Brenner, 'An F Voice?', pp. 118, 125–26).

53. Even Camp critiqued Brenner's reading 'as a trifle forced' (Brenner, 'An F Voice?', p. 118 n. 4).

54. Brenner responded by emphasizing two parameters: (1) the 'muted' or 'doubled' voice discernible in possible F texts and (2) the amplification of a norm beyond its reasonable and rational exigency (Brenner, 'An F Voice?', p. 126 n. 13).

lines of gender distinction. And furthermore, why would an F voice need to assume an M voice within the literary, familial setting of the parental education of children?

While historical-critical readings of Proverbs 1–9 approached the text as a mirror to look *behind*, these particular literary-critical readings of Proverbs 1–9, for the most part, approach the text as a mirror to look *beyond* as it reflects back that which looks into it. No small wonder then that Proverbs 1–9 should reflect rhetorical features to a rhetorician or misogynist biases to a feminist.

Summary

By surveying modern scholarship of Proverbs 1–9, this chapter highlights the focal concerns of historical and literary critics alike. Objectivist inquiries by historical critics behind Proverbs 1–9 into its sources, genre, social background and redaction have garnered only incertitude and textual fragmentation all the while neglecting the poetic character and function (explicated more fully in the following chapter) of Proverbs 1–9. And, while various literary-critical approaches assumed the textual unity of Proverbs 1–9, they, too, have generally disregarded its aesthetic value as poetry by focusing on ideological concerns. How ironic that both historical and literary critics would acknowledge Proverbs 1–9 as poetry and yet ignore the 'orphan' for its own (aesthetic) value!

An alternative, yet literary, reader-response strategy of semiotics as delineated in the next chapter, however, assumes a study of poetry *qua* poetry. Trible's approach, which departs from the traditional concerns with meter and rhythm, shares a starting point with semiotics and thus begins a move in the direction further advanced by this study. How one begins will undoubtedly determine how one ends up. And my approach is no exception. While semiotics, like all interpretative strategies, has its agenda, it works in symbiosis with the text. The value of a semiotic approach to Proverbs 1–9 hinges not on the failure of previous approaches to ask those questions that semiotics might have, but rather on its capability to focus upon what may have been completely incompatible with previous historical- and literary-critical approaches.

Chapter 2

A THEORETICAL FRAMEWORK FOR A 'POSTMODERN' SEMIOTIC READING OF PROVERBS 1–9

When reading poetry, readers immediately encounter a strange, new world. Transported into a world that demands an orientation unlike that of narrative, readers intuitively sense a world different in form and function. Disjointed syntax, paucity of words and terse, indirect language all mark the visible form of an artistic, yet meaningful, reality. Poetic devices such as rhyme, meter, parallelism, paronomasia, metaphors and metonyms, to name a few, integrate form and function while contributing to *how* a poem means. Although not essentially an interpretative act,[1] poetics provides the grammar to express poetic function. If poetics is the grammar, then reason would demand there be a voice to verbalize this grammar. Semiotics is that voice. But perhaps equally as important, semiotics empowers the reader to articulate experiences in the strange, new world of poetry. Before exploring the framework for a 'postmodern' semiotic theory for reading the poetic world of Proverbs 1–9 as satire, however, a brief primer on poetics is in order.

Poetics

Understood both generally and specifically, the term 'poetics' denotes a 'theory of literature' (i.e. 'theory of literary discourse') and a systematic 'theory of poetry', respectively.[2] Roman Jakobson, whose work provides the linguistic foundation for many semioticians, combines these denotations, stating that poetics is an integral part of linguistics and can be defined as ' "the linguistic study of the poetic function in the context of verbal messages in general and in poetry in particular" '.[3]

---

1. Tzvetan Todorov distinguishes between poetics and interpretation though both share a symbiotic relationship. 'The relation between poetics and interpretation is one of complementarity par excellence... Interpretation both precedes and follows poetics' (*Introduction to Poetics* [Brighton: Harvester Press, 1981], p. 7).

2. This specific denotation entails a distinction between the modes of verse and prose, which Roman Jakobson, who asserts verseform as a constitutive feature of and irrevocable difference to poetry, maintains (Alex Preminger and T.V.F. Brogan [eds.], *The New Princeton Encyclopedia of Poetry and Poetics* [Princeton, NJ: Princeton University Press, 1993], p. 930).

3. Jakobson, *Questions de poètique* (Paris: Seuil, 1973), p. 486 as cited in Jonathan Culler, *Structuralist Poetics: Structuralism, Linguistics, and the Study of Literature* (New York: Cornell University Press, 1975), p. 56. Nevertheless, Jakobson admits of many poetic features belonging to general semiotics, thus possessing pansemiotic qualities. 'Linguistics and Poetics', in Roman

As a 'theory of poetry', poetics functions as a grammar of literature.[4] Poetics is internal in that it seeks its rules from within literature rather than from without. Poetics attempts to define the nature of poetry, its kinds and forms, and its resources of device and structure. In Jakobson's estimation such a linguistic understanding of poetics logically follows since poems are *verbal* works of art.[5] Poetics contributes to the interpretative process in its 'attempt to specify how we go about making sense of texts'.[6] To put it simply, poetics aids interpretation in that the reader attempts to discern the contribution of poetic devices to a text's meaning.[7]

Poetics and Linguistic Studies
Within the past half-century, two formal models of poetics have emerged. First, M.H. Abrams posited four orientations of poetic theories: objective or formalist theories (which focus on the poem as a self-contained unit); pragmatic or affective theories (which focus on the rhetorical effect to persuade audiences); mimetic or realistic theories (which focus on the objective reality of the world and universe represented); and expressive or romantic theories (which focus on the poet's feelings). All theorists acknowledge these orientations with disagreements only over their valuations.[8]

Second, Jakobson mapped out a more complex communication model wherein he identified six components of any verbal discourse: addresser, message, addressee, context, contact and code. Each of these six elements corresponds to one of six functions of language (schematized in Figure 1). At this point, I only wish to summarize briefly each function.[9] The 'emotive' function focuses on the addresser with an aim toward the speaker's attitude. A focus upon the message for its own sake constitutes the 'poetic' function. Orientation toward the addressee, or 'conative' function, expresses itself in the vocative and imperative modes. An orientation toward the context of a message marks the 'referential' function. The 'phatic' function aims at establishing contact between the addresser and addressee with expressions intended to establish, maintain or prolong communication (e.g. 'Hello, do you hear me?' or 'Are you listening?'). And finally, the 'metalingual' function

Jakobson, *Language in Literature* (ed. Krystyna Pomorska and Stephen Rudy; Cambridge, MA: Belknap Press, 1987), pp. 62–94 (63).

4.   Adele Berlin describes poetics as 'the building-blocks of literature'. Yet her explanation of poetics assumes the analogy that as linguistics is to language so poetics is to literature. *Poetics and Interpretation of Biblical Narrative* (BibLit, 9; Sheffield: Almond Press, 1983; repr. Winona Lake, IN: Eisenbrauns, 1994), p. 15.

5.   See Jakobson, 'Linguistics and Poetics', p. 63. Jakobson's emphasis reflects one side of an ongoing debate among poeticists over whether the study of poems should fall under the aegis of science (linguistics) or aesthetics (art). Preminger and Brogan, *New Princeton Encyclopedia*, p. 931.

6.   Culler, *Structuralist Poetics*, p. viii.

7.   Unfortunately, Berlin's comment that poetics makes us aware of *how* texts mean in order to place interpreters in a better position to discover *what* a text means only reinforces the interpretative perspective within biblical studies of meaning as an objectifiable truth awaiting extraction from the text. Berlin, *Poetics and Interpretation*, p. 17.

8.   Preminger and Brogan, *New Princeton Encyclopedia*, p. 930.

9.   For further discussion, see Jakobson, 'Linguistics and Poetics', pp. 66–71.

refers to that operation when the addresser and/or the addressee check on whether they are using the same code (e.g. 'I don't follow you – what do you mean?' or 'Do you know what I mean?').

Context
Referential

Addresser   Message   Addressee
Emotive   Poetic   Conative

Contact
Phatic

Code
Metalingual

Figure 1. *Verbal Communication Model that combines both the necessary components of verbal discourse (addresser, message, addressee, context, contact and code) with their corresponding function (emotive, poetic, conative, referential, phatic and metalingual).* Adapted from Jakobson, 'Linguistics and Poetics', pp. 66, 71.

The linguistic scrutiny of poetry must not limit itself solely to one particular function but must instead take into account all functions. Regardless of how enticing the 'referential' function may be for some, it is not, according to Jakobson, the dominant function. Rather, the poetic function is the dominant, determining function of verbal art.[10] As an indispensable feature inherent in any poetry, the poetic function operates according to two basic modes of arrangement – selection and combination.

> The selection is produced on the basis of equivalence, similarity and dissimilarity, synonymy, and metonymy, while the combination, the build-up of the sequence, is based on contiguity. *The poetic function projects the principle of equivalence from the axis of selection into the axis of combination.*[11]

Words come to relate to one another both syntagmatically (axis of combination) and paradigmatically (axis of selection) by means of phonological identity, grammatical parallelism and semantic synonymy or antithesis. Where similarity is superimposed on contiguity, two phonemic sequences tend to assume a paronomastic function. This equivalence in sound, which, by the way, may be attained by more than just the phonological facets of meter and rhyme subsumed under the umbrella of parallelism by Jakobson, inevitably involves semantic equivalence. According to Jakobson, 'Words similar in sound are drawn together in meaning'. 'Pervasive parallelism', the core of poetic language, 'inevitably activates all the levels of

10. Jakobson, 'Linguistics and Poetics', p. 69.
11. Put simply, one selects from a group of similar or paradigmatic words, and one then arranges the selected item, along with items selected from other groups, into a contiguous or syntagmatic chain (Jakobson, 'Linguistics and Poetics', p. 71; original italics).

language' including phonetic, phonological, lexical and grammatical equivalences.[12] In this broad sense, parallelism alone becomes synonymous with the poetic function.

Poetics and Biblical Studies

Unlike poetics, parallelism is no relative newcomer to the field of biblical studies, which has focused on *parallelismus membrorum* ever since Robert Lowth (c. 1753).[13] Lowth defined parallelism only in terms of semantic and/or grammatical equivalences between two or more consecutive lines, and classified parallelism into three categories: synonymous, antithetic and synthetic.[14] Later, James Kugel attacked the inadequacy of Lowth's system. Despite rejecting the Bible as literature and any distinction between prose and poetry, Kugel, nonetheless, affirmed a continuum of 'elevated style' (which comprises the two elements of terseness and parallelism)[15] and expands parallelism beyond semantics to include syntax and morphology.[16]

Literary approaches to Hebrew poetry have sought to advance the concept of parallelism beyond the line-to-line equivalence adopted in biblical studies. Robert Alter perceives an 'emphatic' or dynamic dimension to parallelism, where B 'intensifies' or 'heightens' A. He moves beyond Kugel to note the extension of this intensification throughout a poem.[17] Berlin adopts Jakobson's encompassing view of parallelism to appeal for a 'global view' that seeks linguistic equivalences anywhere within a text rather than just in adjacent lines or sentences. Although the practical examples of parallelism in her detailed study nullify her appeal,[18] she does move beyond the status quo of semantic equivalences to explore other aspects of parallelism – morphological, syntactical, lexical and phonological. But we can

---

12.   Jakobson, 'Linguistics and Poetics', p. 86, and 'Grammatical Parallelism and Its Russian Facet', in *Language in Literature* (ed. Krystyna Pomorska and Stephen Rudy; Cambridge, MA: Belknap Press, 1987), pp. 145–79 (173), respectively.

13.   Although Lowth was not the first to recognize parallelism, he did provide the authoritative model for subsequent studies of Hebrew poetry. On his forerunners, see James Kugel, *The Idea of Biblical Poetry: Parallelism and Its History* (New Haven, CT: Yale University Press, 1981), pp. 96–286.

14.   Wilfred G.E. Watson added other types and sub-types of parallelism to these three categories in his *Classical Hebrew Poetry: A Guide to Its Techniques* (repr.; JSOTSup, 26; Sheffield: Sheffield Academic Press, 1995 [1984]), pp. 114–59.

15.   That not all poetry is parallelisms and that not all parallelisms are poetry proves no difference between prose and poetry for Kugel. In fact, wherever Kugel does find parallelism, he is forced to call it 'elevated style' since he knows it is not poetry (*Idea of Biblical Poetry*, pp. 70, 85). But his argument only proves that the distinction between poetry and prose cannot be made solely on the basis of parallelism (Adele Berlin, *The Dynamics of Biblical Parallelism* [Bloomington, IN: Indiana University Press, 1985], p. 4). Rather, the predominance of parallelism combined with terseness marks poetry.

16.   For Kugel, the essence of parallelism is 'A is so, and what's more, B is so'. 'B has both *retrospective* (looking back to A) and *prospective* (looking beyond it) qualities', signified by 'A ↔ B' (*Idea of Biblical Poetry*, pp. 8, 16).

17.   See Robert Alter, *The Art of Biblical Poetry* (New York: Basic Books, 1985), pp. 10–11, 18–19.

18.   Berlin, *Dynamics of Biblical Parallelism*, pp. 3, 17.

move even further by exploring parallelism in terms of imagery or concept throughout a poem as exemplified in part by this study.

Semiotics as a Theory of Reading

Etymologically, 'semiotics' has its roots in the Greek words *semeion* ('sign') and *sema* ('signal', 'sign') and shares linguistic associations with terms such as 'semiology' and 'semantics'. Semiotics defined is the study of signs or the science of sign-systems. But semiotics did not emerge as an identifiable discipline until the twentieth century under the auspices of two founding fathers: the European linguist Ferdinand de Saussure, and the American philosopher Charles Peirce.[19] Today, semiotic research is by no means a unified science; its scope is enormous comprising many schools and branches of both theoretical and applied semiotics. One such branch, literary semiotics, acknowledges the significant role that the sign, in addition to speech, plays in writing. Jonathan Culler identifies the goal of literary semiotics as describing 'in systematic fashion the modes of signification of literary discourse and the interpretative operations embodied in the institutions of literature'.[20] By a close examination of the text, some literary semioticians endeavor to uncover coded meanings hidden in symbolic discourse, a hermeneutical presupposition not shared by all literary critics including myself. Nevertheless, the contributions of two modern and influential European semioticians, Umberto Eco and Michael Riffaterre, do prove invaluable in that they sufficiently shape the basic contours of the semiotic theory utilized in my analysis of Proverbs 1–9.

Sign

In *A Theory of Semiotics*, Umberto Eco explicates a theory of codes (semiotics of signification) and a theory of sign production (semiotics of communication). While he fully acknowledges Saussure's dyadic theory of the sign,[21] which he critiques as

---

19. Distinctions between the two founding fathers reflect 'two traditions' of semiology and semiotics respectively. Semiology defines the linguistic tradition of Saussure and the European school of sign study, whereas semiotics defines the philosophical tradition of Peirce and the American school of sign study. While some scholars today still retain distinctions between the two schools, semiotics has generally become the umbrella term for the entire field of research ever since the 1969 International Association of Semiotic Studies. See Winfried Nöth who charts the history of semiotic investigations in his *Handbook of Semiotics* (AS; Bloomington, IN: Indiana University Press, 1995), pp. 14-38; cf. Umberto Eco, *A Theory of Semiotics* (AS; Bloomington, IN: Indiana University Press, 1976), p. 30.

20. Jonathan Culler, *The Pursuit of Signs: Semiotics, Literature, Deconstruction* (New York: Cornell University Press, 1981), p. 12. Susan W. Tiefenbrun further describes the goal of literary semiotics as attempting to determine the ways and means by which messages are communicated to readers ('The State of Literary Semiotics: 1983', *Semiotica* 51 [1984], pp. 7–44 [8]).

21. Saussure understood words to function as signs rather than as symbols corresponding to referents. A sign comprises the inseparability of a signifier (material aspect) and a signified (mental concept). The signifier, either a spoken or written word, entails the signified but only because of an accepted, conventional relationship governed by agreed-upon rules. The sign signifies by virtue of its difference from and its combination with other signs in a system of relations. Semiology, the

vague in its definition of the signified,[22] he clearly favors Peirce's triadic theory as the philosophical scaffold for his semiotic theory.[23] In Peirce's triadic theory, the sign comprises three abstract semiotic entities: Representamen, Object and Interpretant. The Sign/Representamen has a relation to an Object, either Immediate (as represented by the sign) or Dynamic (independent of the Representamen but leading to its production), for which it stands. This relation entails an Interpretant, which refers not to the interpreter but to the 'proper significate effect' within the mind. As a sign in the mind, the Interpretant becomes a further Representamen, which has a relation to a further Object, which, in turn, effects another Interpretant ad infinitum. Peirce designates this action or influence of the cooperation of the Sign, its Object and its Interpretant as semiosis and the potential of the constant production of signs as unlimited semiosis.[24]

For Eco, a sign, or more properly *sign-function*, comprises the constitutive elements of an *expression* correlating to a *content*.[25] The content (sememe) of an expression functions as denotation, and connotation occurs when a sign-function (Expression plus Content) functions in turn as the expression of a further content.[26] Connotation represents the ideal process of unlimited semiosis when every content

preferred term by Saussure, seeks to uncover the linguistic codes and conventions underlying this system of relations consisting of various structural levels explainable in terms of syntagmatic and paradigmatic relations. See Paul Cobley and Litza Jansz, *Introducing Semiotics* (New York: Totem Books, 1997), pp. 12–14; Raman Selden, Peter Widdowson and Peter Brooker, *A Reader's Guide to Contemporary Literary Theory* (London: Prentice Hall, 4th edn, 1997), p. 67; and Tiefenbrun, 'State of Literary Semiotics', pp. 13–14.

Structuralism finds its roots in Saussure's semiology. While both semiotics and structuralism belong to the same theoretical universe, their foci mitigate against synonymity: semiotics focuses more on signs and their meaning while structuralism focuses more on the system of relations, which does not necessarily involve 'signs' as such (see Selden, Widdowson and Brooker, *Reader's Guide*, p. 68, and Nöth, *Handbook of Semiotics*, p. 297). Nonetheless, Culler advocates the inseparability of the two since 'in studying signs one must investigate the system of relations that enables meaning to be produced and, reciprocally, one can only determine what are the pertinent relations among items by considering them as signs' (*Structuralist Poetics*, p. 4).

22.   Saussure leaves the definition of the signified halfway between a mental image, a concept and a psychological reality (Eco, *Theory of Semiotics*, pp. 14–15).

23.   Eco accepts Peirce's definition of the sign as ' "something which stands to somebody for something" ' and Morris's more precise definition of something as a sign ' "only because it is interpreted as a sign of something by some interpreter" ', but modifies them with the proviso that that interpretation by the interpreter 'must be understood as the *possible* interpretation by a *possible* interpreter' (*Theory of Semiotics*, pp. 15–16).

24.   The phenomenon of unlimited semiosis is not uncommon to everyday reality where one sign triggers a chain of associations that seem unrelated to the initial sign in the end. According to Peirce, the entire universe is perfused with signs. See Cobley and Jansz, *Introducing Semiotics*, pp. 18–37; also Eco, *Theory of Semiotics*, p. 15.

25.   Eco, *Theory of Semiotics*, pp. 48–49.

26.   Eco defines denotation as 'a cultural unit or semantic property of a given sememe which is at the same time a culturally recognized property of its possible referents' and connotation as 'a cultural unit or semantic property of a given sememe conveyed by its denotation and not necessarily corresponding to a culturally recognized property of the possible referent'. (*Theory of Semiotics*, pp. 86, 97).

(Immediate Object) of an expression (Representamen) is interpreted by another expression endowed with its own content ad infinitum. Connotations, which can work by neoplastic connotative growth,[27] proliferate principally on the basis of semantic markers (identified by Eco as either denotative or connotative) characterizing both contents of two sign-functions.[28] Unlike traditional semantics, Eco does not regard denotation and connotation as the equivalents of extension and intension, respectively.[29] He rejects the dimension of reference because extension does not belong to the category of a theory of codes; thus he avoids the extensional fallacy.[30] The content, not the referent, of a sign-vehicle is the semiotic object of semantics.

Clearly, Eco's early theory of signification entails a theory of codes. His overemphasis of codes in *A Theory of Codes* (1975) led some critics to suggest his semiotic theory as no significant departure from a decodification semiotics. But after *Semiotics and the Philosophy of Language* (1984), Eco began to move away from a 'decodification' semiotics toward an interpretative semiotics as he pushed for an alternative understanding of the sign. Rather than codes establishing a sign simply on the equivalence between expression and content, Eco argued for the establishment of the sign on inference, interpretation and the dynamics of semiosis. He identified otherness, polysemy and dialogism as other constitutive factors of the sign's identity. Meaning no longer resides in the sign, but rather in the dialogical relation between signs.[31]

Text
Eco defines a text as 'the expansion of one or more sememes' and as 'a network of different messages depending on different codes and working at different levels of signification'.[32] A text's complexity results in large part to *what is not said* at the linear text manifestation (i.e. the surface level of expression). The proper domain of semiotics focuses on the functional shift of a sign's metamorphosis at this lower textual level to a signifying unit at a higher textual level. This surface level, mimetic by nature, is syntagmatic, but the semiotic 'text' is paradigmatic. A text

---

27. A mere phonetic association between expressions may open a pseudo-connotative chain where the content of the new sign no longer depends on the content of the first sign. Umberto Eco, *The Limits of Interpretation* (AS; Bloomington, IN: Indiana University Press, 1990), pp. 30–31.

28. A denotative marker corresponds with a sign-vehicle and is that upon which all other connotations rely. A connotative marker corresponds with a sign-vehicle but establishes a correlation between a sign-function and a new semantic unit. Eco, *Theory of Semiotics*, p. 85.

29. Many semioticians reject the denotation-connotation dichotomy altogether. Eco, however, retains the basic dichotomy but, unlike traditional semantics, does not relegate connotative meanings as secondary in importance to denotative meanings.

30. Semiotics demurs any attempt to take the Object of the Sign as strictly extensional. By assuming the 'meaning' of a sign-vehicle to correspond to its referent, the interpreter immediately succumbs to the referential fallacy (Eco, *Theory of Semiotics*, pp. 60–63).

31. Susan Petrilli, 'Towards Interpretation Semiotics', in Rocco Capozzi (ed.), *Reading Eco: An Anthology* (AS; Bloomington, IN: Indiana University Press, 1997), pp. 120–36 (121–36).

32. Eco, *Limits of Interpretation*, p. 69, and *The Role of the Reader: Explorations in the Semiotics of Texts* (AS; Bloomington, IN: Indiana University Press, 1979), p. 5, respectively.

requires actualization for completeness; it needs someone to help it work. 'Every text, after all', claims Eco, 'is a lazy machine asking the reader to do some of its work'.[33] An 'open' text envisages the reader freely responding with a series of interpretative moves neither infinite nor determinate.[34]

Poetic texts especially create a 'halo of indefiniteness', thus making the text 'pregnant with infinite suggestive possibilities'.[35] Riffaterre comments, 'poetry expresses concepts and things by indirection. To put it simply, a poem says one thing and means another'.[36] This semantic indirection occurs in one of three possible ways (displacing, distorting or creating) and expresses itself in a manner Riffaterre labels as ungrammaticality, which elsewhere may be a sign of grammaticality. The 'poetic sign has two faces: textually ungrammatical, intertextually grammatical'.[37] The dual sign (or lexematic interpretant), one particular ungrammaticality, functions as a pun.[38] The language of poetry employs a variety of puns (e.g. lexical and grammatical puns),[39] broadly categorized by Eco according to two types: (1) contiguity by resemblance of signifiers and (2) contiguity by resemblance of signifieds. The pun works as a result of a forced contiguity between two or more words by identical or similar sounds (phonetics) that conjoin two or more meanings (semantics). This *forced contiguity* elicits a series of possible readings or interpretations. In truth, the force of a pun rests in the fact that prior to it no one had previously grasped the resemblance.

33. Umberto Eco, *Six Walks in the Fictional Woods* (Cambridge, MA: Harvard University Press, 1994), p. 3; see also Eco, 'An Author and His Interpreters', in Rocco Capozzi (ed.), *Reading Eco: An Anthology* (AS; Bloomington, IN: Indiana University Press, 1997), pp. 59–70 (59).

34. In the 'open work', analogous to the rhizome labyrinth, the text leads readers but allows them to make up their mind and to (re)assess prior choices. The 'closed work', analogous to the maze labyrinth, by contrast offers to readers choices between alternative paths of interpretation but ultimately forecloses them. Umberto Eco, *Semiotics and the Philosophy of Language* (AS; Bloomington, IN: Indiana University Press, 1984), pp. 80-81.

35. Poetic works are deliberately based on suggestiveness. They stimulate the private world of addressees in order that they may draw on some deeper response mirroring the subtler resonances underlying the text. Umberto Eco, 'The Poetics of the Open Work', in Eco, *The Open Work* (trans. Anna Cancogni; Cambridge, MA: Harvard University Press, 1989), pp. 1-23 (9).

36. *Semiotics of Poetry* (AS; Bloomington, IN: Indiana University Press, 1978), p. 1.

37. Displacement refers to the shift of one sign from one meaning to another or to one word standing for another as with metonymy. Distortion occurs as a result of ambiguity, contradiction or nonsense. Creating occurs when textual space serves as an organizing principle for making signs out of linguistic items otherwise deemed unmeaningful. See Riffaterre, *Semiotics of Poetry*, pp. 2, 164–65.

38. The function of the dual sign as a pun is appropriate given its total or partial homophony with another word. The dual sign becomes a nodal point where two sequences of semantic associations intersect. As a mediating word, the lexematic interpretant represents both the meaning-conveying and the significance-carrying systems (Riffaterre, *Semiotics of Poetry*, pp. 81–86).

39. Lexical puns turn on ambiguity in wording, while grammatical puns turn on an ambiguity in morphology or syntax (Preminger and Brogan, *New Princeton Encyclopedia*, p. 1005). 'The pun', according to Eco, 'constitutes a particular form of metaphor founded on subjacent chains of metonymies' (*The Role of the Reader*, pp. 72–73).

Reader

However 'open' a text, the author inscribes the role of the reader (Model) within the text as a textual strategy. The Model Reader indirectly plays a collaborative role in the text's actualization insofar as the Model Reader is capable of making interpretative moves corresponding to the generative moves of the author (also a textual strategy).[40] The type of reader (whether naive or critical), however, hinges on the level of competence. A well-organized text presupposes a model of competence from outside the text while also building up, by textual means, such a competence.[41] At any rate, the Model Reader and interpretative choices resemble nothing more than textual strategies.

Like any heuristic construct, Eco's Model Reader has its flaws. First, his construct ultimately results in an asymmetry between author and reader. The 'author' assumes a shadowy presence in Eco's semiotic theory no doubt because of its ambiguous referent: empirical or model. But Eco disabused misapprehensions about his position on the 'author' in the 1990 Tanner lectures at Cambridge University where he stressed that he only introduced the empirical author in order to emphasize its irrelevance and to reassert the rights of the text. The transparent intention of the text (*intentio operis*) lies between the unattainable intention of the author (*intentio auctoris*) and the arguable intention of the reader (*intentio lectoris*).[42]

Second, Eco neither explicates the relation between the empirical and Model Reader nor provides a detailed analysis of the interaction between text and reader and its effects. If, as Eco argues, the text requires the cooperation of the Model Reader, itself a prestructured textual strategy, for its actualization, then it would necessarily follow that the Model Reader, too, must require actualization. After all, any discussion of interpretative cooperation between text and reader, and the decision of whether or not to engage in unlimited semiosis must inevitably revert to an empirical, not a model, reader.[43] Since Wolfgang Iser's 'implied' reader construct bears an affinity to Eco's Model Reader, which Eco himself acknowledges,[44] I will use Iser's detailed analysis of the reading process to fill in the gaps where Eco's model lacks specificity.

---

40. Both author and reader are present in the text as 'actantial roles' of the sentence (Eco, *Role of the Reader*, pp. 7, 10).

41. Eco, *Role of the Reader*, p. 8.

42. 'The text is there, and the empirical author has to remain silent'. Eco does, however, reserve one important function for the witness of the empirical author. The empirical author can help readers to understand the creative process and to gain an appreciation for how a text might produce certain effects upon readers and elicit a variety of interpretations. 'Between Author and Text', in Eco, *Interpretation and Overinterpretation* (ed. Stefan Collini; Cambridge: Cambridge University Press, 1992), pp. 67–88 (84-85).

43. Michael Caesar, *Umberto Eco: Philosophy, Semiotics and the Work of Fiction* (Cambridge: Polity Press, 1999), pp. 127–28.

44. Eco, *Six Walks*, pp. 15–16. Similarities aside, the theoretical constructs of both Eco and Iser do differ, if only in degree. Eco describes the interpretative freedom of the reader in terms of textual inscription whereas Iser lacks this delimitation of text-reader interaction. Cf. Caesar, *Umberto Eco*, pp. 121–22.

Iser does not equate the 'implied' reader with any real reader. Nonetheless, the real reader does play a particular role in Iser's heuristic concept. The 'implied' reader comprises two basic, interrelated roles: as a textual structure and a structured act.[45] As a textual structure, the reader's role is prestructured in part by the vantage point of the fictitious reader. Since the real reader initially occupies a position outside the text, the text must manipulate the reader's position in order to safeguard against any disposition exclusively conditioning textual meaning. The fictitious reader serves to 'fix the position of the real reader, who is given a role to which he then must adapt and so "modify himself"'. As the reader adopts the 'wandering viewpoint', this retroactive effect of continual interplay between the modified expectations and transformed memories of the reader occurs in the 'dynamic interaction between text and reader'.[46]

But the reader's role as a textual structure is fully implemented only if it induces structured acts. Through the 'wandering viewpoint', the reader, guided by the textual signals, forms syntheses whereby to make connections between the signs, which themselves become possible signs for further correlations. The potential correlation between signs makes the gestalt or 'consistent interpretation' possible.[47] In forming the gestalt, readers fill in 'gaps', 'blanks' or 'indeterminacies' within the text.[48] Ideational activity, a structured act, occurs as readers create and build images stimulated by textual signals. Ideation eventually results in the production of textual meaning in that meaning 'requires the creative imagination of the reader to put it all together', that is, the process of concretization.[49]

Interpretation

Riffaterre distinguishes between two stages of reading – heuristic and retroactive – that readers must undergo in order to hurdle the text's mimetic quality. In the heuristic stage of reading, the reader follows the syntagmatic unfolding of the text beginning with the linear text manifestation level before moving to other textual levels and sublevels. When faced with a lexeme (sign/word), the reader must decide which of its semantic markers to *blow up* and which to *narcotize* in order to

---

45.   Wolfgang Iser, *The Act of Reading: A Theory of Aesthetic Response* (Baltimore: The Johns Hopkins University Press, 1978), pp. 34–36.

46.   Iser, *Act of Reading*, pp. 153 and 111–18, respectively.

47.   Readers form passive syntheses as textual signals project themselves into their consciousness. For further discussion on the formation of the gestalt, see Iser, *Act of Reading*, pp. 135–36, 118–29.

48.   As the fundamental asymmetry between text and reader, gaps stimulate the reader to fill them and rectify the imbalance. Success in doing so, however, depends on the textual control of the reader's activity. Only when a reader bridges the gaps does communication begin (Iser, *Act of Reading*, pp. 163–69).

49.   At one point, Iser (*Act of Reading*, pp. 137–42) asserts the necessity of distinguishing between ideation and perception. But, as Stanley Fish aptly notes, 'perception itself *is* an act of ideation'. 'Why No One's Afraid of Wolfgang Iser', in Stanley Fish, *Doing What Comes Naturally: Change, Rhetoric, and the Practice of Theory in Literary and Legal Studies* (Durham, NC: Duke University Press, 1989), pp. 68–86 (80).

actualize the lexeme.[50] The reader inputs the linguistic competence and the literary competence (which would include intertextuality) requisite for textual ungrammaticalities and filling gaps. Eco refers to these interpretative moves as 'inferential walks' since the reader 'walks' outside the text to draw upon verbal, textual and extratextual experiences. The Model Reader cannot avoid this intertextual competence since every text refers to previous texts. The textual interpretant (that fragment of a text actually quoted in or alluded to by a poem) guides the reader to an intertextual focus. Situating the polysemous text intertextually with other texts enables the reader to collaborate in the production of meaning.[51]

The retroactive stage of reading is the locus of the semiotic process, which really takes place in the mind of the reader and not the text. The reader modifies and/or transforms previous understandings in the light of present decoding acts. Eco identifies such an interpretative move in this process as 'abduction', a Peircean term referring to the inferential process of making a hypothesis. On the basis of textual polysemy, the Model Reader interprets abductionally by constructing hypotheses about the sign-function. Thus this normal act of decoding, which leads to the possibility of unlimited semiosis,[52] grasps more than just a lexeme's dictionary meaning.

While openness for Eco encourages the reader's participation in the construction of meaning and thus implies a multiplicity of meanings, it obviously does not legitimate any interpretation; instead, 'the interpreted text imposes some constraints upon its interpreters. The limits of interpretation coincide with the rights of the text'.[53] Likewise, Iser's theory allows, indeed demands, the exercise of interpretative freedom while setting limits to interpretation. Iser grants the reader neither autonomy nor even partial independence from textual constraints.[54] That textual constraint, quite specifically, is internal textual coherence. If the sign fits in with other textual signs, then interpretation does not become an act of overinterpretation. By checking interpretative conjectures about the *intentio operis* via a continual

50. By 'blowing up' a semantic marker, a reader makes certain virtual properties of the lexeme textually relevant or pertinent, which, at the same time, 'narcotizes' other elements that always remain virtual and can be actualized by the course of the text (Eco, *Role of the Reader*, p. 23).

51. Robert Scholes, *Semiotics and Interpretation* (New Haven, CT: Yale University Press, 1982), p. 30.

52. Eco makes great efforts to distinguish unlimited semiosis from hermetic semiosis or drift, an example of which is the Derridean notion of *infinite deferral* taken up by deconstructionists. The paradigm of similarity reigns supreme in hermetic drift as one sign can become a sign for another on the basis of their similarity. See Eco, *Limits of Interpretation*, pp. 23–43, and 'Overinterpreting Texts', in Eco, *Interpretation and Overinterpretation* (ed. Stephen Collini; Cambridge: Cambridge University Press, 1992), pp. 45–66 (50–60).

53. While interpreters cannot determine any interpretation as the privileged one, they can agree that certain interpretations cannot be validated contextually (Eco, *Limits of Interpretation*, pp. 41–42, 6–7).

54. Iser continually states that the subjective element is not 'arbitrary' because it is 'guided', 'prestructured' or 'moulded' by the structures of the text. And yet, readers assume a prominent role in that they carry out the textual instructions in their own way, thus producing a literary work different to that by any other reader privy to the same set of textual directions (*Act of Reading*, pp. 21–24).

back-and-forth or retroactive reading against the text as a coherent whole, internal textual coherence controls the otherwise uncontrollable drives of readers.[55] While one can make an intentionally ambiguous text say many things, one cannot make a text say everything.

Similar to but certainly not as explicit as Stanley Fish, Eco upholds the consensus of the community as a check against overinterpretation. Without the agreement of the community, no given interpretation can acquire a privilege over any other possible interpretation.[56] The reader (one attuned to the semiosic process for this study) sets in motion interpretative strategies shared among members of an interpretative community. Social and conventional, interpretative strategies are the shape of reading and, as such, give texts their shape and produce meaning(s).[57]

Summary

Clearly, a *crux materia* for both Ecoan and Iserian reading theories concerns the issue of control: will texts be allowed to constrain their own interpretation or will irresponsible interpreters be allowed to obscure and overwhelm texts?[58] While semioticians like Eco endow the reading process with value, they clearly never deny the literary text as the ultimate object of attention. Such a stance and its concomitant issue of control vividly bespeak the assumed subjective-objective dichotomy, for which Fish proffers a corrective, undergirding such a reading theory. This dichotomy assumes interpreters and texts as two different kinds of *a*contextual entities. But the dichotomy soon collapses as one realizes the entities of text, reader and author vying for the right to constrain interpretation as essentially being *products* of interpretation themselves. Textual structures, 'gaps' and interpretative strategies exist as part of and not apart from the reading experience. The reader, and not the printed page or the space between the book covers, becomes the locus of all possible significations. Readers create the experience of meaning rather than extract it from a poem like a nut from its shell. Therefore, the question to pose, and to answer, is not 'what do poems (and, by extension, Proverbs 1–9) mean?' but rather 'how do poems mean?'

55. Eco, *Limits of Interpretation*, p. 59, and 'An Author and His Interpreters', in Capozzi, *Reading Eco: An Anthology*, pp. 60–62.

56. Community convention, otherwise known by the Peircean concept of *habit*, fixes the intersubjective character of interpretation, which maintains the lines of distinction between unlimited semiosis and *infinite deferral*. See Eco, 'Reply', in Eco, *Interpretation and Overinterpretation*, pp. 139–51 (144), and Petrilli, 'Towards Interpretation Semiotics', in Capozzi, *Reading Eco: An Anthology*, p. 133.

57. Appearances to the contrary, Fish's argument does not affirm subjectivity since the strategies made, as well as the readers themselves, are social constructs (*Is There a Text in This Class? The Authority of Interpretative Communities* (Cambridge, MA: Harvard University Press, 1980), pp. 331, 336).

58. According to Fish, when the variability of readers seems to threaten the possibility of a reader-centered criticism, that threat has generally been countered either by denying the variability (e.g. Michael Riffaterre and Stephen Booth) or by controlling it (e.g. Wolfgang Iser and Umberto Eco). Fish, *Is There a Text in This Class?*, p. 349.

Principally concerned with 'sign' language, semiotics assumes the centrality of the text by regarding the 'orphan' of Proverbs 1–9 as the ultimate object of attention. But semiotics also engenders interaction between the reader and the text in a symbiosis that makes it conducive for reading poetry. It provides readers the voice enabling them to articulate their experiences of poetry and just how poetry 'means'. Executing various linguistic and literary competences like 'inferential walks' facilitates the semiotic task of abductionally interpreting the sign-function. By focusing on an intensional semantics, the semiotic approach of this study considers the contribution of poetics to meaning as it verbalizes its grammar in order to actualize the potential, poetic function of Proverbs 1–9 as satire. So, just how might the poetry of Proverbs 1–9 'mean' as satire?

Chapter 3

PROLOGUE: A C(L)UE TO (READ) PROVERBS 1–9 AS SATIRE

> Fools are my theme, let satire be my song.
> (Lord Byron)

What is heard but not understood; read but not comprehended? How is a מָשָׁל like an introduction? Both receive scant, if little, attention.[1] Readers quickly hurry past the prologue of Proverbs like 'a highway in the summer desert: one journeys over it as expediently as possible to arrive at his destination'.[2] And most Proverbs' commentaries do little to dissuade such 'speed' reading. But introductions serve an invaluable purpose; they preview plot, significant themes and subject content. In short, an introduction cues the reader on how to read, in a rather broad sense, what follows. For example, a reader would not read Umberto Eco's *The Name of the Rose* as anything but historical fiction after having read its prologue. Like the trailer to a feature movie presentation, the prologue of Proverbs projects what appear to be disconnected images while never 'giving it all away'. This elliptical quality prompts the perceptive mind to slow down and to ponder. To read the prologue and, for that matter, the book of Proverbs otherwise can only elicit frustration.

Reading poetry demands that readers reorient themselves according to a mindset commensurate with poetry's nature: 'poetry expresses concepts and things by indirection. To put it simply, *a poem says one thing and means another*' (italics mine).[3] This semantic indirection expresses itself through certain ungramma-

---

1. Some scholars have focused on the grammatical aspects of the prologue. For example, von Rad describes the introduction as a 'hypnotic piling up of nouns' that have been poetically expressed with a care that 'falls little short of that of the modern scientist' (*Wisdom in Israel*, p. 25). Similarly, and perhaps influenced by von Rad, Crenshaw refers to the prologue as a collection of words 'heaped' together into a 'stereometry'. *Old Testament Wisdom*, p. 23.

Only brief attention has been given to the prologue's unique syntax. Delitzsch observed that, of the fourteen stichoi, eight contain thirteen plus or minus one consonant(s); of these eight, six begin with the preposition לְ and five of them with the לְ plus infinitive. Delitzsch provides a full discussion on the chain of infinitive constructs, which he views as the 'statement of its object' annexed to v. 1 (*Biblical Commentary*, p. 2). Likewise, Scott notes 'the series of clauses is syntagmatically dependent on the title and with it forms a single unbroken sentence' (*Proverbs. Ecclesiastes*, p. 35). McKane attributes the superficial treatment of the prologue to its unusual syntax, which he found lacking in harmony and inner consistency. See *Proverbs*, p. 263.

2. John Johnson, 'An Analysis of Proverbs 1.1-7', *Bsac* 144 (1987), pp. 419–32 (421).

3. Riffaterre, *Semiotics of Poetry*, p. 1.

ticalities (e.g. puns) that elicit interpretative moves to intuit *what is not said* at the text's surface level of expression. The 'postmodern' semiotic approach in this chapter explores *what is not said* in the prologue by reveling in the language-play of its poetic world in order to explore its potential significations and connotative imagery, all of which cue a reading of what follows in Proverbs 1–9 as a satire on Solomon. Prior to analyzing the prologue, however, a brief introduction to satire will prove especially helpful.

Reading Satire

At first hearing, any mention of satire and the Bible in the same breath might sound odd to the ear. Before exploring the relationship of satire and biblical studies though, we must first situate satire against the larger backdrop of literary studies. Despite common perceptions, defining satire has proven ambiguous at best. Definitions contradict and some literary critics highly doubt that an unequivocal definition of satire can ever be achieved, such a prospect being forever resigned to the realm of literary utopia.[4] The literary term 'satire' (Latin *satura*) did not emerge as a designation for a new genre until the second century BCE when, in the Roman period, it denoted poetic or prose compositions ridiculing certain vices or follies. But satire as a literary phenomenon existed hundreds of years before satire as a definable genre in the classical world.

Satire and Literary Studies
Modern literary criticism generally identifies satire in its narrowest sense as a formal genre and in its broadest sense as a work of literature with a critical tone and spirit. But satire is not restricted to any particular literary form; instead, it has from the beginning of recorded literature existed in its own right as a spirit inhabiting a diversity of literary forms.[5] Assuming a variety of forms, satire blends together four constitutive elements: attack or aggression, play, laughter or humor and judgment. Satire ranges through a wide spectrum bounded by pure denunciation ('attack without humour') on the one side and romance ('the humour of pure fantasy') on the other side.[6] But tone or mood is perhaps the most essential feature as it differentiates between satire and tragedy on the one hand, and satire and comedy on the other. With criticism as its content, satire has as its object something concrete,

---

4. H.J. Jensen comments, 'Satire's essence is as illusive as the center of Peer Gynt's onion. It is unlike other important kinds of literature because…so far no one has isolated a general effect closely enough for generic definition'. *The Satirist's Art* (Bloomington, IN: Indiana University Press, 1972), p. ix.

5. See David Worcester, *The Art of Satire* (New York: Russell & Russell, 1960), p. 4; and George A. Test, *Satire: Spirit and Art* (Tampa, FL: University of South Florida Press, 1991), pp. 7-10.

6. Northrop Frye examines both of these extremes in his examination of the three phases of satire in his *Anatomy of Criticism: Four Essays* (Princeton, NJ: Princeton University Press, 1971), pp. 226-36. Worcester offers this colorful description of satire: 'the spectrum-analysis of satire runs from the red of invective at one end to the violet of the most delicate irony at the other' (*Art of Satire*, p. 16).

usually topical but often personal. Satire expresses its censure of wicked or foolish behavior, a person, group or attitude through the language of indirection.[7] Thus the satirist employs wit (satire's principal means) via wordplays and puns, for example, in order to evoke disdain and contempt on the part of the reader and to eradicate foolish behavior. By ridiculing folly or stigmatizing crime, the satirist expects to do some good by warning against social, political and religious peccadilloes. No wonder that satire has from the earliest times tended toward didacticism.

Satire and Biblical Studies
Unfortunately, the term 'satire' has yet to gain any widespread recognition in lit-erary-critical approaches to the Bible though it does appear in the titles of some biblical studies' publications, and certain related subjects have been treated in bib-lical scholarship.[8] This nominal concern no doubt stems in part from an inability to discern satire as a genre within the Bible. Nevertheless, Hebrew lexicons do in-clude such words as byword, scoff, taunt and irony, all of which belong to the same semantic domain as satire.

Ancient humor tended toward a 'laughing at' rather than a 'laughing with'. Brenner observes that numerous passages in the Hebrew Bible 'veer towards the "scorn, ridicule" pole, that is, tendentious and even cruel and bitter rather than the merry facet of humour'.[9] Nowhere else is the tone of ridicule more evident than in prophetic literature where the term מָשָׁל signifies its content as a 'mocking-poem' or 'satire' (e.g. Isa. 14.4; Mic. 2.4) while directing contempt against the foolish, corrupt and greedy.

Acutely sensitive to critiques against satire within the Bible, Ze'ev Weisman adopted a maximalist view of satire in his exploration of political satire in the Hebrew Scriptures. A maximalist view also serves my purposes in demonstrating

7.   Although satire mentions real people by name and/or describes them unmistakably (and often unflatteringly), the honest critique of satire seldom occurs in the sense of forthright expres-sion, especially if it has to do with a powerful individual such as a king (see Gilbert Highet, *The Anatomy of Satire* [Princeton, NJ: Princeton University Press, 1962], p. 16; and Worcester, *Art of Satire*, pp. 8, 16–17). As a result, the indirect language of satire imbues it with a power to conceal its critique from some (most especially its chief target) listening to its discourse. The 1970's Ameri-can TV sitcom *All in the Family* and its subtle satiric critique of bigotry illustrate the point. Not everyone (including Archie Bunker) picked up on the mockery of Archie Bunker because they honestly believed the show advocated bigotry à la its main protagonist.

8.   See the following representatives: Klaus Seybold, *Satirische Prophetie. Studien zum Buch Zefanja* (Stuttgart: Katholishes Bibelwerk, 1985); Thomas Jemielity, *Satire and the Hebrew Prophets* (LCBI; Louisville, KY: Westminster/John Knox Press, 1992); Ze'ev Weisman, *Political Satire in the Bible* (SemeiaSt, 32; Atlanta, GA: Scholars Press, 1998) and my dissertation 'When Is a Wise Man a Fool? A Semiotic Analysis of Proverbs 1–9 as Satire' (PhD dissertation, Baylor University, 2001). For the treatment of related subjects, also see Edwin M. Good, *Irony in the Old Testament* (Philadelphia: Westminster Press, 1965) and Yehuda T. Radday and Athalya Brenner (eds.), *On Humour and the Comic in the Hebrew Bible* (JSOTSup, 92; Sheffield: Almond Press, 1990).

9.   Athalya Brenner, 'On the Semantic Field of Humour, Laughter and the Comic in the Old Testament', and Yehuda T. Radday, 'Between Intentionality and Reception: Acknowledgment and Application (A Preview)', in Radday and Brenner (eds.), *On Humour and the Comic in the Hebrew Bible* (JSOTSup, 92; Sheffield: Almond Press, 1990), pp. 39–58 (42) and 13–19 (18), respectively.

that Proverbs 1–9 can be read *as* satire while keenly aware that such material may not actually *be* 'satire' in the formal sense of genre. An important note to the reader though: satire neither reconciles nor celebrates any resolution; instead, its denouement always remains open-ended. 'A strong sense of the unresolved and incomplete haunts the ending of…satire'.[10]

Reading the Prologue

If poetry is pregnant with an infinite number of suggestive possibilities, then semiotics actualizes those possibilities by inviting readers to imagine 'What if…?' What if these initial lexemes apprise of potential significations beyond their mere denotative value of simply a book title? Imagine that משלי שלמה בן־דוד מלך ישראל signifies more than just 'the proverbs of Solomon, son of David, king of Israel'. As a modern-day deceased poet once said, 'It's easy if you try/…it isn't hard to do'.[11] The semiosic mosaic of the prologue (dis)proves no one perspective; rather, it provokes the imaginative exploration into a potential poetic function heretofore narcotized.

The lexeme משל has as its basic sememe 'likeness' or 'imitation'. Its semantic range extends from 'byword' or 'taunt' to include the genres 'proverb' and 'parable'. But upon closer examination, these denotations prove in essence to be connotations. In the semiotic world denotations exist as nothing more than connotations unactualized. On the one end of the spectrum, 'proverb' functions as a descriptive metaphor imitating direct discourse yet bearing within it the likeness of reality. On the other end, 'byword' imitates approbation if only to bear the likeness of utter contempt and disdain.

And what else within the prologue does משל imitate in both sound and form than שלמה? The juxtaposition of משל with שלמה will not allow its easy dismissal out of hand, but rather forces us to ponder this anagram. Like puns, anagrams link semantic worlds.[12] Indeed, a link does exist between 'proverbs' and Solomon, but that link goes well beyond the traditional line of thought, as evocative interpretants from the semiotic confluence of משלי שלמה shall well attest.

The sign משלי שלמה poses a paradoxical image. Its appearance affirms the reign/dominion of Solomon/peace given the denotation of משל as 'to rule' or 'to have dominion', thus eliciting the connotation of Solomon's reign as a golden age. Yet the sememic quality of משל as 'imitation' also subjacently implies the reign of Solomon as only having the appearance of peace and harmony. All that glitters is not necessarily gold(en). Appearances prove deceptive, even with words. Thus משלי שלמה yields the interpretant of a mock-reign giving the illusion of peace.

The traditional identification of Solomon with 'proverb' tends to occlude yet another possible interpretant. While both the Deuteronomist and the Chronicler

10. For a more thorough discussion of the open-ended nature of satire, see Jemielity, *Satire and the Hebrew Prophets*, pp. 42, 68.

11. John Lennon, 'Imagine', *Imagine* (Apple Records, CDP 7 90803 2).

12. This specific anagram operates specifically on the basis of consonance, which remains unaffected by the silent consonants י and ה, and implies a harmony between the two lexemes.

indeed implicitly associate Solomon with the מָשָׁל (1 Kgs 4.32 [5.12 MT]; 9.7; cf. 2 Chron. 7.20), this traditional association by no means dismisses unequivocally alternative perspectives. In three other examples within the Hebrew Bible (Isa. 14.1–21; Mic. 2.4; Hab. 2.6), the context of מָשָׁל 'anticipates some form of retribution which will make the person or persons concerned an object lesson in the abuse of power'.[13] Within Proverbs, that 'person concerned' would be the 'son', Solomon.[14] Thus מִשְׁלֵי שְׁלֹמֹה yields the second interpretant of a satire on Solomon.

These subjacent interpretants of the sign מִשְׁלֵי שְׁלֹמֹה inform of more than a face-value reading of a literary collection *by* Solomon. Instead, they cue a reading of Proverbs 1–9 as a literary collection *about* Solomon (i.e. *as* satire) whose mock-reign only manifests the illusion of peace. Who could miss such biting irony? What if a literary collection *by* Solomon functions subversively to be a literary collection *about* Solomon? What if the one who composed numerous מְשָׁלִים, and/or patronized such literary activity within the royal court, became a מָשָׁל himself, or better yet, one of his own מְשָׁלִים?

The phonemic contiguity of 'son' (בֵּן) to 'understand' (בִּין), an inclusio of sorts to vv. 1–8 (בֵּן grammatically brackets בִּין, which occurs four times in vv. 2–6), establishes a semantic link with implications for the connotative potential of בֶּן־דָּוִד ('son of David'). A brief overview of two additional poetic texts that echo this interplay between בֵּן and בִּין shall sufficiently reveal the meaningful semiotic connection existing between these contiguous lexemes.

First, the Song of Moses (Deut. 32.5-10) contrasts the distorted and twisted ways of the sons (בֵּן) of Yahweh with the just (מִשְׁפָּט), righteous (צַדִּיק) and fair (יָשָׁר) ways of Yahweh. The 'sons' lack discernment (בִּין) of the ancient traditions and so demonstrate comportment unbecoming of 'sons'. Thus, the ways of the 'sons' typecast them as fools rather than as wise.

Second, the Isaianic poet depicts a special relationship between the Creator and Israel and between Israel and creation (Isa. 1.2-4). The sons (בֵּן) of Yahweh have rebelled and, for all practical purposes, assassinated their true king, Yahweh, in favor of a human successor. Unlike the dumb farm animal that knows where its benefits come from and to whom it belongs, these 'sons' do not. This perception comes into sharper focus through Hebrew wordplay: the verb הִתְבּוֹנֵן ('to understand') 'flaunts a false but poetically apt etymology of *banim*, "sons"', such that v. 3d contains the shadow meaning of '"My people did not act as sons"'.[15] To Isaiah's horror, Israel, the 'son', lacks discernment (בִּין) of their rebellious state

13. Aubrey R. Johnson, 'מָשָׁל', in Martin Noth and D. Winton Thomas (eds.), *Wisdom in Israel and in the Ancient Near East* (VTSup, 3; Leiden: E.J. Brill, 1955), pp. 162–69 (166).

14. The slight homophony, association or location of any proper name (e.g. שְׁלֹמֹה) to another lexeme (e.g. מָשָׁל) effects humor and a satiric tone. Scholars tend to overlook humorous implications within Scripture perhaps because the artfulness of poets and narrators never let us sense that they do not speak in earnest. See Yehuda T. Radday, 'Humour in Names', in Radday and Brenner (eds.), *On Humour and the Comic*, pp. 59–97 (59–66).

15. Alter's (*Art of Biblical Poetry*, pp. 144–45) observation has relevance as well for the semiotic confluence of בִּין with בֵּן in Deut. 32, which also employs the metaphorical 'sons-people' pairing in its thematic movement.

and on how to get fed (cf. Isa. 1.10–17). As a consequence, disobedience renders this 'son' useless in Yahweh's cosmic garden.

Both of these synopses emphasize the lack of understanding and discernment (בִּין) on the part of the 'son' (בֵּן), Solomon.[16] Nevertheless, the homonymic quality of דוד signifies that of which בֶּן־דוד does not lack discernment – that is, love. The Deuteronomistic literature attests Solomon as both the subject and object of love: as subject, Solomon loved many foreign women (נָשִׁים נָכְרִיּוֹת, 1 Kgs 11.1); as object, Yahweh gave Solomon his true patronym, 'Jedidiah' ('beloved of Yahweh', 2 Sam. 12.24–25). Semiotically, therefore, בֶּן־דוד functions as a dual sign. First, its subjacency implies a metaphor for Solomon's insatiable lust; he is a 'son of desire'. Second, the allusion of דוד, satiric in tone, to Solomon's divine patronym 'Jedidiah' signifies his failure to live up to his divine calling. Thus the poetic usage of שְׁלֹמֹה in lieu of יְדִידְיָה has more than just aesthetic significance. Only religious tradition, which tends to obscure reality, made more of שְׁלֹמֹה. But of what exactly the son lacks discernment awaits further elucidation.

And yet, behold the king of Israel! At this point, מֶלֶךְ יִשְׂרָאֵל ('king of Israel') drips with sarcasm as one imagines its utterance with heavy tongue-in-cheek. The subjacent capacity of מֶלֶךְ as an accusing interrogative further reinforces the imagery. A similar phenomenon occurs in Isa. 3.15 where the surface level lexeme מַלְּכֶם reads 'your king' while also forming the interrogative 'What to you?' The poet's artful sign engenders the semiotic intuition of this interrogative critical of the monarch(y) latent within every utterance of מֶלֶךְ.[17] 'King of Israel' simultaneously interrogates 'What to you Israel?' That such a tacit signification of מֶלֶךְ does not violate textual signs only emphasizes, not detracts from, a satiric critique of Solomon.[18] What is Solomon that Israel should lionize the exploits of an

16. By identifying the 'son' with Solomon, I assume no denotative or referential claim. Semiotics eschews the referential fallacy of assuming a direct correspondence of the 'meaning' of a sign-vehicle to its object (cf. Eco, *Theory of Semiotics*, pp. 60–63). Instead, my interpretative association operates solely as a connotative marker at the subjacent level since the surface level of expression indicates the dramatis persona Solomon as the logical antecedent of 'son' (1.1, 8), who clearly lacks בִּין.

Poetry is self-referential, establishing its own context. Thus I posit no historical background against which to read this text, though I do assume the consensus position of scholarship of a post-exilic setting for the book of Proverbs. To read against a particular socio-historical context (actual or hypothetical) guarantees no determinate meaning, but only yields a possible meaning. The universal nature of poetry transcends the necessity of context-specifics for its understanding and enjoyment.

17. This semiotic insight originated in a seminar with Dr James Kennedy ('Selected Documents from the Hebrew Scriptures', Baylor University, Spring 1997) who has provided further clarity of this subjacent critique through subsequent discussions.

18. This critique of Solomon within this collection reflects a larger critique against the monarchy throughout the subjacency of the book of Proverbs. Such an assertion, however, demands further exploration beyond the purview of this study. The association of each collection (with the exception of a few) with a monarch and the subject matter contained therein invite such an entertaining prospect. For example, the second collection treats the subject of social justice and the necessity of its maintenance by the monarch(y) for cosmic harmony (e.g. 14.31; 16.4, 11; 17.5; 22.2).

impostor king? Of course, the interrogative implies its own rhetorical answer within the appositive יִשְׂרָאֵל: God (אֵל), not Solomon, is Israel's true king. Therefore, מֶלֶךְ יִשְׂרָאֵל conveys a dual signification: (1) to mock Solomon as the 'king' of Israel and (2) to affirm God as *the king* of Israel.

The syntax of v. 2 departs significantly from the syntagmatic chain of noun constructs with its unique לְ plus infinitive construct chain. In response to this syntactical disjunction and semantic riddle, most scholars posit an implied 'to be' verb at the end of v. 1. The infinitive constructs in the series of clauses in vv. 2–6 then refer back to the 'to be' verb while declaring the objectives of the מָשָׁל for its subject pupil ('The proverbs of Solomon, son of David, the king of Israel *are* for the purpose of...').[19] Yet another alternative broaches the disjunction from the altogether different perspective of poetics, which retains the expected, yet meaningful, poetic phenomenon of syntactical disjunction. This elliptical syntax structurally mirrors the מָשָׁל functioning poetically to mock syntactical harmony while reflecting the image of structural order.[20] Form mimics content; syntax echoes satire.

Immediately we learn that what the 'son' lacks knowledge (ידע) of is wisdom. On occasion, ידע in the Hebrew Bible connotes an intimate knowledge of a sexual nature. When coupled with חכמה, personified as Woman Wisdom, this connotation cuts against the grain of tradition. Why should the wise Solomon need Wisdom? Did he not already have an intimate knowledge of wisdom? This poetic imagery of an intimate knowledge of Wisdom starkly contrasts with Solomon's (in)discretions with the נשׁים נכריות ('foreign women')[21] to foreshadow the later erotic conte(s)(x)t between Woman Wisdom and Woman Folly (Prov. 9), both of whom vie for his devotion. Such highly suggestive poerotica would certainly catch the attention of the sexually libidinous.[22]

In addition to wisdom, the 'son' also lacks מוּסָר ('discipline', 'instruction'). The twice-repeated collocation חכמה ומוסר (vv. 2, 7) in the prologue emphasizes their distinct correlation.[23] Moreover, the syntactical parallelism of the second colon of

---

19. See McKane, *Proverbs*, p. 263, and Renfroe, 'Effect of Redaction', p. 291.

20. Such an observation comes about only through creative musing, an exercise that the poetic persona of Ps. 1.2 enjoins upon its reader vis-à-vis divine wisdom (ובתורתו יהגה יומם וליל ה, 'let him meditate upon his [Yahweh's] instructions day and night').

21. The preponderance of feminine nouns in such a compact space (e.g. חכמה, בינה, v. 2; מזמה,דעת,ערמה, v. 4; תחבלות, v. 5; מל יצה, חידה, v. 6) underscores Solomon's (in)discretions. The appellation נכריה occurs elsewhere throughout Prov. 1–9 (2.16; 5.20; 6.24; 7.5) as does its lexical parallels אשׁה זרה (2.16; 7.5) and זרה (5.3, 20).

22. Having seven hundred wives and three hundred concubines most likely speaks to the symbolic potency of Solomon with a large harem than to his sexual prowess. But sex, often the grist of the critic's mill to discredit prominent leaders, must not be completely ruled out. The claim (perhaps boastful) by the legendary basketball player Wilt Chamberlain to have slept with one thousand women does come to mind.

23. Scholars have generally regarded חכמה as the subject or goal of education in the Wisdom school with *moral discipline* (מוסר) as its method and process (e.g. Scott, *Proverbs. Ecclesiastes*, p. 36). Similarly, Richard Clifford suggests that מוסר refers both to process and to content in his *Proverbs: A Commentary* (OTL; Louisville, KY: Westminster/John Knox Press, 2nd edn, 1999), p. 35.

v. 2 correlates מוסר with אמרי בינה ('insightful words'), a metonym foreshadowing both the ensuing instructions and discourses of Woman Wisdom. Their discernment, however, especially within satire, by the 'son' requires an ability to read
between the lines. The effect of the satiric edge of these lexemes interpellates the
'son' to assume the position of an attentive and receptive subject to the following
discourses, Wisdom's מוסר.

Given the natural predisposition of the monarch 'to take', the poet advises
Solomon 'to take' מוסר (v. 3). The king, as portrayed by the Deuteronomist, repeatedly 'takes' and 'takes' from his subjects. When that is not enough, he 'takes' some
more, and then 'takes' again (cf. 1 Sam. 8.11, 13-17). Never does the monarch
'take' instruction. In an ironic twist, the one who 'took' gets 'taken' as the later connotation of לקח ('seduction', 6.24-25) by the נכריות will bear out. The alternative
sememe of לקח as 'instruction' further presses the necessity of the מוסר of Wisdom
as *the* object of Solomon's continual taking. Satire has subverted tradition in that
Solomon, who should 'know' wisdom, appears the fool in dire need of Wisdom
and her instruction.

If Whybray's assessment that מוסר השכל 'refers to the training of the perceptive
and intellectual faculties' holds value,[24] then the discipline of insight (שכל) implies
an intelligent assessment of situations, which can lead to practical decisions. The
semiotic confluence of the paragram כסל ('to be foolish') and שכל ('to act pru-
dently') and the homophone סכל ('to act foolishly')/שכל concurrently establishes a
paradigmatic axis of behavioral orientation (i.e. folly and wisdom) while reinforcing the subjacent critique of Solomon as a fool. The continual 'taking' of Solomon
only accentuates his lack of insight, which, had he possessed, would have spared
him from being 'taken'.

The enjambing nouns צדק ומשפט ומישרים ('righteousness, justice and equity',
v. 3) seem out of place in that they break with both the consonant and the ל plus
infinitive schemas (see n. 1). Despite the ostensibly acontextual relation of these
enjambing nouns,[25] they do connect both to what precedes and to what follows.
This same collocation appears in Prov. 2.9 where the appropriation of 'wisdom'
(חכמה) and 'knowledge' (דעת) into one's being empowers one to discern righteousness, justice and equity. Moreover, the (pre)(ab)sence of righteousness, justice and
equity indicates the means whereby one demonstrates כל(ש)(ס), respectively. Unfortunately for Solomon, these words incriminate. When a king does משפט, one
should expect that which would enhance the stability and harmony of the kingdom.
Instead, the משפט of the king continually exploits. The משפט of Solomon demonstrates a lack of insight and an imprudent ability to rule with righteousness, justice
and equity, thus signifying implications of disharmony both within the 'united'
monarchy and within the cosmos. Therefore, the syntactical parallelism of צדק
ומשפט ומישרים with v. 1 echoes the subjacent critique of Solomon's 'reign of
peace'.

---

24. R. Norman Whybray, *Proverbs* (NCB; Grand Rapids: Eerdmans, 1994), p. 32.
25. Renfroe claims that an editor interpolated these nouns to assuage concerns about the secular
character of vv. 2a-4b, especially the practically unethical emphasis on 'cunning' as the key to
success ('Effect of Redaction', p. 292).

The poet additionally characterizes the implied subject of the prologue as 'naive' (פְּתָאיִם) and 'young' (נַעַר). The connotative marker of פְּתִי as 'naive' generally refers to youths with an inexperience of life. Their openness to influence, whether good or bad, bespeaks both their immaturity and their willingness to learn. Such openness, unfortunately, can result in their easy deception, hence the often-negative association of foolishness with youth. The naive 'son' demonstrates foolishness when, seduced by the smooth talk of the נכריות (Prov. 7), he acts upon impulse and disregards the voice of Wisdom. Naivetè renders vulnerable the young man whose proclivity for folly bespeaks a dire need for 'prudence' (עָרְמָה) and 'discretion' (מְזִמָּה), Wisdom's roommates (8.12).

This irony reveals itself in the oftentimes-impugning usage of עָרְמָה ('cunning') and מְזִמָּה ('shrewdness'), despite their otherwise ethical neutrality. Their connotations, whether good or bad, hinge on intent and mark those activities as either 'wisdom' or 'folly' as signified by the homophone כל(שׂ)(ס). Rather than disavowing cunning and shrewdness, the poet cunningly tempers these traits with the ethical compass of righteousness, justice and equity. By turning a deaf ear to the instruction of Wisdom, Solomon perpetuates the מִשְׁפָּט of the monarchy characterized as folly (סכל). But by making his ear attentive to Wisdom (2.2), discretion, the better part of valor, will protect this foolish and naive 'son'.

A significant shift in syntax from infinitives of purpose to imperfects (understood jussively) occurs in v. 5. Scholars tend to overlook this particular disruption either by ignoring it or explaining it away. According to Johnson, the interpreter faces a syntactical conundrum: either opt for a governing 'to be' verb assumed at the end of v. 1 or for a governing verb (יִשְׁמַע) following the infinitives to which they connect. With the latter option, the preceding infinitives with ל receive special emphasis.

> To be intimately acquainted with wisdom (v. 2), to discern wisdom's language
> (v. 2b), to develop moral insight (v. 3) and to move from immaturity to maturity
> (v. 4), one must be willing to 'hear', to be receptive.[26]

That the lexeme שׁמע resounds throughout this collection (and the book of Proverbs for that matter) only underscores Johnson's salient insight about the necessity and benefit of 'hearing' (e.g. 1.8, 33; 4.1, 10; 5.1, 7; 7.24; 8.6, 32-34; 19.20, 27; 22.17; 23.19, 22). But the either/or solution to the syntactical conundrum betrays certain redactional presuppositions, which allow Johnson to dismiss out of hand the parenthesis as an adequate explanation due to its intrusiveness. As a non-intrusive literary device, however, parenthesis enables the poet to emphasize the necessity of instruction ('Let the wise one listen and gain instruction').[27]

But why would a wise person require instruction? Perhaps this parenthesis, as some have suggested, simply refers to those naive youths with the propensity for wisdom. Or perhaps this parenthesis alludes to a wise person who, in fact, is not

---

26. Johnson, 'Analysis of Proverbs 1.1-7', p. 429.

27. A writer will often use parenthesis as a means to qualify or to add to previous statements. See J.A. Cuddon, *Dictionary of Literary Terms and Literary Theory* (London: Penguin Books, 3rd edn, 1992), p. 681.

wise. This latter alternative would certainly allow the satiric tone within the prologue to deride, if only implicitly, the 'wise' Solomon. Although Solomon received wisdom as a gift from Yahweh (1 Kgs 3.12), that gift required maintenance and cultivation. For others, the acquisition of wisdom can become a lifelong process. Wisdom requires a trained ear and a heart inclined toward instruction. Listening sounds simple, but is difficult to achieve. Any optimistic hope for the instruction of Solomon quickly dissipates with the connotation of לקח as 'seduction', which only reiterates the subjacent critique of the 'wise' one whose (in)discretions render him no better than a naive and foolish youth. Like the Isaianic poet's imperative ('Keep listening but do not understand', 6.9), this poetic parenthesis ('Let the wise one listen…') also evokes the expectation that, as was the case with Israel, such a plea will fall upon the deaf ears of this 'son' too.[28]

If listening can garner instruction, then insight can provide guidance. The cognate relation of תחבלות ('guidance', v. 5) to other nouns of the same verbal root (e.g. חֶבֶל 'rope', חֹבֵל 'mast' and חֹבֵל 'sailor') underscores its denotative value of nautical expertise, such as steering a ship. This denotative marker readily lends itself as a guidance metaphor with the image of navigating one's way successfully through life via instruction. Similarly, McKane posits the metaphorical image of negotiating skills 'which discern the beginning and the end of a problem and perform each operation in the right place at the right time', hence his translation with the well-known metaphor 'learning the ropes'.[29] But certainly the divinely gifted 'wise' and 'discerning' Solomon needs neither instruction nor guidance. After all, foreign rulers come from afar to marvel at his wisdom. This satiric tone infuses the descriptors 'wise' and 'discerning' with a sarcastic edge, mocking Solomon whose navigational (in)ability resulted in the dissolution of his kingdom. Even the 'wise' and 'discerning' one can benefit from the procurement of instruction and guidance in order to safeguard against a kind of pseudo-wisdom. If Solomon is truly wise, then he will accept wise counsel.[30]

Listening (or reading as the case may be) closely becomes requisite to discerning the instructional quality of satire (מֹשֵל), mocking allusions (מליצה) and riddles (חידה). Though initially posing a barrier to intelligibility requiring an effort of intuition to surmount, the מֹשֵל intends to illumine despite its enigmatic quality. Riddles and proverbs, like satire, possess an innate power in that, paradoxically, they initially conceal what they ultimately reveal.[31] In the only other occurrence of this juxtaposition of מֹשֵל, מליצה and חידה in the Hebrew Bible (Hab. 2.6), they connote the subsequent poetic material as 'satire' or 'mocking-poem'. Such poetry uses indirect language to mock that to which it alludes.[32]

---

28. Reinforcing this expectation are the oft-recurring imperatives 'hear' and 'listen' that appeal for the attentiveness of the 'son' at the beginning of each of the instructions in Prov. 1–9.

29. McKane, *Proverbs*, pp. 266 and 265, respectively.

30. The truly wise are open to instruction. If the wise person were to fail to listen, then he would only be as one 'wise in his own eyes'. Roland E. Murphy, *Proverbs* (WBC, 22; Nashville, TN: Thomas Nelson, 1998), pp. 4-5.

31. Preminger and Brogan, *New Princeton Encyclopedia*, p. 1071.

32. Brenner ('On the Semantic Field of Humour', p. 54) notes the indeterminacy of whether מליצה denotes 'riddle, proverb' or, within the semantic field of humor, 'satirical song, taunt'.

Quite literally, the markers of מליצה emulate the indirection through which satire achieves its desired effect. Its denotative indeterminacy surfaces in the semiotic confluence of מל יץ ('a slippery saying') and ליץ ('to speak indirectly', 'to scoff'), both of which elicit the connotations of allusion and taunt, respectively. Likewise, חידה, too, implies indirect or obscure language characteristic of the nature of riddles. Discerning riddles requires a keen wit and sharp mind because their meaning remains hidden and mysterious; it does not lie at the surface. The language of indirection reverberating throughout the subjacency of the prologue sharpens the intuitive capacity of its reader to discern the instruction embedded within such language. The poet's artful satire crafting words like knives, sharp and cutting, hinges on the language of indirection, the nature of which empowers the משל, מל יצה and חידה to engender thought. In *The Name of the Rose* a monk named Venantius offers an observation clearly apropos here, 'The question, in fact, was whether metaphors and puns and riddles, which also seem conceived by poets for sheer pleasure, do not lead us to speculate on things in a new and surprising way'.[33] Thus the language of indirection as reflected in the paradigmatic lexemes משל, מל יצה and חידה functions to recapitulate the initial cue to read Proverbs 1–9 as satire on Solomon.

The prologue reaches its climax with the image of a contrastive choice (details of which derive in part from *what is not said* at the text's linear manifestation level) between wisdom and folly (v. 7) allegorized in Proverbs 9. Fools scorn the 'fear of Yahweh' (occurring six times in Proverbs 1–9 – 1.7, 29; 2.5; 3.7; 8.13; 9.10), a necessary quality for the inception of enlightenment. But the connotation of the 'fear of Yahweh' as a disposition evades its relegation simply to just that of an emotion or reverential attitude. Rather, in the ancient Near Eastern milieu 'fear' of a god connoted the specific disposition of obedience to the god's commands.[34] An attitude of fearing (the) god(s) demonstrated knowledge of one's place within created order, which enabled one to live happily and to avoid trouble. To 'fear Yahweh', therefore, is tantamount to doing one's duty. But what constitutes the duty of the 'son' whereby to model the 'fear of Yahweh'?

The recurrence of 'wisdom and instruction' (חכמה ומוסר) to parallel the 'fear of Yahweh' recapitulates the necessity of its acquisition. By 'taking' חכמה ומוסר, Solomon models the 'fear of Yahweh'. But even this observation lacks the specificity the aforementioned question demands. So how exactly does taking wisdom and instruction specifically constitute the duty of the 'son'? An inferential walk through the Deuteronomistic tradition, which conceptually echoes the union of

---

Nevertheless, some situation and word contexts indicate a 'mock' signification either on the denotative or connotative level.

33. Umberto Eco, *The Name of the Rose* (trans. William Weaver; San Diego, CA: Harcourt Brace & Co., 1983), p. 82.

34. Such an attitude especially characterized Mesopotamia and the Levant. Humans were created as the gods' servants and 'had to learn to live optimally within a hierarchized world where the gods occupied the highest tier and human beings the lowest, as slaves of the gods' (Clifford, *Proverbs*, pp. 35–36).

'fear of Yahweh' and education,[35] will prove informative. The Deuteronomic code for kingship explicitly outlines the monarch's duty as primarily that of a chief archivist. First, the king should ensure a copy of the Torah to be written in the presence of the Levitical priests (perhaps intended as surety against scribal changes that might sanction illegitimate activities by the monarchy). Second, the king should read this copy of the Torah all the days of his life (Deut. 17.18–19). Like every other Israelite, the king, too, was subject to the תורה ('instruction') of Yahweh. By embracing Yahweh's instruction, the king performs his duty and demonstrates 'fear of Yahweh', the path to wisdom. Nonetheless, affinities between the משפט of the king and Solomon's 'ways' imply his failure to perform his divinely appointed duty. That Solomon lacks discernment of the תורה of Yahweh and flouts divine guidance demonstrates itself by his exploitative acquisitions and continual (in)discretions. The absence of the fear of Yahweh results in the negation of wisdom. The wise king has become a royal fool.

Summary

'Before' (*pro*) a 'word' (*logos*), words like hors d'oeuvres whet the reader's appetite for the main (dis)course of Proverbs 1–9. Such 'beginning words' form the touchstones to a labyrinthine subtext of significations actualized by semiosis. What the linear manifestation level of the prologue may present as harmless instruction of an immature youth, its textual signs render as a subtext of satire on Solomon whose reign, ironically, only gave the illusion of peace. Upholding this satiric censure of Solomon are two points of critique (made more explicit by inferential walks through the Deuteronomistic literature).[36] First, Solomon's continual politico-economic exploitations only reflect a reign sans righteousness, justice and equity by a less than benevolent despot. Second, Solomon's numerous sexual (in)discretions with the נשים נכריות demonstrate his naiveté and foolishness typical of an immature and sexually impulsive youth.

Kings have long had their critics who have made them easy targets for the laughter of attack characteristic of satire. 'All kings', observed Huckleberry Finn, 'is mostly rapscallions',[37] and Solomon was no exception, as we will see more clearly in the following chapter. According to the value system of ancient Near Eastern royal ideology, sex and wealth functioned as commodities exchanged for

---

35. Note, e.g., Deut. 4.6; 6.4; 14.23; 17.19; 31.12–13 as well as the frequent injunction to 'fear Yahweh' in the Holiness Code (Lev. 17–26), which, argues Dermot Cox, emphasizes a close connection between the fear of Yahweh and education. These texts insist that the fear of Yahweh, a fruit of מוסר, can be instructive. See 'Fear or Conscience? *Yir'at YHWH* in Proverbs 1–9', *StudHier* 3 (1982), pp. 83–90 (87–88).

36. An intertextual dialogue with the Deuteronomistic portrayal of Solomon (1 Kgs 1–11) in the next chapter will further reinforce this satiric censure by concretizing and expounding upon these points of critique.

37. Mark Twain, *Adventures of Huckleberry Finn* (New York: Chas. L. Webster & Co., 1885; repr. Berkeley, CA: University of California Press, 2001), p. 199.

or demonstrated as proof of wisdom contra the perspective of the Torah.[38] In Solomon's case, wealth and sex, the subject focus for the remainder of Proverbs 1–9, had displaced wisdom. Consequently, the prologue cues its readers to view the once-traditional literary collection *by* Solomon now as a literary collection *about* Solomon. Satire subverts in order to mock the 'wise' king now-turned royal fool. As Wallace Stevens once wrote, 'The poem is the cry of its occasion,/Part of the res itself and not about it'.[39] And as part of the *res*, the *torah* of Proverbs 1–9 with its subtle attempts to reorient its thematic royal fool to embrace Wisdom and her *torah* forms the cry of this משל and its occasion.

38.   See David Jobling, ' "Forced Labor": Solomon's Golden Age and the Question of Literary Representation', *Semeia* 54 (1991), pp. 57–76 (64-66).

39.   *The Collected Poems of Wallace Stevens* (New York: Knopf, 1954; repr. New York: Vintage, 1990), p. 473.

Chapter 4

THE 'WISDOM' OF SOLOMON

Histories make men wise.
(Francis Bacon)

In the preceding chapter a semiotic analysis of the prologue revealed a subjacent satire of the 'wise' Solomon on the basis of two points of critique reinforced principally by the Deuteronomistic portrait of Solomon. Now some might question, Why not take the Chronicler's portrayal (1 Chron. 28–2 Chron. 9) of Solomon into consideration? The obvious (but surely not the least) reason of the Chronicler's glaring, overtly theological bias comes to mind. Moreover, that narrative provides nothing substantive about the reign of Solomon apart from his temple-building activity. Only the Deuteronomistic narrative sketches the reign of Solomon out more roundly, fleshing out the specific nuances of those points of critique alluded to in Proverbs 1–9. This chapter concerns itself solely with the first point of critique (i.e. Solomon's reign of injustice, unrighteousness and inequity) with an eye to ascertaining the true nature of Solomon's 'wisdom'. Therefore, the first part of this chapter will provide a précis of the intertext 1 Kings 1–11 focusing especially on its concrete details of socio-economic injustice. The second part analyzes Proverbs 1.8–19 as a poetic metaphor for social injustice emblematic of that subtly critiqued in 1 Kings 1–11. Finally, the third part analyzes Proverbs 3.1–12 as the poet urges the 'son' to reorient himself to the monarch's task – that is, to observe Torah.

An Inferential Walk in the Woods of 1 Kings 1–11

The indeterminant narrative of the intertext 1 Kings 1–11 provides concrete examples of Solomon's unjust socio-economic policies while illumining the true nature of Solomon's 'wisdom'.[1] This section identifies those examples via a brief over-

---

1. The textual indeterminacy of 1 Kgs 1–11 yields four major opinions on Solomon's characterization. First, the consensual position, which assumes 1 Kgs 1–11 as a chronology of the 'rise and fall' of Solomon, maintains an unambiguous portrait of a 'golden age' as late as ch. 10 with a disparaging assessment in ch. 11. Gary Knoppers regards Solomon's accumulation of wealth, horses and chariots as signs of divine favor since the Deuteronomist only explicitly condemns him for his accumulation of many wives (11.2–8). But such an argument disregards any critical ability on the part of the reader who possesses knowledge of the Deuteronomic code ('The Deuteronomist and the Deuteronomic Law of the King: A Reexamination of a Relationship', *ZAW* 108 [1996], pp. 329–46).

view of those narrative blocks contiguous to four narratorial comments (3.28; 4.29–34; 5.12; 10.23–25) about Solomon's wisdom.

The first narratorial comment concludes narratives that, on the basis of five details, cast suspicion upon Solomon. First, David's voice is the first to call Solomon 'wise'. While on the threshold of death, David veils parting advice concerning Joab, Barzillai and Shimei with oblique references (e.g. 'act therefore according to your wisdom', 2.6, and 'you are a wise man; you will know what you ought to do to him', 2.9) that assume young Solomon to be shrewd enough to read between the lines. After David's death, the narrator indicates that the kingdom of Solomon 'was firmly established' (v. 12b). Nevertheless, Solomon demonstrates his 'wisdom' to read between the lines by piling murder upon unnecessary murder as he summarily dispatches with Adonijah (vv. 13–25), Joab (vv. 28–34) and Shimei (vv. 36–46a). Now the 'firmly established' kingdom (v. 46b) bears the imprint of Solomon's bloody hand. This demonstration of 'wisdom' establishes the expectations of readers as noted by Eslinger: 'the implication of the dry comment on Solomon [in 2.46] is that…this *modus operandi* are what can be expected under this administration'.[2]

Second, after 'establishing' the kingdom, Solomon expeditiously secures a political alliance via marriage to Pharaoh's daughter (3.1), a blatant contravention of Deut. 7.3-5. The lexeme יתחתן ('became son-in-law') generally carries negative connotations: (1) either the Israelite man is subservient to his father-in-law, or (2) he is subject to his wife's harmful influences (e.g. Gen. 34.9; Deut. 7.3; Josh. 23.12).[3] Solomon's marital union connotes his 'foreign abominations' (11.7) as well as his subordination to Pharaoh who conquers and gives his daughter a city within Solomon's own boundaries (9.16).

Third, the telling significance of Solomon's building projects (3.2) lies in the construction of the royal palace taking precedence over that of the temple, a point stressed by the narrator in two ways: (1) the narrator anachronistically interrupts the account of the temple construction (chs. 6–7) with a digression on the con-

---

Second, a minority position views the entire account as anti-Solomonic throughout. See Lyle Eslinger, *Into the Hands of the Living God* (JSOTSup, 84; Sheffield: Almond Press, 1989), pp. 123–76.

Third, a few positions mediate between the two aforementioned extremes. Kim Parker ('Solomon as Philosopher King: The Nexus of Law and Wisdom in 1 Kings 1–11', *JSOT* 53 [1992], pp. 75–91) views ch. 9 as the turning point whereas David Jobling ('"Forced Labor"', pp. 57-76) regards chs. 3–10 as basically positive with the surrounding chs. 1–2 and 11 as more negative.

Fourth, an alternative position acknowledges both positive and negative characteristic traits throughout 1 Kgs 1–11. Jerome Walsh (*1 Kings* [BerO; Collegeville, MN: Liturgical Press, 1996], pp. 34-156, and 'The Characterization of Solomon in First Kings 1–5', *CBQ* 57 [1995], pp. 471-93) notes the narratorial strategy of characterizing Solomon positively on the surface but negatively through a definite pattern of gaps, ambiguities and verbal subtleties. But how positive can Solomon's characterization be when such ambiguities cast a dark shadow upon his characterization?

2.   Eslinger, *Into the Hands of the Living God*, p. 129. Cf. Jerome Walsh ('Characterization of Solomon', p. 483) who hypothesizes that the young Solomon's insecurity perhaps drove him to systematically eliminate any perceived threat to him as he ruthlessly strengthened his hold on an already firmly established throne.

3.   Walsh, 'Characterization of Solomon', p. 486.

struction of the royal palace (7.1–12); and (2) the narrator juxtaposes statements on the length of both building projects in such a way as to reveal Solomon's priorities – 'He was seven years in building [the temple]. Solomon was building his own house thirteen years' (6.38b–7.1).

Fourth, the people sacrifice at the 'high places' (3.2–4) because Solomon had not yet built the temple.[4] The needs of the royal subjects rate last on Solomon's list of priorities. Such negligence jeopardizes Israelite devotion to Yahweh given the 'high place' as a metonym for idolatry throughout the Hebrew Bible. Solomon, too, sacrifices at the 'high places', but the narrator offers no mitigating excuse for his behavior as the next scene reveals a more appropriate cultic site in Jerusalem for offering sacrifices to Yahweh (3.15). His cultic practices only blacken devotion to Yahweh.

Solomon's fornication with other gods at the high place at Gibeon occasions the first of two appearances by Yahweh to Solomon in dreams, which have as their purpose to reprove him for his devotion to other gods (11.10). Solomon's wives may have turned his heart completely away from Yahweh in his old age, but his idolatrous ways had long been in existence. Instead of granting Solomon what he wants ('a listening heart and the ability to discern between good and evil', 3.9), Yahweh gives him what he sorely needs ('a wise and discerning heart', 3.12).[5] Upon awaking, Solomon immediately returns to the more appropriate cult site in Jerusalem to offer sacrifices (3.15), which begs the question, Does Solomon's sudden orthodoxy reflect genuine repentance of idolatry or does his orthodoxy simply mean to manipulate divine favor for the guarantee of his dynasty?[6]

Fifth, Solomon gets the opportunity to demonstrate 'a wise and discerning heart' in the renowned tale of the two prostitutes. Instead, he exhibits 'a listening heart' as he parrots the words of the two mothers (3.22–23). But he is unable to discern the true mother from the testimony alone. Faced with a new problem, Solomon does what he always does when faced with a problem. He hands down a verdict of execution, which, whether a psychological ploy or not, only the true mother over-turns. Of course, the populace (not privy to the proceedings) naturally hails Solomon for his divine wisdom. Perhaps most striking, though, is their reaction to Solomon's judgment, which does not elicit love, admiration or even praise of Yahweh, but rather fear.

The second narratorial comment on Solomon's wisdom (4.29–34 [5.9–14 MT]) concludes the narrative about the economic burden of support through taxation

---

4. Note the adversative רק ('only', v. 2) for the implication that such religious behavior would soon cease once Solomon had built the temple. Walsh, 'Characterization of Solomon', p. 487.

5. God sees right through Solomon's innocent guise and childlike naiveté, which masks his true desire – i.e. to rule (2.12, 46) and to know good and evil. Moreover, God adds wealth and honor to Solomon's boon as a means of temptation. See Eslinger, *Into the Hands of the Living God*, p. 137. Cf. Stuart Lasine who broaches the similar concern of such gifts making the king insatiable and sinful. 'The King of Desire: Indeterminacy, Audience, and the Solomon Narrative', *Semeia* 71 (1995), pp. 85–118 (85, 105–13).

6. Eslinger (*Into the Hands of the Living God*, pp. 144–50) pursues this line of investigation in-depth as he probes the purpose behind Solomon's prayers.

imposed upon the royal subjects. By realigning the kingdom into twelve districts of Israel, each responsible for the royal provisions one month out of the year, Solomon's bureaucratic efficiency flouts northern sacral traditions. He aggravates the economic strain upon Israel's material productivity with the additional burden of forced labor (5.13–18), foreshadowed in the list of high officials (4.16). And yet, presumably, such oppressive taxation elicited joy, peace and security in Israel (4.20–21, 24–25)! These verses juxtapose the peace and security of Judah and Israel with Solomon's dominion while concurrently bracketing a litany of the daily quota for the royal court (vv. 22–23). Certainly the narrator speaks with heavy sarcasm for even at face value such a statement cannot ameliorate the exorbitant cost of such joy and the attendant expenses of a vast chariot corps.[7] The necessity of such an armed force implies brute strength as the source of the people's security and their exacted tribute. Thus the narrator's comment about the divine gift of wisdom to Solomon implicitly critiques him for its misappropriation.

The third narratorial comment on Solomon's wisdom (5.12 [5.26 MT]) both succeeds and precedes narratives that further denigrate Solomon. In the preceding narrative, Solomon tenders a business proposal to Hiram to construct the temple with the misleading reason that he is neither beset by an 'adversary' (שׂטן) nor 'the stroke of misfortune' (פגע רע, 5.4). Despite Solomon's blithe denial, adversaries such as Hadad of Edom (שׂטן, 11.14) and Rezon of Damascus (שׂטן, 11.25) dogged him all of his days. Also, if Solomon has no 'evil stroke', it is only because Benaiah's ready 'strokes' eliminated them. Indeed, Solomon's kingdom bears nothing but the bloody imprint of a Macchiavellian 'evil stroke' (פגע רע, 2.25, 29, 31, 34, 46).

Perhaps Hiram, too, could read between the lines since he firmly rejects and renegotiates the terms of Solomon's proposal to his own advantage. Solomon's acquiescence places him in a position to Hiram similar to that of his own subjects toward him. Moreover, the extravagant expenditure of grain and oil (on an annual basis) only increases the burden upon Israel and her material resources. Never again does the narrator mention joy in Israel during Solomon's reign. The 'wise' Solomon gets no bargain, hence giving some irony to Hiram's remark about Solomon's wisdom (5.7). Even the narrator indulges in a bit of irony with a sarcastic comment about Solomon's business acumen (5.12): 'And Yahweh gave Solomon wisdom [but he certainly didn't use it]'![8]

In the subsequent narrative (5.13–18), Solomon again makes good use of his gift when he conscripts forced labor (מס, v. 13) out of 'all Israel'.[9] Solomon's 'bargain'

7.　Walsh, *1 Kings*, pp. 89–90.

8.　The narrator only says that Yahweh gave Solomon wisdom, but never that he made good use of that gift. Walsh, *1 Kings*, p. 99, and 'Characterization of Solomon', pp. 491–92.

9.　Attempts to (re)cast Solomon's image in a positive light focuses on two points: (1) the one month on-two months off work shift for the מס, and (2) the distinctive contrast between the מס and the מס עבד ('slave labor'), to which the Israelites were not subjected. The first point neglects the misleading phrase 'at home'. While 'at home' those two months, the Israelites worked in 'his house' (5.14 [5.28 MT]), most likely the temple. The second point assumes the מס and the מס עבד as two different systems of periodic forced labor and perpetual slavery, respectively. Our limited information about conscripted labor systems, however, militates against such an assumption. But

proves worse than before: he not only pays an exorbitant annual sum to Hiram but he also provides a vast amount of the labor that Hiram should have supplied. Solomon's discriminatory policies exacerbated by his son eventually drove Israel to reject the Davidic dynasty *in toto* after his death.

The fourth narratorial comment on Solomon's wisdom (10.23–25) likewise succeeds and precedes damning evidence against Solomon. In preceding material (9.15–19) the corvée undoubtedly persisted so long as the whims of administrative policy dictated the necessity of numerous building projects (e.g. the 'storage cities', 'chariot cities' and 'cavalry cities', v. 19). Storage cities (מסכנה) were only a necessity because of Solomon's (extorted) accumulated wealth and material resources, which were obviously of great benefit (סכן) to Solomon but a symbol of impoverishment (סכן) to the people. The mention of 'chariots' subtly critiques for where there are chariots, horses stand nearby. And Yahweh's king is not allowed to have a standing army.

The international renown of Solomon's 'wisdom' piques the curiosity of the Queen of Sheba (10.1–13). Apart from the ubiquitous opulence within this narrative, its telling significance rests in the ironic contrast between the queen's observations (vv. 4–5) and her response (vv. 6–9). Ironically, she proclaims what Solomon's wisdom should do for Israel – that is, 'execute justice and righteousness' (v. 9) – but obviously does not given their conspicuous absence from the fruits of Solomon's 'wisdom' (vv. 4–5).[10] The ubiquitous opulence within this narrative inextricably binds wealth with wisdom to unequivocally bespeak wisdom as merely a means to an end for Solomon. Wisdom becomes barter for exchange.[11]

Solomon persistently amasses wealth, horses, chariots and numerous foreign wives, all of which directly violate the Deuteronomic code (Deut. 17.16–17). The encyclopedia of Solomon's un–deuteronomic marriages (11.1) bombards the reader who, if dull to the narrator's clues thus far, should certainly get the point now with an explicit cross–reference to Deuteronomy in v. 2. Solomon's 'clinging in love' to these foreign women signifies his idolatry[12] (of which Yahweh had twice forewarned him) made more explicit with a pun: the heart of Solomon (שלמה) was not true (שלם) to Yahweh (v. 4).

Appearances notwithstanding, the narrator's repetitive comments about Solomon's 'wisdom' pique the reader's suspicion that, from his dubious characterization, the narrator speaks with heavy tongue-in-cheek. Similarly, Whybray remarks:

> the author was well aware, as were the authors of Proverbs, that not everything which passes for wisdom should be accepted at its face value, and also that wickedness can assume the character of wisdom for its own purposes.[13]

even if two different systems did exist, that reality would not ameliorate Solomon's unjust economic policies toward Israel (Walsh, *1 Kings*, p. 100, and 'Characterization of Solomon', p. 481 n. 20).
  10. Eslinger, *Into the Hands of the Living God*, p. 151.
  11. Jobling explores the potential system of economic exchange between wealth and wisdom where the latter becomes just one of many commodities (' "Forced Labor" ', pp. 64–66).
  12. The ambiguous pronoun 'these' (v. 2b) may equally have both the 'gods' and the 'foreign women' as its antecedent. Walsh, *1 Kings*, p. 135.
  13. Whybray, *Intellectual Tradition*, p. 90.

With every move of Solomon, he demonstrates his firm stance in the monarchical mainstream and reveals his 'wisdom' as that of ancient Near Eastern royal ideology.[14] From such a perspective, sex and wealth may either demonstrate proof of wisdom or be commodities received in exchange for wisdom. As for Solomon, sex and wealth displaced wisdom. In short, Solomon disdained divine wisdom in favor of royal 'wisdom', the brutal nature of which the intertext of 1 Kings 1–11 discloses. Through 'wisdom', Solomon flouted his duty as proscribed in Deuteronomy by implementing policies of socio-economic injustice to exploit his subjects via oppressive taxation and the corvée for his own personal wealth and aggrandizement. The military threat of the royal army would surely have insured compliance to these policies by preying upon the fear of Israel if they did not. Indeed, 'what to Israel' is this 'son' of Yahweh whose imprudent ability to rule with justice, righteousness and equity bled the innocent dry without cause?

Murder and Metaphor: Social Injustice in Proverbs 1.8-19

In the first poem of Proverbs 1–9 the poet sets the tone by ascribing primacy to the imperative שְׁמַע (v. 8), which intensifies the jussive form in v. 5. As a result, the poetic reprise emphatically reiterates the immediacy of listening on the part of the 'son'. (Com)(de)mand from the outset quickly displaces the previously implied request.

The phrase 'my son', which occurs frequently throughout chapters 1–9 (1.8, 10, 15; 2.1; 3.1, 11, 21; 4.10, 20; 6.1, 3, 20; 7.1), evokes the image of close, familial relations. Nevertheless, this expression may function, as Newsom points out, to interpellate and continually reinterpellate the son (and reader) to assume the position of a willing recipient to the authoritative father's instruction.[15] The lack of specificity with בְּנִי elicits a variety of relational dynamics (e.g. father–son, teacher–pupil). Thus, the semiotician may also perceive a subjacent allusion to Solomon since the only linear-sequential antecedent to בֵּן is Solomon ben-David.

The ancient Near East regarded the monarch in some mystically conceptual manner expressed variously from the king as divine in origin (Egypt) to the king as sacral in nature and function (Mesopotamia).[16] In both Egyptian and Mesopotamian literature, one finds references to the king as the 'son' of a respective god. Similarly, Hebrew literature refers to the Israelite king as the 'son' or 'firstborn' of Yahweh, and Yahweh as the 'father' of the king (Pss. 2.7; 89.27; 2 Sam. 7.14; cf. Isa. 9.6). All arguments over such an ideological claim aside, however, this study need only demonstrate the plausibility of the semiotic intuition of the 'son' as Solomon.

---

14. Extra-biblical parallels illumine the monarchic ideology of the ancient Near East and its heavy influence upon Solomon. See Lasine, 'King of Desire', p. 99.

15. See her 'Woman and the Discourse of Patriarchal Wisdom', pp. 143–44.

16. For further descriptions of both Egyptian and Mesopotamian concepts of the monarch, see Henri Frankfort, *Kingship and the Gods: A Study of Ancient Near Eastern Religion as the Integration of Society and Nature* (Chicago: University of Chicago Press, 1948), pp. 5–55 and 224–301, respectively.

The Israelite conception of the monarch embraces mythical significance.[17] Israel did not understand her king as divine in origin or nature. Rather, she regarded her king in terms of a metaphorical 'father–son' relationship to express the special bond between Yahweh and the king formed at the king's accession to the throne. The application of holy oil transformed the king into 'the anointed of Yahweh' (1 Sam. 10.6).[18] As 'the anointed of Yahweh', the king was Yahweh's son and a potent extension of the divine personality, that is, as sacrosanct.[19]

Despite Henri Frankfort's contention that the transcendentalism of Hebrew religion hindered the ability of Israelite kings to integrate society and nature,[20] the king did assume a supremely crucial role in the social and cosmic order (cf. Ps. 72). The king was to embody righteousness. By seeking the economic well-being and vitality of the nation rather than his own self-aggrandizement, the king ensured a sound moral order and a corresponding stability within the cosmos by his righteous rule.[21] But the right exercise of power by the monarch depended upon fidelity to Yahweh and to the Torah. Failure by the adopted 'son' of Yahweh to attain this ideal would result in his death like that of a mere mortal (Ps. 82). Therefore, the mythico-religious symbolism of the monarch as 'son' legitimates the semiotic intuition of בן as Solomon.

Given such symbolic data, the logical apprehension of אב as a sign of the paternal figure Yahweh naturally follows. Might we not then discern within the paralleling maternal figure (אם) an allusion to personified Wisdom since her instruction to the 'son' occupies such a prominent role in Proverbs 1–9?[22] Watson demurs this possibility claiming that אם occurs merely for the sake of parallelism; thus, 'only the first element is intended'.[23] The parallelism of אב and אם, both of whom the poet associates with מוסר ('discipline') and תורה ('instruction'), emphasizes both אב and אם as the poetic totality of parental instruction, that is, a merismus.[24] Torah, and not the parents, is the focal point for the son (and reader). James Williams astutely notes that the figure of the parents, who may simultaneously represent

17. The innocent story of Abishag (1 Kgs 1.1–4) alludes to the widespread practices in the ancient Near East of testing the waning virility of the old monarch, who embodied the nation's potency and fertility. William Irwin also cites the example of Jeremiah, who refers to public lamentations at the death of a king such as clearly relate them to the ritual of the fertility god (22.18). 'Nation, Society, and Politics', in Henri Frankfort *et al.*, *The Intellectual Adventure of Ancient Man: An Essay on Speculative Thought in the Ancient Near East* (Chicago: University of Chicago Press, 1946), pp. 326–60 (347).

18. Irwin, *Intellectual Adventure of Ancient Man*, p. 347.

19. Aubrey R. Johnson, *Sacral Kingship in Ancient Israel* (Cardiff: University of Wales Press, 2nd edn, 1967), p. 14.

20. According to Frankfort (*Kingship and the Gods*, pp. 342–43), keeping the covenant of Yahweh relinquished the harmonious integration of man's life with that of nature.

21. The righteous rule of the king parallels the Egyptian concept of *Ma'at*, often personified as a goddess. See Johnson, *Sacral Kingship in Ancient Israel*, pp. 3–7, 20–21, 90, 127–28.

22. In Egyptian thought the throne, which made the gods, is referred to at times as the ruler's 'mother' (Frankfort, *Kingship and the Gods*, p. 44).

23. Watson, *Classical Hebrew Poetry*, p. 139.

24. By contrast, Clifford uses the term 'merism' in reference to the 'totality of people intent on hindering the quest for wisdom' (*Proverbs*, pp. 37–38).

leader, teacher, counselor *et al.*, only embodies the tradition, which the poet enjoins upon the 'son'. The 'son' maintains tradition via Torah observance, 'which is related to the ancient wisdom principle of maintaining proper order in one's personal life', in society and, by extension, the cosmos.[25]

In v. 9 the lexeme לויה ('wreath', 'garland') occurs three times in the Hebrew Bible, all within Proverbs (1.9; 4.9; 14.24). This lexeme, which parallels ענק ('neck-pendant', 'ornament', Judg. 8.26) here and עטרת ('crown') in 4.9, reveals itself as part of the royal apparel.[26] The connotations of both 'garland' and 'crown', deriving from the sememe 'to surround, encircle', project the imagery of the crown, which alludes to Solomon as the poet shifts this imagery into a metaphorical dimension. But does the 'crown' imagery function as a metaphor for Torah or fidelity to parents? Clifford assumes the latter,[27] but the parents are only the medium of the instruction. The poet's emphasis upon Torah observance suggests that by complying with the מוסר of the father (Yahweh) and the תורה of the mother (Wisdom), Solomon dons the proper insignia of royalty. Torah becomes the royal crown and symbol of wealth that shall surround the monarch and protect him. Only the emperor's new clothes of instructional discipline can garner the authority and honor truly befitting 'the anointed of Yahweh'.

As parental instruction commands the son's attention again in order to urge him to resist interpellation by a rival discourse, this poem continually stresses its conative function. The second occurrence of בני (v. 10) introduces a dramatic scenario of evil (mis)adventure, the consequences of which receive fuller elaboration after the third occurrence of בני (v. 15).

The conditional sentence אם־יפתוך חטאים אל־תבא ('if sinful men entice you, do not follow') expresses a generalized, yet realistic, behavioral possibility. The root פתה in the protasis re-emphasizes Solomon's lack of wisdom as it echoes the implicit naiveté of the פתי at a subjacent level. The naiveté of the 'son' engenders his enticement by sinful men. But for the seduction to occur, these men must stand in some close relation to the king. Perhaps they are advisors who have his confidence and respect to the point that they can effectively persuade his decision-making. At any rate, these deceiving men pose a hindrance to Solomon's acquisition of wisdom. The poet promptly presents the son with a choice: either heed the call of parental instruction, which foreshadows the ensuing calls of personified Wisdom, or heed the call of sinners, which foreshadows the later calls of Woman Folly.

The protasis of the father's second conditional sentence (אם־יאמרו 'if they say', v. 11), the apodosis of which does not appear until v. 15, upholds speech as the means of enticement by the sinful men. The imagery of the scenario reveals a group of criminals who try to persuade the 'son' to join them in a plot to shed innocent blood. As the dramatic scenario unfolds, robbery appears secondary and murder primary. The murderous intentions of these sociopaths to waylay innocent victims simply 'for the hell of it' (חנם) yields some reward. The connotation of צפן ('to

25.   James G. Williams, *Those Who Ponder Proverbs: Aphoristic Thinking and Biblical Litera-ture* (BibLit, 2; Sheffield: Almond Press, 1981), p. 41.

26.   'Wreath' in 1.9 anticipates the gift bestowed by Wisdom in 4.9. Murphy, *Proverbs*, p. 9.

27.   'The attractive jewelry symbolizes fidelity to parents…' (Clifford, *Proverbs*, p. 38).

treasure up'), which anticipates the spoil (שׁלל) mentioned later in v. 13, intimates the potential of gain shared by all as a direct result of this murderous scheme.

But what actually entices: the speech (of the criminals? of the father?), the criminals' schemes, the potential for lucrative gain or perhaps just the whole enterprise? And what relation do the criminals have with the 'son'? Unlike the father, they certainly do not stand in any hierarchical relation to the 'son'. Neither do they appear as rank strangers as the pervasive first common plural ('we', 'our', 'us') suggests.[28] Rather, the intimacy of such language indicates a close group of peers. By association, the father implicates his 'son'.

Within the father's depiction of the criminals lies an ironic paradox. The criminals' expertise in hitting their 'mark' belies the connotative symbol of their name (חטא 'to miss the mark') and yet their success demonstrates a failure 'to miss the mark'. The father waxes hyperbolic in his description of the criminals, who speak metaphorically when identifying their goal and themselves with Death. The metaphor of Sheol as a hungry monster, opening wide its mouth and never satisfied, finds its parallel in Canaanite mythology. Mot (Death) is the god with the gaping throat and the insatiable appetite, and it is through his gullet that the living must pass into the underworld of the dead.[29] Likewise, the appetite for innocent blood never satisfies, and it is through the חטאים that the נקי ('innocent') must pass into the underworld of the dead. Lest we forget, the father exercises complete control over the speech and description of the criminals as he infuses an element of reality into a hypothetical scenario, which smacks of more than just youthful temptation. First, youthful temptation generally succeeds because of the enticing power of subtlety (completely absent in these criminals' appeal) and/or peer pressure. Second, murderous brigands would not conceive of themselves in such metaphorical terms. The question then follows: what does such metaphorical imagery evoke in ideative activity?

The eager anticipation at the prospect of wealth climaxes the persuasive appeal by the criminals (vv. 13–14). The spoil they expect, however, derives not from warfare, but rather from innocent victims. Such imagery of murderous greed echoes the identical metaphorical image within the book of Isaiah. Within the vineyard, itself a metaphor, Yahweh expected to find justice and righteousness, but alas, only bloodshed (5.7), described thusly by the poet: 'What do you mean by crushing my people/by grinding the face of the poor?' (3.15). Of course, what else does ground meat yield but blood, and fat (wealth)?[30] Rather than maintaining justice and righteousness within the vineyard, the Judean nobility instead exploit it with their

---

28. Newsom, too, notes the featured cohortative speech rather than the direct imperative. Verse 14 especially makes more explicit the egalitarian subtext. But her patriarchal agenda limits her view of the subtext's concern over a division of power between older and younger men in patriarchal society ('Woman and the Discourse of Patriarchal Wisdom', p. 145).

29. McKane, *Proverbs*, p. 269; cf. Scott, *Proverbs. Ecclesiastes*, p. 38.

30. 'Oil' and 'fat' function as metonyms for the wealth of the nation in the book of Isaiah. Wealth does not ameliorate destruction (1.6). In fact, wealth invites destruction as it serves to lure imperialist predators (cf. 39.2). 'Oil' cannot soften the blow because the nobility has taken it. Rural areas of production and urban areas of commerce and trade no longer function (1.7).

insatiable appetite to amass land and property (5.8), gold and silver and the spoil of the poor, which they greedily hoard away in their houses (3.14). After all, filling houses with gold and silver is exactly what royalty does (Job 3.14–15). Thus the Isaianic poet uses the imagery of murder as a metaphor for social injustice. But only the appetite of Sheol can match and surpass that of the Judean nobility. Sheol enlarges its appetite to accommodate those who pervert justice (Isa. 5.14–17; cf. 14.9–11). This Isaianic intertextual echo illumines the father's instruction about murderous greed as a subjacent metaphor for social injustice by the חטא׳ם and, by association, the 'son'.[31] By devouring, they are devoured. Sheol swallows itself up.

While there may be no honor among thieves, there is certainly a common purse (כ׳ם, v. 14).[32] The purse generally carried either money or weights used in daily commerce by Israelite merchants, but the usage of כ׳ם elsewhere in the Hebrew Bible also connotes unethical and dishonest business practices (Deut. 25.13; Mic. 6.11). Only in relation to Yahweh does כ׳ם bear a positive symbol for just, economic exchanges. The sage emphasizes this point later through the explicit pun of כ׳ם and כסא ('throne', 16.11–12), which, nevertheless, does occur, albeit subtly, within the syntagm כ[׳ס] [ס] [א]חד ('one purse'). This pun forces an associative connotation by implying that, in contrast to Yahweh, the monarchy symbolizes social and economic injustice (16.11–12), which undermines the very foundation and stability of the throne, that is, righteousness. The pursuit of כ׳ם by Solomon and his administration only effects the 'kiss' of death. Any counsel to such a life-pursuit unwittingly proves the undoing of this royal conspiracy.

The lexeme בנ׳ in v. 15, which reprises vv. 8 and 10, both rhetorically reclaims the attention of the 'son' and syntactically introduces the delayed apodosis. Also, the assonantal feature of the suffixal *-am* ending with both colons of vv. 11 and 15 conjoins the apodosis to its protasis. Subsequent imagery of vv. 15–19 works to undo the intentions of the חטא׳ם via the recurrence of the lexemes הלך (vv. 11, 15), חנם (vv. 11, 17) and דם (vv. 11, 16).[33]

The dramatic scenario gives way to a negative command preventing a specific action. The lexical parallelism of דרך ('way'), which occurs over seventy times,[34] with נתיבה ('path') and the foot imagery metaphorically signify a way of life or means of conducting oneself. Besides feet, this poem also mentions other body parts, namely the head and neck. The head and neck steer the body while the feet move it in the direction that it goes. If 'where the head and neck go, the body is sure to follow', then the תורה crown upon the head of the 'son' will guide his footsteps in righteous conduct.

The instructional discipline of the 'son' induced by grave circumstances dismisses normal conventions. Generally, only one כ׳ clause follows a warning such

---

31. McKane (*Proverbs*, p. 269) disagrees: 'I cannot believe that it is justifiable to introduce so much subtlety into the interpretation of these verses'.

32. Murphy (*Proverbs*, p. 9) views the connotation of 'lot' as the common share from evil adventure as blasphemous given its function to determine God's will (16.33).

33. Clifford, *Proverbs*, p. 37.

34. Note other paradigmatic lexemes in Proverbs – e.g. הלך בדרך (6×), ארח (20×) and נתיבה (6×). Clifford, *Proverbs*, p. 38.

as that in v. 15, but the twice-repeated כִּי in vv. 16–17 forms the exception to the grammatical rule.[35] By appropriating the preceding foot imagery in v. 15 with the catchword רגל, the father's vivid description poetically complements the metaphorical imagery in vv. 11–12. The verbatim echo of רגליהם לרע ירוצו וימהרו לשפך דם ('their feet rush to evil/they hasten to shed blood') in Isa. 59.7 further reinforces these metaphorical images decrying the murderous nature of social injustice rampant in Israelite society. These criminals have made their path so crooked that no one knows peace (שלום, 59.8), most especially the innocent. If, however, these criminals abstain from evil (רע), then they will be despoiled (59.15), no doubt an unsettling prospect for this group. But does not the poet then condone that for which he condemns the monarch? Absolutely not, since to refrain from evil concurrently implies the re-establishment of justice so that everyone shares in the basic necessities of life without fear of exploitation and deprivation. But of course, greed, which initially procured the spoil, would naturally forestall, if not prohibit, any course of action risking the loss of such spoil. Moreover, the hastiness with which the חטאים rush to 'shed blood' signifies their impetuousness and blatant disregard for human life with no thought to the consequences.

Despite appearances to the contrary, the shift to third person reference to the criminals in v. 16 does not exonerate Solomon. Much like the use of indirect language by Nathan the prophet to confront David with his sin, so the sage's subjacent metaphor indirectly critiques Solomon and his royal advisors for their implementation of sanguinary, domestic policies. Their bloodthirsty exploitation flouts human dignity by bleeding dry those basic life necessities that provide humanity its sense of dignity. By observing Torah, though, Solomon begins to disassociate himself from the חטאים and to discern justice, righteousness and equity.

Ambiguity enshrouds the metaphorical image of v. 17. According to McKane, the interpretative crux lies with מזרה,[36] which interpreters have denotatively fixed as either 'to throw high' or 'to spread out'. Both denotations work because of the semiotic confluence of זרה and מזר in מזרה.[37] In ancient Palestine, hunters would capture birds by placing two vanes of netting on either side of a clearing (זרה) or over a hole strewn with bait (מזר) while they hid behind a wall and held onto the cord. When a bird landed, the hunters would then quickly pull the vanes toward each other.[38] The historical data thus substantiates either rendering of מזרה and so allays any perceived interpretative crux.

Verse 17 yields two potential readings: (1) the parenthetical remark implies that the trap fails because the bird sees the net being baited and avoids it, and (2) the

---

35. Clifford (*Proverbs*, p. 39) suggests v. 16 as a secondary explanation of v. 15 because a copyist did not understand v. 17 (cf. Murphy, *Proverbs*, p. 10). But the suggestion of a gloss only absolves interpreters of any consideration to the poetic function of v. 16.

36. McKane, *Proverbs*, p. 270.

37. Clifford objects to the misinterpretation of זרה as casting a hunting-net over birds. Yet, in his preference for the denotation 'to throw high', he makes the unsubstantiated claim of the piel passive participle מזרה as a ' "divine passive", a customary way of stating divine or customary agency' (*Proverbs*, p. 39).

38. See Othmar Keel, *The Symbolism of the Biblical World: Ancient Near Eastern Iconography and the Book of Psalms* (New York: Crossroad, 1978), pp. 89–95; also Clifford, *Proverbs*, p. 39.

parenthesis suggests that the bird sees the net but, unable to control its appetite, plunges into it. Moreover, both readings share a symbiotic relationship with what Murphy observes as ambiguous referents.[39] Metaphorically, the first reading assumes the 'son' as the referent, in which case, any trap set for him will fail either because he can avoid the too obvious trap or because he receives good advice. Despite its modicum of possibility, this reading naturally assumes the addressee and the referent as the same.[40] While the entire instruction of 1.8–19 undoubtedly addresses the 'son', the context of this poem has the nefarious activity of the הטאים as its object of discussion. In addition, such a reading inadequately fits as an apposite metaphor for the self-destruction of the criminals described in vv. 18–19. Nevertheless, this interpretation does indicate, at least subjacently, the veiled potential for the deliverance of the 'son'.

The second, and most common, reading best honors the textual signs. The folly of the criminals is inferred from the folly of the bird. Like the bird's inability to control its appetite, so, too, the הטאים, unable to control their appetite, foolishly rush into the trap of their own downfall.[41] The immediacy of חנם ('without cause', v. 17) following upon the heels of לשפך־דם ('to shed blood', v. 16) recapitulates the imagery of malicious intent by the הטאים, whose ambush of the innocent with a net (vv. 11, 18) indelibly stamps itself into the reader's mind.[42] Thus the imagery of v. 17 becomes metaphorically illustrative of v. 18.

The lexemes דם...ארב in colon A and צפן in colon B of v. 18 reprise those in v. 11. These recurring lexemes bear out the conceptual parallelism between these two verses and further reiterate the malevolent plot of the הטאים. The twice-repeated suffixal endings *-am*, which find their grammatical parallelism in v. 15,[43] incorporate v. 15 into the conceptual parallelism, but also pose a grammatical ambiguity. Why does the poet use plural suffixes for a singular antecedent (נקי)? The singular antecedent נקי functions collectively to denote the sum total of individuals belonging to the same class.[44] Yet the grammatical incongruity of the plural suffixes also allows for the הטאים as their antecedent. In an ironic twist the blood for which these criminals lie in wait turns out to be 'their' blood; the lives for which they hide in ambush are 'their' own lives (v. 18).[45] Thus the grammatical incongruity of the ambiguous plural suffixal *-am* endings allows for both the נקי and the הטאים as their antecedents. The pathway of an imperial policy sanctioning social

39. Murphy, *Proverbs*, p. 10.

40. Jakobson's communication model distinguishes between a text's 'referent' (or context) and its conative (or addressee) function ('Linguistics and Poetics', in *Language and Literature*, p. 66).

41. McKane, *Proverbs*, pp. 270–71. Clifford (*Proverbs*, p. 39) elaborates upon זרה as a 'divine passive' by paraphrasing v. 17: 'God does not hold up to the view of the wicked the net set to entrap them. Divine retribution ("a net") operates invisibly'.

42. The paralleling wordplay of hiding 'without reason' (חנם, v. 11)//holding up high a net 'without reason' (חנם, v. 17) reinforces the imagery.

43. Clifford, *Proverbs*, p. 39.

44. This grammatical phenomenon in the Hebrew language generally accounts for any grammatical or syntactical incongruities, especially with regard to verb-subject agreement.

45. The evil designs of the הטאים turn against them and bring them down. See Murphy, *Proverbs*, p. 10.

injustice only accentuates its cold-blooded nature. Murder, a most apt metaphor for socio-economic injustice, best characterizes a domestic policy, which, for all intents and purposes, portends the fateful demise of the monarch(y). The nefarious policies of Solomon and his administration shall recoil upon them.

In the more prosaic v. 19, the metaphor for social and economic injustice broaches crystallization.[46] The lexeme ארח ('way') functions in paradigmatic relation to the lexemes דרך and נתיבה, all of which connote a way of life or a manner of conduct that the poetically sensitive reader has previously discerned. The 'way' as one of social and economic injustice gains in significance with the verbal syntax בצע בצע ('greedy for gain'). In other texts with a similar syntactical construction (e.g. Prov. 15.27; Jer. 6.13, 8.10; Ezek. 22.27; Hab. 2.9), בצע bears the dual signification of greed for gain and extortion (with the further connotation) by violent means. The continual unjust procurement of gain by means of violence metaphorically depicts the 'way' of the חטאים. Although their way seems politically expedient and right, it only accrues the reward of death.

The emphasis upon life in colon B makes the pursuit of wealth pale in comparison. Nevertheless, wealth does have its significance. As the life of the נקי was taken just 'for the hell of it', so now wealth takes the life of its owner, but with just cause. In an ironic twist, the wealth possessed (dis)possesses its possessor (cf. Prov. 10.2; 11.4).[47] By 'blowing up' another sememe of בעל ('Baal'), though, we can further nuance the descriptive metaphor of exploitation. 'Baal', a metonym for idolatry, directly pertains to wealth unjustly gained. Cultic images in the ancient Near East functioned as a channel through which large amounts of material productivity were funneled into the control of the priestly and royal classes.[48] The deleterious collusion of the priesthood and royalty customarily implemented idolatry as a religious dictum and tool for the socio-economic exploitation of the lower classes. Idolatry enhanced the accumulation and control of material resources by the ruling elite as aptly depicted by the pun of בעל upon בלע ('to swallow up', 'to devour', v. 12). By repudiating the cultic image, Israel sought to rid itself of an important source of wealth for the ruling classes. Therefore, the metonymic בעל illumines a subjacent allusion to the religious problem sanctioning the Solomonic regime's unjust domestic policies. Get rid of the בל/ע/בעל, and get rid of the socio-economic exploitation! Ultimately, the main issue inferred concerns a choice between two paths lying before Solomon: one leads to death, the other to life.

In summary, this poem's linear text manifestation portrays parental instruction to a 'son' advising against his participation in a violent plot to murder innocent victims. But semiotic analysis, supported by various historical and intertextual data, evokes a poetic metaphor for socio-economic injustice at a subjacent level of

---

46. By changing 'way' (ארח) to 'end', scholars do little to retain the metaphor when 'way' best fits the figurative language. Murphy, *Proverbs*, p.10.

47. Contrast with the view of Murphy (*Proverbs*, p. 10) who maintains the subject of 'it' to refer 'in a general way to the pursuit of the unjust "gain" '.

48. For further discussion on the role of the cultic image in the ancient Near East, see James M. Kennedy, 'The Social Background of Early Israel's Rejection of Cultic Images: A Proposal', *BTB* 17 (1987), pp. 138–44.

this poem. As a poetic metaphor for social injustice, this poem picturesquely emblematizes the first point of critique (i.e. Solomon's imprudent ability to rule with justice, righteousness and equity) in the Deuteronomistic literature, most especially that of the intertext 1 Kgs 1–11. Murder graphically depicts the greedy despoliation of the innocent by Solomon whose administrative policies sanctioned by the religious dictum of idolatry bled the innocent dry of their material resources. But the accumulation of wealth only profits death. While rival voices entice with persuasive speech, only (the) 'father' knows best. By embracing Torah, the 'son', too, may know best the life-path of righteous conduct.

Divine Censure and Monarchical Duty: Torah Reorientation in Proverbs 3.1-12

The poem in 3.1-12 resumes the theme of the book's motto (1.7) with additional parental instruction in the face of rival voices. Both the חטאים (alluded to in 2.12–15; 4.10–19) and the אשה זרה (2.16–19; 5.1–23; 6.20–35; 7.1–27; 9.13–18) function as poetic antagonists to the 'father' and 'mother' (1.8) by their deceptive speech and 'smooth words'. This dark merismus of *a*parental instruction summon the 'son' to a (self)destructive course in life and so hinder his acquisition of wisdom.[49] Only Yahweh can grant wisdom (2.6) and that only if Solomon 'stores away' (צפן, 2.1) the commandments,[50] a metonym for Torah. The poet emphasizes Torah as *the* means in the acquisition of wisdom and insight with the usage of paradigmatic lexemes such as מוסר and תורה (1.8), אמר and מצוה (2.1), and תורה and מצוה (3.1).

The parallelism of מצוה//תורה (3.1) as well as the language and imagery of vv. 1–4 foreshadow 6.20–22 and, more significantly, echo the Torah, specifically Deut. 6.1-15. Like Israel, the 'son' must bind (קשר, v. 3; Deut. 6.8) the instruction of Yahweh around his neck and write (כתב, v. 3; 6.9) them upon his heart (על-לבב, v. 3; 6.6), no doubt to safeguard against forgetting (שכח, v. 1; 6.12) the commandments (מצוה, v. 1; 6.2). If heeded, the commandments will give the 'son' (בן, v. 1; 6.7) long life (ארך ימים, v. 2; 6.2) and well-being.[51] Such strong echoes reinforce the ideation of the monarch's duty to 'fear Yahweh' through his duty to Torah. Torah, the medium of wisdom and insight, shall protect the receptive heart (נצר, 2.2, 11; 3.1) of the 'son' to Wisdom just as Yahweh safeguards the paths of justice (נצר, 2.8).

The metaphor of Yahweh as 'father' re-emerges with the promise of 'long days' (ארך ימים) and 'peace' (שלום, v. 2). Who else could lengthen life and guarantee well-being but the 'father'? The promise of 'long days' (ארך ימים) and 'well-

---

49. Compare the similarities between the deceptively inviting speech of the חטאים and the אשה זרה – 'Come!' (1.10; 7.18); 'to lie in wait' (1.10, 18; 7.12); and 'to find' (1.13; 7.15).

50. The poet starkly contrasts what Yahweh 'stores away' (צפן, 2.7), wisdom, with what Solomon 'stores away' (צפן, 1.11, 18), wealth.

51. This striking concentration of parallels and the similarity of Deut. 8.5 to Prov. 3.11–12 prompt Whybray (*Proverbs*, p. 60) to suggest a dependence of the book of Proverbs upon Deuteronomy.

being' foreshadows those gifts proffered by Wisdom (3.16–17). The promise also recalls Yahweh's blessing (ימים ארך, 1 Kgs 3.14), contingent upon the king's observance of Yahweh's (not David's) statutes and commandments.[52] Regardless of that blessing, the name (שלמה) that should have been emblematic of peace (שלם) ironically knew no peace either politically or religiously! Solomon's abandonment of Torah resulted in his disorientation. He assumed a course of violence that rendered him no better than an immature fool who, with a gift that could have helped him successfully navigate between the paths of good and evil, instead squandered such a gift by a corrupt usage of it. Perhaps Yahweh did not honor Solomon's initial request because he already had that which would enable him 'to discern between good and evil' (1 Kgs 3.9). Only by reorienting himself to Torah can the 'son' experience deliverance from his crooked path of evil (2.12-15) and reverse his downward spiral to Sheol.

The negative (de)(com)mand of v. 3, different in structure,[53] calls attention to itself and reaches its climax with the isolated third colon. Previously, however, the poet associates Yahweh's תורה with two rich lexemes in the Hebrew Bible. Regardless of the diverse renderings of אמת ('fidelity') and חסד ('loyalty', 'kindness'), they generally connote the quality of relations both between God and humans as well as between humans.[54] As the intertextual data bears out, the son's quality of relations is much less than stellar. He has neither demonstrated fidelity to God nor kindness to his royal subjects, especially Israel. To state the negative command positively, remembrance of Yahweh's תורה implies a demonstration of fidelity and kindness, attributes which parallel יראת יהוה ('fear of the Lord') in Prov. 16.6. This confluence of חסד ואמת with both תורה and יראת יהוה reiterates the semiotic quality of יראת יהוה as a sign of the monarch's duty. Internalizing the Torah has as its external complement the visually practical expression of fidelity and kindness.

The poet illustrates by expanding upon a previously constructed metaphor. In addition to phraseology redolent of תורה, the metaphor utilizes two images involving different parts of the human body. The first image recalls that of the first poem (1.9) where the royal crown functions metaphorically for the תורה. Now, the metaphor subtly shifts with fidelity and kindness as the neck-ornament.[55] The lexeme 'bind' veils a contrast between what Solomon should bind upon himself and what, as its connotation 'alliance' implies, he does bind upon himself. By

---

52. That Solomon lived to an old age confirms in the minds of some that he indeed observed the statutes and commandments of Yahweh as his father David had. But the verbal ambiguities within 1 Kgs 1–11 suggest otherwise.

53. This verse's different structure of three colons rather than the usual two has elicited various responses, all of which disregard literary integrity. Although many commentators regard the third colon as a gloss introduced from 7.3, Whybray (*Proverbs*, pp. 60–61) proposes the first colon as the gloss arguing that elsewhere (6.21; 7.3; cf. 1.9; 3.22) the father's (or parent's) teachings are to be bound or written on the heart.

54. Scott (*Proverbs. Ecclesiastes*, p. 47) cites as examples the relationship of the true son to his father (Gen. 47.29), of Yahweh to his people (Exod. 34.6) and of a covenant of friendship (Josh. 2.14).

55. Another shift occurs in 3.22 and 6.21 with תושיה ('wisdom') and מצוה/תורה respectively as the royal necklace.

binding חסד ואמת around the neck, the 'son' adorns himself with a splendor truly befitting Yahweh's anointed and keeps his royal duty close to heart.

The second image has its echo in a later poem where, instead of fidelity and kindness, the poet advises the 'son' to engrave מצוה and תורה upon the 'tablet of the heart' (על לוח לב, 7.3), a rare syntagm which occurs only three times in the Hebrew Bible. The graphic character of this metaphor embeds within itself an image of permanence in that a writer permanently inscribed literature upon clay tablets by using a metal stylus. Likewise, the 'son' should permanently inscribe upon his heart fidelity and kindness such that it becomes intrinsic to his own disposition as his own heart is to his body. Satiety of Solomon's entire being with תורה internally and חסד ואמת externally suppresses satiety for wealth and (foreign) women. The poet's graphic metaphor makes its impression, too, by allusion to the permanence of Torah and its manifestation as fidelity and kindness.

The pervasiveness of fidelity and kindness throughout Solomon's entire being could only bode well for him as he would certainly not need to protract his quest for 'acceptance' (חן) and 'success/insight' (שׂכל טוב) amongst God and humans (v. 4). McKane comments that 'the ability to get on well with people, the possession of an attractive personality (חן) and the enjoyment of reputation and success are highly prized'.[56] 'Success' and 'insight' correlate with one another in that the Hebrew mind closely linked insight or competence with the success that normally fol-lowed.[57] But the homophonic quality of (ס)(שׂ)כל only underscores the folly of Solomon who has fallen into disfavor with both God and Israel. So, the 'father' pursues a quest to restore his 'son' to a favored status. If Solomon reorients himself to תורה, then he will curry the favor of Yahweh and live up to his divine patronym Jedidiah ('beloved of Yahweh').

The structure of vv. 5–10 comprises three quatrains, all admonitory in tone and similar in form. Each admonition states a request (either expressed with imperatives or the imperfect with אל) followed by a promise, but only the first two, which are less specific than the third (vv. 9–10), possess positive and negative elements.

The first admonition (vv. 5–6) gets to the heart of the matter. Solomon has demonstrated a mindset completely incompatible with the proper attitude that an Israelite monarch should have toward Yahweh. Trust (בטח) in the Lord requires wholehearted commitment, not mixed devotion. As an act of religious expedience, Solomon sacrifices at the high places and at the royal cultic site when it seems convenient or advantageous to do so. He circumvents the necessity of undivided loyalty as he attempts to garner divine surety. Adulterous relationships, however, evince no security (בטח).

The command 'trust in the Lord with all of your heart' semantically parallels 'do not rely on your own understanding' (v. 5b). For the Hebrews, the heart was the seat of the intellect. The expression in v. 5b assumes a metaphorical dimension in that it connotes a sense of independence. Although the mass populace might per-ceive the Israelite monarch as the embodiment of independence, the monarch can

56. McKane, *Proverbs*, p. 292.
57. Whybray, *Proverbs*, p. 61.

neither stand independent of Yahweh nor depend on his own intellectual prowess. To do so would be tantamount to the blind leading the blind since the 'son' (בֵּן) of Yahweh demonstrates an absence of (in)sight (בִּין). By relying upon his own (royal) insight,[58] this 'son' ironically reveals his own deficiency. Regardless of the royal authority with which the masses may have empowered Solomon, the poet instructs the 'son' to abandon his independence *of* for a dependence *on* Yahweh. Only undivided loyalty to Yahweh can ensure the security that a formidable chariot corps, immense wealth and incomparable 'wisdom' cannot.

The poet moves toward a less implicit critique in v. 6 with a denunciation of the ways of the 'son'. By now, of course, the ways of Solomon remain no mystery. Guided by royal 'wisdom', Solomon's ways murderously exploit Yahweh's vineyard of her material wealth for his own self-aggrandizement. Solomon's ways increase the oppressive burden imposed upon his subjects because of his imprudent business negotiations. In short, Solomon's ways reflect a discernment of רָע ('evil') because he stands bereft of an intimate knowledge of Yahweh. The connotation of יָדַע as intimate knowledge also alludes to Solomon's ways of an intimate knowledge with foreign women. Moreover, the semiotic confluence of דָעָה ('to seek') with יָדַע in דָעֵהוּ reiterates the necessity of Solomon to acknowledge his ways and to desire (a knowledge of) Yahweh.

The poet holds out the restorative promise that no matter how crooked Solomon has made his paths, Yahweh, and Yahweh alone, can straighten them (v. 6b). Yahweh can right the wrong of Solomon's unjust, unrighteous and inequitable policies. But Solomon must seek Yahweh wholeheartedly. By 'storing away' the תורה of his 'father', only then will he truly discern the paths of justice, righteousness and equity (2.9). Ultimately, the poet offers Solomon the opportunity to discern between good and evil.

The second admonition (vv. 7–8) compresses its directive in favor of a picturesquely metaphorical promise. The negative form 'Do not be wise in your own sight' (v. 7a) chiastically parallels 'do not rely on your own understanding' (v. 5b). The metaphoric image of 'wise in one's own sight' reverberates throughout Proverbs ('There is a way that seems right to an individual/but its path is the way of death', 14.12; and 'The way of a fool seems right in his own sight/but the wise one listens to advice', 12.15). But the clearest expression occurs almost verbatim in Isaiah ('Woe to those who are wise in their own sight/and perceptive in their own opinion', 5.21). 'Wise in their own sight', the Jerusalem nobles sanctioned the socio-economic rape of the Lord's vineyard. As bloodshed reigned in lieu of righteousness, royalty misguidedly viewed evil (רַע) as good (טוב) because they had rejected Yahweh's תורה (Isa. 5.20, 24). How 'wise', too, must Solomon have seemed in his own sight with his political alliances, with his administrative realignment of the kingdom's districts, with his domestic policy of the corvée, with his military buildup of chariots and horses and with his financial stockpile of gold and silver! As Solomon's reputation for 'wisdom' spread internationally (perhaps

---

58. McKane argues that בִּינָה, now no longer primarily an intellectual virtue, is used pejoratively of 'a sinful *hubris* which is incompatible with trust in Yahweh' (*Proverbs*, p. 292).

helped along by political spin doctors), he came to believe too much of his own press. So the poet offers a reality check: 'Do not be wise in your own sight', Solomon, for your way, though it may seem right to you, is the way of a fool.

What our reading has inferred thus far, the poet makes explicit, that is, Solomon's way is one of evil (רע). As with the ways of the monarch(y) in the book of Isaiah, the self-deluded Solomon perceives his royal policies as 'wise' because he, too, has rejected Yahweh's תורה. The command 'fear Yahweh' (ירא יהוה) echoes the earlier mentioned primacy sign יראת יהוה ('fear of Yahweh'), which signifies the monarch's duty to Torah. The poet counsels the 'son' to 'turn away' from (a way of) evil to Yahweh rather than 'turning away' from Yahweh to (a way of) evil. If Solomon heeds such advice, then he will no longer continue to play the fool. Through Torah devotion, he gains the intimate knowledge of Yahweh requisite for rightly discerning between good and evil. But will Solomon continue along the path of evil (רע) or will he 'walk in the way of good' (טוב, 2.12, 20)?

The syntactical and grammatical parallelism of both colons in v. 8 entwines their semantic worlds. As a result, a semiotic light illumines two rare lexemes in the Hebrew Bible (שר and שקוי occur three times) that might otherwise remain contextually enigmatic. Poetry prompts its readers to explore potential connotations when, as with the instance of שר ('navel', 'umbilical cord'), denotation alone makes no sense syntactically. Upon first sound, לשר bears a phonemic contiguity to בשר ('flesh', 'skin'), which we would naturally expect to parallel עצם ('bone'). After all, both lexemes parallel one another quite frequently in the Hebrew Bible. The lexeme שר also puns אשר ('flesh', 'body') and further underscores the potential connotation of שר as 'flesh' or 'body'. Thus this connotation would suggest the denotative marker 'navel' as a synecdoche for the body. The imagery of שר, which signifies the exterior of the body, and עצם, which signifies the interior of the body, complementarily emphasize the entirety of the body. Furthermore, this signified imagery of the body's exterior and interior conceptually parallels the exteriority and interiority of Torah vis-à-vis the human body as locus.

The second rare lexeme שקוי denotes 'drink' and, like שר, makes no sense by its denotation alone ('a drink for your bones'?). Yet its parallelism to רפאות ('healing') in the first colon yields the possible connotations of שקוי as 'refreshment' or 'medicine'.[59] Yet the context of this poetic instruction reveals no physical illness from which Solomon needs healing. So how might this verse mean? In some occurrences of רפא in the Hebrew Bible, this lexeme assumes the metaphorical intent (usage) 'to restore'. Since physical healing seems less plausible in this poem, the poet, therefore, uses the vehicle of physical healing to convey the tenor of the complete restoration of the 'son' to his 'father'.[60] Only the 'fear of Yahweh' proves a necessary and beneficial therapy for Solomon and his entire being.

Provocative insights emerge at the subjacency of v. 8, which simultaneously remind us of the satiric nature of this poetic critique of 'wise' Solomon. The

---

59. Whybray, *Proverbs*, p. 63.

60. 'The reward for following the father's advice…is the well-being of the whole person…and not only physical health' (Whybray, *Proverbs*, p. 63).

homophonic pun שָׁרַק ('hissing', 'whistling') on שָׁרַק imposes its connotation of 'mockery' or 'derision'. Rarely ever do poets satirize people of impeccable and respectable character. The poet, however, is not alone in his mocking, for Woman Wisdom also derides and laughs at Solomon who, in essence, rejected her when he rejected the 'fear of Yahweh' (יראת יהוה) and her reproof contained therein (1.26-30). The derision of Solomon arises in part from his fundamentally mixed devotion to Yahweh, that is, idolatry. The polysemic lexeme עצב ('idol'), which puns עצם, connotes idolatry as the illness from which he needs healing. The semiotic confluence of עֵץ ('tree') and מות ('death') embedded within עצמות signifies the idol as a 'tree of death'. This imagery foreshadows its stark contrast with the beneficent Wisdom as a 'tree of life' (3.18). Seizing (חזק) Wisdom strengthens (חזק) life whereas a (death)grip on idolatry deadens. Therefore, the poet extends the prospect of a complete recovery of Solomon from the disease of idolatry (and from satire), but he must embrace the therapeutic תורה of Yahweh.

Material wealth returns to the fore in the poet's third admonition for the 'son' 'to honor (כבד) Yahweh' (vv. 9–10) with his 'wealth' (הון), 'revenue' (תבואה), 'storehouse' (אסם) and 'vat' (יקב), all of which confirm his prosperity. Nevertheless, the conspicuous absence of generosity towards the poor indicates a significance of no small degree. A predominant view among scholars maintains this third admonition as advice to pay sacrificial dues.[61] But the language and context of v. 9 do not have in view the religio-cultic sacrifices as perceived by interpreters.[62] Instead, the tenor of v. 9 evokes a metaphorical image of sacrifice. In a sense, the poet indeed counsels the 'son' to sacrifice as a means of ascribing honor to Yahweh, but that sacrifice, as the ensuing paragraphs shall argue, is one of a socio-ethical rather than a religio-cultic nature.

When actualized, the two narcotized sememes of כבד ('to be heavy', 'burdensome') and הון ('to be easy', 'light') provide a telling contrast in the first colon of v. 9. The sufficient wealth (הון) of Solomon no doubt came to him with relative ease. His light regard for the dignity of his subjects became a heavy burden for them. The lexeme הון flashes back to the first poem where it lexically parallels שלל ('spoil', 1.13), the object of the murderous exploitation of the innocent. Thus, הון becomes a lexematic interpretant of socio-economic injustice. But the ease of Solomon's wealth from socio-economic exploitation burdened Yahweh as well. Consequently, a paradox emerges: If Solomon's wealth burdened Yahweh, how can he honor Yahweh from his wealth? Solomon honors Yahweh by redistributing the 'fat of the land' for the benefit of all within the kingdom, not just for the monarch(y).[63] Like

---

61. According to Whybray (*Proverbs*, p. 63), this passage is the only one in Proverbs that positively enjoins sacrificial offerings such as those prescribed in the Pentateuchal laws. Cf. McKane, *Proverbs*, p. 293.

62. The lexemes כבד ('heavy'), הון ('wealth') and תבואה ראשית ('best produce') never occur in any explicit context of offering sacrifices to Yahweh. In the closest example, a man of God condemns the high priest Eli who honored (כבד) his sons above Yahweh because he withheld the choicest (ראשית) parts of sacrifices devoted to Yahweh (1 Sam. 2.29).

63. The functionary effectiveness of an Egyptian king hinged on his ability to produce the 'fat

Eli, Solomon had dishonored Yahweh by withholding the *crème de la crème* of his material gain (תבואה), not animal sacrifices.

The phonemic contiguity of תבואה with תבונה ('understanding') further reiterates the subjacent mocking of Solomonic discernment. While the best of Solomon's intellectual acumen generated valuable revenue, it only brought dishonor to Yahweh. And what good is Solomon's best if it only brings out the worst? The pun of תבונה upon תבואה foreshadows that in 3.13–14 where the embrace of Wisdom concurrently embraces understanding (תבונה) and revenue (תבואה) far more beneficial than gold. By comparison, Solomon's gold is nothing more than a valueless pile of metal. Therefore, the poet implicitly mocks Solomon's mental prowess and its worthless yield.

The surface level of expression with lexemes like אסם ('storehouse') and תירוש יקב ('wine-vat') also connotes Solomon's produce (תבואה) as agricultural. A significant portion of his wealth (aside from the gold, silver and precious jewels) comprised the agricultural stockpile in the royal granaries and wineries. Rather than the normally anticipated אוצר ('storehouse'), the poet uses the obscure lexeme אסם, which occurs only twice in the Hebrew Bible. In its only other occurrence, אסם denotes an earthly storehouse in contrast to its heavenly counterpart (אוצר), without which the earthly storehouse would stand empty (Deut. 28.8–12). The poetic significance of the paucity of אסם depreciates human, and more specifically Solomon's, wealth in comparison to that of Yahweh. The abundance of Solomon's storehouse and wine-vats did not derive from his devotion to Yahweh, but rather from his trampling of the vineyard, as the embedded sememe 'to dispossess' within תירוש signifies. 'Wine', as the intertexts Isaiah 3 and 5 intimate, functions as a metaphor for the blood of the poor oozing through the pores of their crushed and ground faces. Solomon increases his wine holdings as a result of his ruthless dispossession of wine vineyards and their yield.

As a natural consequence of a surface level reading of vv. 9–10, two problems appear. First, the poetic promise of material prosperity presents an ethical dilemma. Whybray comments that 'this is the most blatant expression in the Old Testament of the principle *do ut des* – the offering of gifts to God solely in order to elicit material rewards from him'.[64] Second, the promise of an overabundance of grain and wine can only subvert the desired response from Solomon to honor Yahweh. After all, his abundant wealth initially impeded his devotion to Yahweh. How would an overabundance not impede his honor of Yahweh that much more? Both of these problems emerge, however, due to the misguided notion of reading poetry simply at its literal surface expression. Conversely, a literary-semiotic analysis discerns beyond the surface of poetry its metaphoric quality and its labyrinthine significations. Such poetic sensitivity hones the ability to intuit such indirect language associated with agricultural prosperity as a poetic metaphor for the prosperous wealth of Wisdom. As the 'son' reorients himself to his duty and 'honors'

---

of the land' as well as his ability to distribute this bounty for the benefit of all his subjects. Frankfort, *Kingship and the Gods*, pp. 34–36.

64. Whybray, *Proverbs*, p. 63; see also Murphy, *Proverbs*, p. 21.

Yahweh, he embraces Wisdom and its concomitant benefits of inner contentment, insight, honor and life (3.13-18).

The final command of this poem in v. 11 mentions no rewards, only Yahweh's educative discipline (מוסר) and reproof (תוכחת).[65] This (com)(de)mand echoes that in 1.8. 'Listen to the discipline of your father' (1.8) and 'do not reject the discipline of Yahweh' (3.11) simultaneously imply 'Yeah Solomon, don't be a fool' because we all know that fools despise wisdom and discipline (1.7). Although the poet strictly associates מוסר with the 'father', now explicitly identified as Yahweh, תורה is common to both mother and father (1.8; 4.2). The discipline (מוסר) and reproof (תוכחת) of Yahweh becomes an attempt to reorient the 'son', who, by implication, has already rebuffed Wisdom's reproofs (תוכחת, 1.23, 25, 30).[66] The lexeme מאס ('to reject') puns the obscure אסם in the previous verse to reiterate the storehouse as a symbol of Solomon's wealth. While the poet's appeal to the 'son' might seem to imply 'rewards-righteousness', the acceptance of Yahweh's discipline defies any quantification. Accepting divine censure garners no material rewards, for it is itself the reward.

The poet bases his metaphor of Yahweh as a father reproving his son upon the simile of a human father disciplining his son out of love. This analogy further confirms the previously asserted hypothesis of the 'father' as Yahweh and the 'son' as Solomon at the beginning of this chapter. The clause in v. 12 recalls the close relationship between Yahweh and the Davidic king. Like any responsible and loving father, Yahweh reproves (יכח) his 'son' when he does wrong (2 Sam. 7.14). The king enjoys no immunity from Yahweh's discipline, especially if he abandons the תורה (Ps. 89.27–32). Whybray (mis)reads this metaphor in 3.11–12 when he concludes that 'the Lord's discipline and reproof are not seen as punishment for disobedience, but as meted out simply for the good of the recipient'.[67] He disregards the semantic implications of יכח, which, as a legal term, denotes an ability to argue one's case so convincingly as to win.[68] Thus, Yahweh's reproof of the 'son' indeed stands justified because Solomon has abandoned תורה and deserves Yahweh's reproof.

---

65. Scott (*Proverbs. Ecclesiastes*, p. 47) claims that this fourth admonition is a necessary corrective to the mistakenly derived principle 'that prosperity will always accompany piety'. Whybray (*Proverbs*, p. 64) echoes Scott's claim with the observation that experience does not always bear out the traditional view that the righteous shall be rewarded.

66. Ultimately, the interchangeableness of the paradigmatic lexemes תורה, מוסר and תוכחת, all of which converge in Prov. 6.23, defy any gender exclusivity in their relation to either 'father' or 'mother' in Prov. 1–9.

67. Whybray (*Proverbs*, p. 64) bases his conclusion on similar 'discipline' passages in Proverbs (19.18; 23.13; 29.17) that do not suggest the child as having done anything deserving of punishment. But this reading falters since Solomon has acted disobediently, for which he incurs the discipline of Yahweh.

68. In one example, Job imitates Eliphaz by throwing his language back at him, strenuously contending that he could successfully win his case against Yahweh were he to take the Deity to court (יכח, 22.4; 23.7). For the connotation of יכח and its cognates, see James M. Kennedy, 'The Structural Semantic Analysis of Selected Biblical Hebrew Words for Punishment/Discipline' (PhD dissertation, Drew University, 1986), pp. 164–96.

Far more disturbing about Whybray's poetic inacuity, however, is the warped implication from his (mis)reading of this analogy. What kind of a father would discipline a child when that child has not acted disobediently?[69] Only an abusive father would discipline a child, even if educative in intent, when that child has not disobeyed. But our semiotic analyses of this poem have revealed Yahweh's disciplinary reproof of Solomon as justified. Yet for all the discipline, Yahweh never withdraws steadfast love from the 'son'. The divine discipline is beneficent. But if Solomon spurns Yahweh's disciplinary reproof, he signs his own death certificate (Prov. 6.23).

Summary

So what exactly is the nature of Yahweh's educational discipline that the poet enjoins upon the 'son'? What do the textual signs signify as Yahweh's reproof that Solomon should willingly embrace?[70] Semiotic analyses of the indirect language in these poems found in Prov. 1.8–19 and 3.1–12 invite the reader's intuition of the nature of Yahweh's discipline as that of תורה. The paradigmatic relationship of מוסר, תוכחת and תורה as well as the poetic injunction for the 'son' to embrace instructioñ (תורה, 3.1) bolster this intuitive hypothesis. Therefore, the lexeme תורה signifies more than just the Torah.

Semiotic analysis discerns a poetic metaphor of socio-economic injustice within Prov. 1.8–19. By depicting the 'son' and his political advisors murderously plotting to bleed the innocent dry of their material wealth via the religious dictum of idolatry, this poem's graphic imagery picturesquely illuminates those concrete details pertaining to Solomon's inability to reign with justice, righteousness and equity in the intertext 1 Kings 1–11. With every political move to amass wealth, horses, chariots and numerous foreign women, Solomon demonstrates his 'wisdom' to be that of royal ideology rather than that of Torah. Solomon flouts his proscribed duty in a tyrannous reign of oppressive taxation and the dreaded corvée for his own self-aggrandizement. As one 'wise in his own sight', Solomon unwittingly exchanges טוב for רע, justice for injustice and wisdom for wealth.

The poem in Prov. 3.1–12 attempts to reorient this disoriented 'son' to his duty to תורה, which itself functions as a medium for the divine (and poetic) censure of this royal fool. This poetic chastisement of Solomon functions as a medium of Yahweh's discipline. Only a fool would continually subject himself to such satiric critique when he could take the divine reproof and shape his conduct accordingly.

---

69. The example of Job immediately comes to mind. But such an example proves to be the exception rather than the rule. Only Job's friends, whom Yahweh rebukes in the end, identified Job's unnecessary suffering as Yahweh's reproof of him.

70. For the sake of clarity, the continual interchange between 'son' and Solomon throughout this study does not intend to confuse. Neither does this association, and here I hasten to re-emphasize the point, assume any referential claim on my part. Instead, this semiotic identification explicitly unstated at the text's surface level of expression only intends to keep the subjacent allusion to Solomon ever-present before the reader by the designation 'son'.

Due to their instructional nature, these poems in Proverbs 1–9 constitute a surrogate תורה and the poet a surrogate father like Moses to Israel. Therefore, we may conclude that the sign תורה conveys a dual signification: (1) the Torah narrative of Genesis-Deuteronomy and (2) the torah poetry of Proverbs 1–9.

Chapter 5

THE (IN)DISCRETIONS OF SOLOMON

Things sweet to taste prove in digestion sour.

(Shakespeare)

Enticingly (e)(pro)vocative, nothing (ex)(in)cites and captivates (the imagination) like sex. Sex sells, as the advertising slogan goes. But like a double-edged sword, sex also fells, and none have fallen harder than the mighty. Many careers of promi-nent, political leaders have met with an untimely demise because of certain sexual indiscretions, and, in some instances, because of the mighty pen of the critic. This chapter focuses its attention upon Solomon's numerous sexual (in)discretions, the second point of critique against this 'wise' king, by illumining the high irony of the poetic material in Proverbs 5 and 7, which reads differently than prior material in that the spotlight primarily shifts away from the 'son'. Admittedly, the intertextual data between these chapters and Solomon à la 1 Kings 1–11 are not as strong. But the sharp irony in these chapters, their associative chain of lexemes interconnected within a semiotic web, and the prologue's cue, nevertheless, establishes a relation to Solomon that affirms the 'satire' interpretant. Therefore, the first part (5.1–23) of this chapter analyzes the poetic description of an erotic conte(x)(s)t within which to advise the 'son' against sexual relations with (an)Other Wom(a)(e)n (אשה זרה). As the second part of this chapter (7.1-27) (re-)emphasizes vis-à-vis an explicitly graphic vignette, Solomon should instead pursue and 'enjoy' Woman Wisdom since illicit relations with the אשה זרה only conceive death.

Eroticism and Proverbs 5: Fatal Attraction for Bitter Honey

The parental instruction in this chapter divides into four sections (vv. 1-6, 7–14, 15–19, 20–23)[1] with various word repetitions providing it its unified coherence – for example, 'my son' (vv. 1, 7, 20); 'to incline the ear' (vv. 1, 13); 'strange/other woman' (vv. 3, 10, 17, 20); 'outcome/fate' (vv. 4, 11); 'to take hold of' (vv. 5, 22). This poem's dominant and central imagery contrasts the Other Woman (vv. 1–14) with the right woman (vv. 15–19). But the Other Woman is no stranger. As the second of four warnings against the אשה זרה (2.16–19; 5.1–14; 6.20–35; 7.1–27), this poem develops in detail the seductive threats of the Other Woman, upon which

---

1. According to Clifford (*Proverbs*, p. 69 n. 4), 'my son' (vv. 1, 7, 15 [implicitly], 20) naturally divides these four sections. The imperative of v. 15 links it with vv. 1, 7 and 20.

the last two warnings further elaborate. Emphasis of this theme, however, does not surprise given Solomon's addiction to the נכריה (1 Kgs 11.1, 8).

With language highly reminiscent of 2.1-2, the father describes his instruction in uniquely personal terms such as '*my* wisdom' and '*my* understanding' (v. 1).[2] As a result, some commentators emend the text by deleting the possessive pronoun.[3] But 2.2 and similar verses identify 'wisdom' and 'understanding' with the 'words' and 'commandments' of the father. Textual emendation, therefore, stands unwarranted, as other reasons shall later reveal.

The poet advises the 'son' to guard knowledge with his lips (v. 2), which, according to Clifford, rings nonsensical. Convinced that elsewhere in Proverbs, the heart, not the lips, keeps and guards knowledge, Clifford proposes to emend the text, which, unfortunately, totally eclipses the poetic contrast between the 'lips' of the 'son' and those of the אשה זרה.[4] How ironic that the one from whose lips freely dripped three thousand proverbs, one thousand and five songs, and an almost ency-clopedic breviary of natural and animal life should exercise a discretionary tight-lippedness about his knowledge! But Solomon's speech (and actions) belies wisdom as he parlayed that divine gift into an occasion for intellectual grandstanding before visiting dignitaries. Thus discretion becomes the better part of Solomon's valor for, as he guards knowledge, knowledge and discretion shall, in turn, guard him (2.10–12; cf. 4.5–9).

Although the poet associates various attributes with wisdom, we must not mistakenly identify those attributes as different personifications. Rather, as Gale Yee astutely observes, Knowledge, Discretion and Understanding 'form a poetic cluster that points to one figure, namely Wisdom'.[5] Likewise, the poet uses a variety of paradigmatic lexemes to convey a cluster of descriptions for the contrastive figure Folly.[6] Equally significant for my purposes, the lexical parallelism of אשה זרה with נכריה in three texts (2.16; 5.20; 7.5) forms an associative chain rendering אשה זרה as a paradigmatic code. With each mention, this code epitomizes the high irony of this poetry by simultaneously correlating the son's (potential) *affaire d'amour* with the אשה זרה to Solomon's (in)discretions with the נכריה (Other Wom(a)(e)n) within a semiotic subtext.

Despite the divergent conclusions of Yee and Camp, the climax of Proverbs 1–9 suggests that Woman Folly, not the אשה זרה, rivals Woman Wisdom (9.1–18), while the Other Wom(a)(e)n (אשה זרה), symbolized by Folly, functions as the

---

2.   Nowhere else does the father refer to 'my' wisdom, though he earlier claimed to teach his son 'in the way of wisdom' (4.11) (Whybray, *Composition*, p. 23).

3.   See Toy, *Proverbs*, p. 101.

4.   Clifford suggests the deletion of שפתיך as 'the most economical solution to the textual problem'. Thus v. 1 'probably urged the learner to heed the words of the father, and v. 2 to memorize them in the heart' (*Proverbs*, p. 67).

5.   Gale A. Yee, ' "I Have Perfumed My Bed with Myrrh": The Foreign Woman ('*iššā zārâ*) in Proverbs 1–9', in Athalya Brenner (ed.), *A Feminist Companion to Wisdom Literature* (FCB, 9; Sheffield: Sheffield Academic Press, 1995), pp. 110–26 (112).

6.   For example, נכריה (2.16; 5.10, 20; 6.24; 7.5); אשה זרה (2.16; 5.3, 20; 7.5); אשת רע (6.24) and אשת כסילות (9.13).

negative antithesis to the wife, personified by Wisdom.[7] Semiotically, therefore, the descriptors of vv. 1–3 signify and foreshadow their interpretant made more explicit in the climactic ch. 9.

In a metaphorical sense, the father urges devotion to Wisdom within vv. 1–2. From a preceding instruction (4.1–4), the father models the same pedagogical tradition by passing on to his son what his own father passed on to him. The (grand)-father's speech employs bridal imagery with its language of love and marriage.

> Get wisdom; get insight.
> Do not forsake her, and she will keep you;
> love her, and she will guard you (vv. 5–6).

The bridal imagery highlights an appeal to the 'son' to embrace Wisdom (4.8) as a bride and as a lover.[8] The poetry in 4.5–9 juxtaposes its economic code with an erotic code. Wisdom is to be 'found' (מצא, 3.13; 8.17, 35) much as one 'finds' a good wife (18.22; 31.10).[9] Moreover, an easily overlooked, yet noteworthy, poetic image is that of Wisdom as the daughter of Yahweh. From infancy through childhood, the young girl Wisdom was the apple of her father's eye (8.22–31). Now Wisdom has come of age, as has Folly, both of whom ultimately become rival lovers of the 'son' in an erotic conte(x)(s)t. Solomon's betrayal of the most precious gift of the 'father' prompts the paternal counsel for the 'son' to channel his erotic affections appropriately.

Fatal attraction to the Other Wom(a)(e)n provides the motive for parental instruction. From the length and intensity of the attack upon her, she clearly figures as the father's chief pedagogical antagonist as she misleads the naive 'son' with her instruction (לקח), a term of reference for the father's instruction as well (4.2). In contrast to the cautionary advice to the 'son', the 'lips' of the Other Woman ooze sweet words (5.3). Elsewhere, the poet describes her thus: 'a smooth tongue' (6.24), 'smooth words' (7.5) and 'smooth lips' (7.21). Although a real smooth-talker, her

---

7.   See Yee, ' "I Have Perfumed My Bed with Myrrh" ', p. 112, and Camp, *Wisdom and the Feminine*, pp. 115–17, respectively. Against Yee and Camp, see Newsom, 'Woman and the Discourse of Patriarchal Wisdom', p. 155, and Arndt Meinhold whose allegorical reading of Proverbs 5 views the 'fremde Frau…als Symbol für die Torheit…, den die Weisheit gegenüber steht' and the love for one's own wife as an analogy (*Vergleich*) to the proper relationship to Wisdom (*Die Sprüche*, I [ZBK, 16; Zürich: Theologischer Verlag, 1991], p. 101). Scholars have regarded the identity of the אשה זרה variously: a foreign harlot, a foreign devotee of a foreign god, a foreign goddess, a social outsider, a native prostitute or Other (for a brief summary, see Lang, *Die Weisheitliche Lehrrede*, pp. 87–99, and Fox, *Proverbs 1–9* [AB, 18a; New York: Doubleday, 2000], pp. 134–41, 252–62). Nevertheless, her poetic role logically identifies her as another man's wife. She also functions as a type-figure for any adulterous woman. Although a minority view, my position evolved quite independently of that by Fox.

8.   On the bridal imagery, see Camp who notes that חבק ('to embrace') in the piel form always refers to an erotic embrace when applied to a man and a woman (Song 2.6; 8.3; Prov. 5.20). *Wisdom and the Feminine*, pp. 93–94, 100.

9.   The poet emphasizes this point via the literary device of antanaclasis when Wisdom claims, 'Whoever finds (מצא) me finds (מצא) life' (8.35). See Roland E. Murphy, 'Wisdom and Eros in Proverbs 1–9', *CBQ* 50 (1988), pp. 600–603 (601); also, A.R. Ceresko, 'The Function of *Antanaclasis* in Hebrew Poetry, Especially in the Book of Qoheleth', *CBQ* 44 (1982), pp. 551–69.

speech alone does not seduce; her beauty captures the eye of its beholder (6.25). Her batting eyelashes hook while the seductive charms of her speech draw her victim in with the almost irresistible prospects of mystery, excitement and delight.[10] Smooth and deceptive, her speech proves fatal. But perhaps the most fatal danger that the insidious nature of this *femme fatale* poses is that she couches her seductive speech in words similar to those Wisdom herself addresses to the 'son'.[11] Necessity for discernment by the 'son' grows more urgent since beauty and seductive speech form a deceptively deadly duo.

The poet repeatedly intertwines speech and sexuality with the closest association appearing in the most explicitly erotic descriptions 'her lips drip with honey' and 'her mouth is smoother than oil' (v. 3).[12] This erotic imagery echoes Song of Songs 4.11 where the lover proclaims to his beloved, 'Your lips drip honey, my bride'. This expression, however, connotes kisses rather than just mere words (cf. Song 7.9). In fact, the 'interverset progression' inward from lips to palate remind of tongued kisses. Alter notes, 'The honey and oil at the beginning [of chapter 5] refer metaphorically to beguiling speech and metonymically to luscious kisses'.[13] The same imagery also applies to Wisdom (24.13–14a; 8.6–8). Yet even though both the lips of Wisdom and the אשה זרה drip honey, only honey from the latter leaves a bitter taste.

The latent eroticism grows more sexually explicit in the double entendre 'lips' (שׂפה, v. 3). A growing knowledge of cognate languages such as Ugaritic and Akkadian help to reveal hidden puns in Hebrew poetry. The following Akkadian text brings out the double meaning of 'lips'.

> May my lips be lallaru-honey,
> may my hands be all charm,
> may the *lips of my pudenda* be lips of honey.[14]

Obviously the female body contains more than one pair of lips. The eroticism persists at the semiotic level with the pun of חק ('lap') upon חך ('palate'), the force of which becomes more apparent later (cf. v. 20). The pun of 'lap', a euphemism for the pudenda, suggests the 'palate' 'as an adumbration by way of analogy of the other orifice where oil-smoothness will turn into a double-edged sword'.[15] Ordinarily, the 'lips' naturally guard the orifice from any penetrative force, but not so with the Other Woman. Given Solomon's addiction to the נכריה, no other advice could be more apropos for this womanizing monarch with one thousand Other Women in his harem who could gratify his sexual desires when the mood struck. Indeed, Solomon 'knows' and 'discerns' the ways of eros (with [the] Other Wom(a)(e)n), as the Song of Songs, traditionally attributed to Solomon, graphically attests.

---

10. McKane (*Proverbs*, p. 314) attributes the seductiveness of her speech in part to her foreign accent.

11. The next chapter shall closely compare/contrast the words and demeanor of Woman Wisdom with the *femme fatale* a.k.a. Woman Folly.

12. See Newsom, 'Woman and the Discourse of Patriarchal Wisdom', p. 153.

13. Alter, *Art of Biblical Poetry*, pp. 181–82.

14. As cited in Watson, *Classical Hebrew Poetry*, p. 247; original italics.

15. Alter, *Art of Biblical Poetry*, p. 182.

The smooth demeanor of the אשה זרה exudes a sensuality that both captivates the imagination and elicits desire. She knows how to get what she wants; and what she wants she gets initially by word ('smoothtalking'). Yet, her 'lip-action' only engenders a destructive rather than a constructive life-course for both her and her partner(s).[16] Sweet to eat, cunnilingus with the אשה זרה leaves a metaphorically bitter aftertaste described by two similes: (1) 'bitter as wormwood' and (2) 'sharp as a double-edged sword'. The first simile works on the basis of wormwood (*Artemisia*), a Palestinian plant-like shrub with a bitter taste, hence the connotation of the Other Woman as a deceiver who ends up something other ('bitter') than what she passes herself off as ('sweet'). The lexeme מרה ('bitter') also signifies the rebellious or obstinate nature of this poetic persona, for whom the poet holds no hope for rehabilitation. Thus the poet addresses the 'son' whose life-orientation conversely can change.

The second simile 'sharp as a double-edged sword' (v. 4) echoes the symbolic 'mouth' imagery in v. 3 on the basis of the implied literal rendering 'lipped-sword'. The אשה זרה poses a danger in that 'behind that reassuring smoothness, that visible absence of the phallus, there lurks something "sharp as a two-edged sword"'. Furthermore, 'the fantasy is that she not only possesses a hidden super potency but that it is a castrating potency as well'.[17] But Newsom's observation has more to commend than her pejorative label 'fantasy' implicitly disavows.[18] This *femme fatale* reveals her symbolically castrating potency through her seductive charms. After all, the 'lips' of a sword eat people (cf. Isa. 1.20). Therefore, we may construe vv. 3–4 as the answer to its own riddle: What is sweeter than honey, smoother than oil, bitter as wormwood, sharp as a sword?[19]

All speech aside, the Other Woman and the 'criminals' (חטאים) share much in common. In addition to enticing with their lips, both share the same fate as a result of their treachery. The poet's description of the אשה זרה in terms of her sole

---

16. Whybray ignores the ambiguity of the feminine suffix ending, unequivocally claiming that '"the end" is not the fate of the woman but of the young man' (*Proverbs*, p. 85).

17. In patriarchal thought woman's lack of a phallus and the privilege the male associated with the phallus grounded feminine inferiority. Newsom, 'Woman and the Discourse of Patriarchal Wisdom', p. 153.

18. Unfortunately, feminist readings of Prov. 1–9 tend toward broad sweeping generalizations. These ideological critiques decrying misogynist biases conveniently overlook the textual signs of two distinctly contrasted female types. Surely feminists would not maintain that all women reflect the same ideal; some women are actually sexually promiscuous and that has nothing to do with misogyny. In a similar, yet independent, critique, Fox concludes that the Strange Woman 'represents the class of women who behave like her... And, contrary to what Camp seems to believe, some do'. A married feminist would find nothing savory about (an)Other Woman committing adultery with her mate. For any (wo)man, another spouse other than one's own is, in a sense, considered '(an)other' ('Every wife is an *'išša zārâ* to all men but her husband'), but certainly not 'strange' (Fox, *Proverbs 1–9*, pp. 261 and 140, respectively). Thus Fox's descriptor for the אשה זרה (Strange Woman) should be consistent with his view of her identity. Therefore, the characterization of the Other Woman in Prov. 1–9 is less an instance of misogyny and more the poetic counterpart to harmonious marital relations.

19. See Alter, *Art of Biblical Poetry*, p. 180.

capacity to speak and to walk – that is, as all 'lips' (vv. 3–4) and 'feet' (vv. 5–6) – leaves the graphic ideation of a walking vagina. As smooth and deceptive as is her speech, her lifestyle proves equally deceptive. Amidst whispers and mannerisms of sweet love, the Other Woman only provides a roll in the hay for she can offer nothing more substantive, say (a) life, because with her every step she descends deeper into the abode of the dead. The heaviness of her anklets (צעדה), a subjacent pun alluding to the royal harem, around her feet weighing her down connotatively accounts for that 'sinking' feeling. While a literal rendering of colon B in v. 5 ('her steps grasp Sheol') may not semantically parallel colon A, it does reflect an apt meta-phoric descriptor for the lifestyle of the אשה זרה. Unknown to her, her insidious activity recoils upon herself just as with the 'criminals'. Ironically, the imagery of vv. 4–6 reverses the devouring role of the feminine (ק)(ך)ח in that 'the woman who wishes to control the youth is not the one actually in control of events; her words and actions have consequences of which she is unaware'.[20] Just as the Other Woman would have drawn men deeper into her, thus swallowing them up, so Sheol analogously draws her deeper into it with her promiscuity, thus swallowing her up.

The poet sharpens the contrast on the imagery of death and the path to Sheol with its binary opposite 'the path of life' (v. 6). Nonetheless, the 'son' cannot reach 'the path of life' through any erotic encounter with the אשה זרה. The grammatical ambiguity with the verbs תפלס ('she/you observe') and לא תדע ('she/you do not know') allow for both readings of a continuation of the description of the 'steps' of the Other Woman (v. 5) and/or a direct warning to the 'son' about the wandering ways of the Other Woman.[21] Poetic signs cue us to imagine the untoward orienta-tions of both the אשה זרה and the 'son' as so routine to warrant the mundane description of a 'rut' (מעגלה). Such ruts leave a distinct weaving (נוע) pattern much like that of drunkards who stagger due to their inebriated state (נוע, cf. Isa. 28.7; 29.9). The 'son' and the Other Wom(a)(e)n stagger(s), too, but their intoxication results from the lightheaded euphoria of their sexual (in)discretions rather than from strong drink. What knowledge the אשה זרה possesses ultimately proves false because she lacks any cognizance of her unstable lifestyle or of the ramifications of her words and actions. The choice before Solomon clearly begins to emerge more explicitly as one either of life or death. Wisdom symbolizes life, whereas Folly vis-à-vis the אשה זרה symbolizes death. By embracing Wisdom, Solomon escapes the אשה זרה in favor of (the good) life; conversely, by embracing the אשה זרה, Solo-mon betrays Wisdom in favor of death.

The direct address of the parental admonition resumes in v. 7, but with the plural form בנים ('children', 4.1; 7.24; 8.32) rather than the customary singular form בני ('my son').[22] This anomalous plural remains at odds with the singular forms else-where throughout the poem. Most interpreters explain the plural as originally an

20. Clifford, *Proverbs*, p. 70.
21. See Murphy, *Proverbs*, p. 32.
22. Prov. 7.24 and 8.32 reprise verbatim the first colon within Prov. 5.7 (ועתה בנים שמעו־לי 'Now listen to me children'). Moreover, the second colon of 4.1 merges with that in 5.7 to form the syntagm והקשיבו לאמרי־פי ('pay attention to my words') in the second colon of 7.24.

enclitic *mem* erroneously read as a plural.[23] The enclitic *mem*, an archaism that poetic language tends to use more so than prose, conveys a 'venerable and authentic quality'.[24] But whether read as a plural or not, the surface level of expression by no means demurs the subjacent allusion to Solomon within בנים.

In v. 8 the poet particularizes his audience and continues the warning that began in v. 3. The fatherly advice to the 'son' ('keep your way far from her') implies a vivid contrast between keeping the father's instruction close (v. 7b) while keeping the אשה זרה far off at a distance. In doing so, the 'son' avoids any direct exposure to her seductive wiles. But the closer the 'son' draws near (קרב) to the אשה זרה, he 'comes' into the empty grave (קבר) of death, underscored by the pun of קרב upon קבר. This forbidden fruit, pleasing to the eye, deceptively kills. The syntagm 'entrance (פתח) to her house' portends the ominous fate with her.[25] Yet this syntagm, a double entendre, also reasserts the erotic code with its sexual overtones. This sexual connotation for the vaginal opening gains emphasis with the embedded lexeme פת ('female pudenda'). Moreover, the pun of פתה ('seduce', cf. 1.10) upon פתח subjacently alludes to Solomon's sexual (in)discretions, which ultimately render him no better than a naive youth susceptible to the meretricious charms of (the) Other Wom(a)(e)n. Such semiotic insights stress the ideative role reversal that, unlike most women whose womb would naturally function to reproduce life, the (dys)functional womb of the אשה זרה only breeds barrenness in its cavity of death.

In vv. 9–11 the focal subject shifts away from the Other Woman to the deleterious effects of sexual relations with her, graphically depicted in terms of depletion. If the 'son' refuses to listen, he risks the loss of power (v. 9a), years (v. 9b), wealth (v. 10a) and the fruit of hard-earned labor (v. 10b). Sexual intercourse with the אשה זרה precisely conceives a loss of dignity for the 'son'.

An erotic liaison with the אשה זרה drains away both the power (הוד) and the best years of the 'son'. The lexeme הוד generally denotes 'splendor' or 'majesty' but, by extension, connotes 'power' and 'vigor'. And it is the power and vigor of the 'son' that (the) Other Wom(a)(e)n siphons off to (t)he(i)r own kind, the Others.[26] The poet never explicitly defines the 'strangers' (זרים) and the 'foreigners' (נכרי), but, as some scholars suggest, perhaps has in mind for the 'cruel' one (אכזרי) an outraged husband.[27] But what exactly constitutes the 'power' and 'vigor' of the king? Of course, the mythic symbolism of royalty regarded the king's sexual potency as a metaphorical symbol of his power and vigor. Yet how to make sense of this symbol alone vis-à-vis the community of foreign males proves most difficult.

---

23. Cf. Whybray (*Proverbs*, p. 87) who regards the verse as a gloss. See also Clifford, *Proverbs*, p. 67.

24. Watson, *Classical Hebrew Poetry*, pp. 38, 46–49.

25. See this phrase also in 2.18; 7.8, 11; 9.14.

26. Newsom comments on this social element, which overwrites 'an obvious element of psychosexual fantasy', of depletion: 'The others/the merciless/the strangers/the foreigner who are the devourers here are all masculine nouns and imply the community of males to whom the woman belongs' ('Woman and the Discourse of Patriarchal Wisdom', p. 154).

27. See Murphy, *Proverbs*, p. 32.

Another symbol for royal power surfaces in the lexeme כֹּחַ (v. 10), which, though denoting 'strength' and 'power', extensively connotes wealth. The lexical parallelism of כֹּחַ to עֶצֶב ('labor') reinforces the connotation. Solomon's wealth, however, derived not from *his* hard-earned labor, but rather from that of his subjects. Moreover, the embedded sememe 'idol' within עֶצֶב subjacently recalls the religious dictum whereby Solomon procured his wealth. But now through his manly vigor with the אִשָּׁה זָרָה, a paradigmatic code for all Solomon's foreign wives, the satiety of Solomon's house becomes that of the foreigner's house via large dowries and outlandish expenditures. Solomon's numerous exogamous relationships introduce insalutary influences (e.g. idols), which only precipitate his downfall. 'Exogamy becomes deplorable because it results in the alienation of wealth'.[28] Erotic trysts with (the) Other Wom(a)(e)n leave Solomon completely spent.

Others, total strangers, now reap the benefit from Solomon's profits. His naiveté and (in)discretions unwittingly conspire with the Others who, in all effects, unobtrusively fleece him without a second thought to the consequences. Wasted away to practically nothing, a physically and economically drained Solomon can only groan (הנם, v. 11) over his predicament. The phonemic contiguity of הנם ('regret') to הנם underscores his fate as one deserving of only pity. Now the 'son' has only regret as his constant and intimate companion. Solomon's end (אחרית), whether that of life or that of an affair matters not, echoes that of the אִשָּׁה זָרָה (v. 4) in that it, too, becomes a bitter pill difficult to swallow. As Solomon entertains illicitous relations with the אִשָּׁה זָרָה, his life can only ebb further away into the abode of the dead. Only later can he discern the true nature of the אִשָּׁה זָרָה as a seducer, a deceiver, a manipulator, a user and, himself, a fool. Unfortunately for Solomon, by the time that he comes to his (cognitive) senses and arrives at such an insight, it will be too late.

From a state of depletion, the 'son', in an *imagined* soliloquy, expresses the rueful admission of his failure over his exogamous sexual escapades (vv. 12–14), which flouted instruction (תּוֹרָה) to the contrary. Within this soliloquy, the poet places upon the lips of Solomon incriminations thus far only implied by the poet. Solomon's self-reproach, especially when juxtaposed with previous comments, admits of his own folly.

...fools despise (בוז)...discipline (מוּסָר) (1.7).

...

[fools] scorn (נאץ) reproof (תּוֹכַחַת) (1.30).

...

How I hated discipline (מוּסָר),
and I despised (נאץ) reproof (תּוֹכַחַת) (5.12).

This semiotic convergence, which accentuates the paradigmatic relationship between נאץ and בוז, discloses Solomon as the fool who had spurned discipline and reproof, in other words, Wisdom. In short, this soliloquy validates the poetic satire of Solomon as a fool.

The introspection of the 'son' only acknowledges himself to blame as *the* determinant factor engendering his downfall. The discipline and reproof that he spurned

28. Newsom, 'Woman and the Discourse of Patriarchal Wisdom', p. 154.

was that of the instruction of his teachers (מורה, v. 13). Such instruction would have included the Torah (תורה) given its lexical and phonemic contiguity to מורה. Solomon admits his folly of inattentiveness (לא־הטתי אזני 'did not incline my ear'), which harks back to the necessity of the father's urgent imperative (הט־אזנך 'incline your ear') in v. 1. But only in retrospect will he realize the deleterious ramifications of his folly. His poor judgment and immoral behavior result in a great loss of wealth, but also in great harm to his reputation within the community. The qualification 'almost' (כמעט, v. 14), however, may indicate only a temporary ostracism by 'the assembly and congregation' (most likely a hendiadys) who lets him off with a caution.[29] Nevertheless, Solomon's repudiation of Torah and numerous sexual liaisons with (the) Other Wom(a)(e)n will only leave him with a depleted state of wealth, power, resources and life.

By contrast, vv. 15–20 affirm appropriate sexual relations, which 'have a centripetal direction',[30] in an intriguing, if not arousing, manner. Within these verses, the poet constructs a metaphor for sexual relations by means of the erotic imagery of water contained and dispersed. The father urges the 'son' in v. 15 to 'Drink water (מים) from your own cistern (בור)/flowing water (נזלים) from your own well (באר)'. Such imagery echoes the metaphorically descriptive language in Song of Songs 4.12, 15 by the groom who cherishes his bride as an enclosed garden, 'a garden fountain, a well of living water (באר מים חיים), and flowing streams (נזלים) from Lebanon'.[31] That a cistern was usually privately owned further buttresses this metaphorical image of a woman as a spring satisfying sexual thirst. By infusing an erotic interpretant into 'water', the poet advises the 'son' to quench his sexual thirst in a genuine relationship with his wife rather than in illicit relations with (the) Other Wom(a)(e)n. By maintaining that genuine relationship, the 'son' neutralizes the seductive temptations of the אשה זרה.

The water imagery in v. 16 ('let your springs flow into the streets', MT) poses great difficulty for interpreters. Its apparent contradiction to the aim of v. 15, which restricts sexual relations to one's wife, has induced three major interpretations: (1) '(and so) your springs will flow…'; (2) 'Lest your springs overflow in public/like rivulets in the open streets'; and (3) 'Should your springs flow into the streets…?'[32] The first, and most unlikely, interpretation affirms that the husband, who has intercourse only with his wife, shall have numerous progeny. The second interpretation maintains that the wife, provoked by her husband's adultery, will commit adultery. The third, and most common if not most probable, interpretation rhetorically implies the husband's abstention from sexual intercourse with women other than his own wife. 'Springs' (מעין) and 'streams' symbolize the male semen spent outside the domestic sphere. But this same imagery, albeit in the singular, applies elsewhere to the woman (מעין, Song 4.12, 15). Therefore, this ambiguous imagery confirms the last two mutually reciprocal interpretations: if the 'son' reserves his 'springs' for

---

29. Whybray (*Proverbs*, p. 89) offers this explanation if only to take it back.
30. See Newsom, 'Woman and the Discourse of Patriarchal Wisdom', p. 154.
31. Yee, ' "I Have Perfumed My Bed with Myrrh" ', p. 118.
32. For a fuller explication of these arguments, see Clifford, *Proverbs*, pp. 67–68.

his wife alone, then he does not neglect his 'spring' who might otherwise seek comfort elsewhere.

The poet again uses the water image ('fountain', v. 18) for the woman now identified as 'the wife of your youth' (Song 2.17). Her uniqueness peers forth with her comparison to an animal, a quite conventional device in love poetry. In the Song of Songs the woman is called a dove (5.2) and the man a gazelle (2.9, 17). Nonetheless, according to Murphy, the poetic metaphors of 'a lovely hind' (אילה, v. 18; cf. Song 2.7; 3.5) and 'a graceful doe' (יעלה) 'symbolize womanly attractiveness and beauty'.[33] If the 'son' would 'rejoice in' (שׂמח) his wife, erotic language which in Song 1.4 compares to 'the physical pleasure of gastronomical excess',[34] then the attractions of (an)Other Wom(a)(e)n will disappear. The poet drives the point home with all of these erotic images by means of a linguistic chiasm.

> Let (your wife's) *breasts* fill you at all times
> In her love be seduced (*tišgeh*) always
> Why be seduced (*tišgeh*), my son, by a *zarâ*,
> and embrace the *bosom* of a *nokrîyâ*? (5.19b–20)[35]

The implied milk of the wife's breasts form the counterpart to the honey and oil dripping from the seductress's 'lips', itself a euphemism for the pudenda as alluded to by the framing pun חכך/חיק ('palate'/'bosom', vv. 3, 20). The conjugal well, which by contrast offers pure, running water that alone nurtures and never runs dry, becomes a source of blessing and fertility. Its enjoyment sates to the point of sexual inebriation, a connotation of שׁגה ('go astray'). Such a concrete reference to love play intimates 'that there is something nurturing in the delights of this conjugal love'.[36]

A teasing question arises, though: Just who is the wife of Solomon's youth? The answer lies within the sign חבק ('to embrace'), which, in its only other occurrence in Proverbs (4.8), signifies an erotic passion for Wisdom. Such comparative love language within this allegorical metaphor confirms that a love relationship with the wife, a symbol personified by Woman Wisdom, becomes the antidote against the enticements of the 'fremde Frau', a symbol personified by Woman Folly.[37] The 'son', however, has foolishly betrayed his 'wife' to pursue erotic affairs with her (poetic) antagonist, (an)Other Woman. Given the inimical consequences of such foolish (in)discretions, the poet's rhetorical question advances a lucid thought heretofore oblivious to the naive 'son', Why be seduced, my 'son', by a *zārâ* and embrace the bosom of a *nokrîyâ*?

As conclusion, vv. 21–23 summarize the entire poem of Proverbs 5. Why be enthralled with (an)Other Woman when it entails such great risk? Regardless of how clandestine Solomon's erotic encounters with (the) Other Wom(a)(e)n, they are not hidden from the eyes of Yahweh. Yahweh observes (פלס, v. 21) every person's way, unlike the אשׁה זרה who cannot even see (פלס, v. 6) her own path.

---

33. Murphy, *Proverbs*, p. 32.
34. See Clifford, *Proverbs*, p. 72.
35. Yee, '"I Have Perfumed My Bed with Myrrh"', pp. 118–19.
36. See Alter, *Art of Biblical Poetry*, p. 182.
37. Meinhold, *Die Sprüche*, p. 105.

One's misdeeds carry within them the seeds of their own consequences: for the אשה זרה, death; for the 'son', regret and, ultimately, death. As the footsteps of the Other Woman firmly take hold (תמך, v. 5) in Sheol, so misconduct with her firmly holds (תמך, v. 22) one within her grasp on the way to Sheol. Although sex with (an)Other Woman entices and intoxicates (שגה, v. 23), such (in)discretions ('sin', חטאת) only prove fatal for both partners entrapped by the power of seduction. Death only results where the 'son' lacks (self-)discipline (מוסר, v. 23). From a metaphorical perspective, Solomon must reconcile with his estranged wife Wisdom who alone can liberate him from his fatal attraction to (the) Other Wom(a)(e)n.

Eroticism and Proverbs 7: A Twilight Tryst at the House of Sheol

The poem in Proverbs 7 brings the four explicit warnings against the אשה זרה to a climax. Its first three verses form a tightly knit unit with the recurrence of שמר ('to guard', vv. 1a, 2a) and מצוה ('commandment', vv. 1b, 2a). The tone of the parental injunctions now shifts in emphasis from the necessity of an attentive posture to a defensive posture. Even the anagram (ק)שרם and pun of אמר on שמר (vv. 3–4) subtly urge the 'son' to be *en garde* for the sake of his own life.[38] In order to guard 'words' (אמר), commandments (מצוה) and instruction (תורה), the 'son' must devote his entire being to Torah vividly depicted in the imagery of v. 3 ('Bind them around your fingers/write them on the tablet of your heart'), which echoes the Deuteronomistic tradition (e.g. Deut. 6.6–9; 11.18), Prov. 3.3 and 6.21 respectively.[39]

> …tie them around your neck,
> write them upon the tablet of your heart.
> …
> Bind them upon your heart continually,
> tie them around your neck.

Furthermore, the simile of guarding the Torah like the 'pupil of the eye' (v. 2) builds upon the metaphor in Prov. 6.23 ('For the commandment (מצוה) is a lamp/and instruction (תורה) a light') to connote the Torah as a precious medium of illumination. Without such light, the monarch lacks the religio-ethical compass for his imperial duty.

Verses 4–5 alert to the ensuing erotic conte(x)(s)t as the father exhorts, 'Say to Wisdom, "You are my sister"'. The lexeme 'sister' occurs in Hebrew and ancient Near Eastern love poetry as an expression of love.[40] Although not explicitly bridal

---

38. The poet 'dramatizes the choice between life and death' with the imperative חיה ('to live', v. 2a) at the center of vv. 1–3 (Clifford, *Proverbs*, p. 87).

39. Verbs such as 'store', 'keep' and 'bind' underscore 'a tenacity of memory and unbroken concentration and attentiveness' while 'write them on the tablet of your heart' suggests 'an inward assimilation of the tradition…as a way of life'. See McKane, *Proverbs*, pp. 332–33.

40. The Song of Songs uses the term 'sister' as an exchange name for 'bride' (4.9–10, 12; 5.1–2; 8.8). In the Ugaritic Aqhat epic, the goddess Anat expresses her desire for the young man Aqhat as her lover when she states, 'you are my brother/and I [your sister]' (*ANET*, p. 152). See also Meinhold (*Die Sprüche*, p. 125) who argues 'sister' as a name for 'wife' since 'bride' represents a status of wife (Tob. 7.15).

language, the parallel lexeme מדע ('kinsman'), which occurs elsewhere only for Ruth's husband Boaz (Ruth 2.1; 3.2), does suggest an intimate confidant. Embracing Wisdom as an intimate companion and lover protects the 'son' from the אשה זרה. The right woman, Woman Wisdom, guards against (the) Other Wom(a)(e)n whose seductive charms and flatteries would otherwise prey upon the fatal attraction of the 'son'. Yet the 'son' must *declare* his love to Wisdom,[41] for in not doing so, silence and passivity typecast him as the naive, young lad in the subsequent vignette.

The vignette of vv. 6–23 is but one of seven contexts in the Hebrew Bible where the phrase בעד החלון or בחלון ('through the window') accompanies the particular type-scene of a figure at a window looking out.[42] Scholars naturally disagree over the exact identity of the figure in v. 6 even though most maintain the reading of the Septuagint and the Syriac, both of which switch the first person singular to the third person feminine singular to conform to the 'woman and the window' motif.[43] The ambiguous allusion to the 'woman and the window' type-scene within the Masoretic text indeed admits of the maternal presence with the father in this parental instruction while not exclusively identifying the speaker as the mother.

Equally important to this vignette is its setting. The lexeme בית ('house'), which occurs six times in this poem (vv. 6, 8, 11, 19, 20, 27), reveals the hotbed of activity within this scene. From within their house, both father and mother espy the deleterious results of a late-night sexual tryst with the נכריה/אשה זרה at her house. In this particular type-scene, sexual attraction or its potential frustration accompanies the use of deception by some character and the ominous threat of death lurking in the background.[44] These distinctive isotopies become increasingly self-evident as this drama unfolds.

At the window the poet peers out over the streets below to observe a group of young men milling about. But one young man catches the poet's watchful eye not because of any noticeable difference, for both he and his peers alike are no better than naive simpletons (פתאים). Openness to easy enticement epitomizes their

41. Wisdom reciprocates such ardor as she openly declares, 'I love those who love me' (8.17). Murphy, 'Wisdom and Eros', p. 602.

42. While the majority of these seven contexts reveal the type-scene as predominantly that of the 'woman and the window' (e.g. Josh. 2.15, 18, 21; Judg. 5.28; 1 Sam. 19.12; 2 Sam. 6.16; 2 Kgs 9.30, 32), the contexts of Gen. 26.8 and Prov. 7.6 defy such exclusive categorization.

43. The classical position identifies the figure as a woman, an alien devotee of the cult of a foreign goddess, most likely the Phoenician Astarte. Against this backdrop, John Barclay Burns ('Proverbs 7,6–27: Vignettes from the Cycle of Astarte and Adonis', *SJOT* 9 [1995], pp. 20–36) focuses on the portrait of the young man as a type of the Phoenician god Adonis and his relationship with the goddess Astarte. McKane (*Proverbs*, pp. 335–36) speculates upon the figure as Wisdom, portrayed as a queen, looking out of the window because of: (1) the narrative motif in the Old Testament of the queen looking through the window (Judg. 5.28; 2 Sam. 6.16; 2 Kgs 9.30) and (2) archaeological evidence of a window and lattice arrangement as an architectural feature of a royal palace.

44. Of the seven contexts with this type-scene, some involve explicit sexual attraction (Gen. 26.8; Prov. 7.6) whereas in others menacing circumstances frustrate a potential for sexual attraction (e.g. Josh. 2.15, 18, 21; Judg. 5.28; 1 Sam. 19.12; 2 Sam. 6.16; 2 Kgs 9.30, 32) (Robert H. O'Connell, 'Proverbs VII 16–17: A Case of Fatal Deception in a "Woman and the Window" Type-Scene', *VT* 41 [1991], pp. 235–41 [236]).

naiveté, and perhaps accounts for their close proximity to this 'red-light district'. Nonetheless, the poet fixes his gaze upon this young lad who lacks common sense (חסר לב), a descriptor with which the father previously typified the adulterer (6.32). No doubt this lad's character evaluation derives in retrospect from his foolish actions soon recounted. Such purposeful descriptors, though, suggest a subjacent association between this vignette's second primary character and Solomon. Through his actions, this young lad reflects to Solomon a mirror image of himself: a naive, court fool without a lick of common sense.

Despite his naiveté, this young lad's compulsiveness abandons any prior contentment with loitering. While he may lack (common) sense, he, unlike the others of his subculture, does not want for a keen sense of direction. With resolute gait, he traverses the street near her corner and ambles up a slightly ascending path toward 'her' house (v. 8).[45] How this young man knows the way (a well-worn path? local gossip? frequent visits?) or why he strolls to her house remains open to various hypotheses. Does a voyeuristic whim to glimpse the אשה זרה propel the sure steps of this naive, innocent lad who, in the end, winds up in the wrong place at the wrong time? Or does an unrestrained sexual passion for the נכריה drive this fully willing and knowing participant to engage in an erotic tryst such that he, in effect, belies his unsophisticated façade?

The young lad's action occurs within the darkness of night (v. 9). In fact, the poet's syntagmatic enjambment of paradigmatic lexemes – נשׁף ('twilight'), ערב יום ('evening time'), אישׁון ליל ה ('middle of night') and אפל ה ('deep darkness') – engages in a bit of overkill so that even the first-time reader could not misapprehend. The lexeme נשׁף calls to mind its anagram נפשׁ, which has as its narcotized sememes 'desire' and 'passion'. 'Night', the time of desire for the lover, appears prominently as a motif in erotic poetry (Song 3.1, 8; 5.2).[46] Normal people generally remain home in the darkness of night, but normal people are not in question in this scenario. The echo of אישׁון (vv. 2, 9) illumines the affinity between this lad and the 'son'. That this lad holds precious (אישׁון) the potential for sexual gratification under the dark cover(s) of night insinuates the sexual (in)discretions of Solomon, for whom the poet urges to regard Torah instead as precious (אישׁון). This poetic enjambment of paradigmatic lexemes then signifies more than just a time-marker: the ensuing sexual (in)discretion shuns the light of day. Thus, this young man out on a midnight stroll for some night-time action indeed repudiates his portrayal as a naive unsophisticate.

The drama gains in tempo as the third, and final, character, the אשׁה זרה, enters the scene from behind the dark shadows of night. She emerges for the quite specific

---

45. Note the Arabic connotation of צעד ('to step', 'to march') as an ascent to one's steps. Whybray's (*Proverbs*, p. 113) reading differs as he unequivocally concludes that 'her' (v. 8) anticipates the 'woman…dressed as a harlot' who, directly introduced in v. 10, cannot be the same as the 'loose woman' of v. 5. Yet the ambiguity of v. 10 mitigates against such an ironclad conclusion, easily allowing for the אשׁה זרה (v. 5) as the antecedent to both 'her' and the 'woman' (אשׁה, v. 10).

46. Clifford, *Proverbs*, p. 87.

intention of an encounter, not mere happenstance, with this young lad.[47] Moreover, the sememe 'to call' (קרא) elicits the ideation of an explicit summoning of this lad, perhaps even by name. Nevertheless, this midnight rendezvous unites more than two presumably, anonymous individuals; rather, two resolute purposes, driven by sexual passion, come to a climactic head.

With a rather prolix depiction of the style and demeanor of the אשה זרה (vv. 11–13), the poet unmistakably aligns her with the appearance of what is illicit and with concealment.[48] Her public debut, like her speech, proves deceptive in that she appears as a prostitute by donning the attire of the harlot. Even the lexeme נצר underscores her secretiveness, which extends deep beyond her attempt to mask her identity to a close guarding of the true intentions of her heart. But what exactly does she protect in the hidden chambers of her heart? Does she conceal an emotional (de)privation in a marriage far from blissful? Or does she simply desire to conceal her clandestine activit(y)(ies) from her husband?[49] She definitely has no plans of concealing her sexual desire for this young lad. And as she implements her designs upon him, her emergence with the night seems perfectly apropos since she becomes the living personification of dark night. Now, only the young lad remains 'in the dark'.

The comportment of the אשה זרה equally corresponds with her fashion-style, that is, loud and boisterous. The two descriptors 'boisterous' (המיה) and 'rebellious' (סררת) aptly epitomize her demeanor and reiterate her symbolic association with Woman Folly (cf. 9.13). Both of these participial adjectives bear the connotation of instability and inconstancy exemplified in her adulterous behavior and her lack of devotion to her family and her society.[50] A sexual encounter without the encumbrance of emotional strings attached could only entice this young lad that much more. But one wonders how she can hope to retain even the slightest modicum of anonymity, regardless of her attire, with such rebellious behavior? How can she honestly hope to keep her illicit, sexual relations a secret from her husband?

The poet's observation that the אשה זרה cannot stay at home certainly comes as no shock. Its mention recalls the differences and similarities between herself and Woman Wisdom. Both carry on in the streets crying out loudly (המיות, 1.20–21), but the similarities in demeanor end there. In stark contrast to the אשה זרה whose feet do not stay (שכן) at home, Wisdom does stay (שכן) at home (8.12). The infidelity of the אשה זרה disdains social convention; after all, respectable (and married) women do not loiter in the street late at night.

Not only can the אשה זרה not stay at home, she cannot even stay put long enough when outside the home. The restlessness in her movement that would

---

47. The usage of קרא, in contrast to קרה, generally does not connote a chance meeting. Although its occasional usage does suggest a chance meeting, the infinitive of purpose (לקראתו 'to meet him') in v. 10 clearly indicates an expected rendezvous.

48. Newsom, 'Woman and the Discourse of Patriarchal Wisdom', p. 156.

49. See Whybray, *Proverbs*, p. 114.

50. Her adulterous activity especially threatens the social structure by jeopardizing paternal and inheritance rights. For further discussion on the ramifications of her adulterous activity, see Camp, *Wisdom and the Feminine*, pp. 116–18, 256–82.

exhaust the typical mortal marks both her private and public affairs. With a shuffle of the feet, she is here, she is there, she is everywhere, or so it seems. Flitting about, one moment she canvasses the streets while the next moment she peddles her wares in the market square(s) (v. 12). Her boisterousness wastes no time, as this street-corner girl gets busy. Despite the appearance of an erratic meandering, her frenetic pace indeed has an aim in mind. The madness of her bus(y)(i)ness lacks no shortage of targets in her bus(i)(y)ness. One might even surmise that her unsuspecting prey come to her as she frequents every street corner where, patronized by potential clientele à la the young lad (פנה...אצל, vv. 8, 12), she soon finds a victim. The brief moment though that she does stay still, she does so only to 'lie in wait' (ארב), to set up as it were an 'ambush', a predatory quality shared in common with the חטאים ארב, 1.11, 18) and made explicit in vv. 22–23. Such method to her madness elicits the perception of her as a stalker. While the darkness of night might well veil her midnight rendezvous, it cannot suppress her reputation.

The juxtaposition of the description of the אשה זרה in these verses with the open, universal style of Wisdom's poem (Prov. 8), perhaps a précis of her oft-repeated invocations, provides the vivid contrast between these two figures. In addition to the aforementioned difference that the אשה זרה (unlike Wisdom) finds no solace at home, two other noticeable exceptions surface. First, and yet non-tangential, the אשה זרה conveniently stands 'beside' (אצל) every street corner for easy accessibility whereas Wisdom assumes a place close 'beside' (אצל) Yahweh (8.30). Although both women stand out in public loudly summoning passersby, they, nevertheless, view their roles in the town square much differently. For the אשה זרה, the street becomes the locus to invite sexual unrestraint; for Wisdom, the street becomes the locus to invite sexual restraint. Second, the *modus operandi* of Wisdom need not resort to ambush tactics. Rather, her confidence derives from the substance of her polished, rhetorical speeches. No doubt the stalking maneuvers of the אשה זרה make up for what her appeals lack in substance. By depicting Wisdom and the Other Woman with similar terminology, the father emphasizes that the greatest seduction to evil consists in inviting the foolish with similar words that summon one to good.[51]

With a bold forwardness uncharacteristic of proper decorum befitting modest women, the אשה זרה slinks out from behind the dark shadows with an aggressive, and almost brutal, greeting. Unable to contain herself any longer, this huntress on the prowl forcefully seizes her young paramour with a grip from which he would not easily extricate himself even if he wanted. She then brazenly 'kisses' (נשק, v. 13) the young lad while at the same moment unabashedly 'handling' (נשק) him, with care of course, in full view of all.[52] The impropriety of such a shameless display indeed requires brazenness. Her impudence graphically reveals the conse-quences for the 'son' turning a deaf ear to this parable: his silent passivity to seize Wisdom for his wife (3.18; 4.5; 5.15–20) can only result in his seizure by (the) Other

---

51. See Jean-Noël Aletti, 'Séduction et parole en Proverbes I–IX', *VT* 27 (1977), pp. 129–44 (133).

52. The graphic and phonemic contiguity of נשקה ('to burn') to נשקה ('to kiss') underscore the burning desire of the אשה זרה for this young lad.

Wom(a)(e)n whose interests are clearly self-indulgent. Next, she quite smoothly runs her lips to his ear to breathe an explicit, erotic proposition that would cause anyone else, but her, to blush. That the poet could not possibly have overheard such intimate dialogue from a window down the way might otherwise raise suspicions.[53] But the poet's interpretation naturally follows given her aggressive style and shameless comportment.

Initially, the midnight rendezvous begins with all talk comprised of obscure references and ambivalent symbols. Perhaps the most obscure reference is her mention of fulfilling obligatory vows concerning peace offerings. Her first words, which ostensibly do not fit the context, puzzle readers who have proffered a variety of interpretative responses. The first response understands her words ('I have offered sacrifices/today I have paid my vows', v. 14) to convey the intent to offer a sacrifice of well-being to Yahweh in fulfillment of a vow (cf. 2 Sam. 15.7).[54] But the youth would have understood 'Today I fulfill my vow' as an invitation to a feast with meat (from an animal killed in fulfillment of a vow) on the menu. The woman's frankness in disclosing her intentions (vv. 16–20), however, denies her invitation as simply that of sharing a communal meal.

A second response views her words as those of a foreign woman, who, worshipping her own divinity, participates in sacred prostitution associated with pagan cults.[55] She lures the young man into her lair for the sake of 'devotion' in order to fulfill her obligatory vows. Such a passing reference, though, seems to be a rather odd means of enticing the youth, and certainly does not easily fit the story. A corollary of this interpretative response uncritically assumes an Israelite woman engaging in cult prostitution. Yet the association of sexual intercourse, which renders one ritually impure by Israelite standards, with 'peace offerings', not to mention the untenable assumption of cult prostitution in Israel, seems incomprehensible in the light of Lev. 7.19–21.

The third, and perhaps equally inexplicit, response regards the אשה זרה as enjoying a bit of 'religious camouflage'.[56] Just in case the young paramour might develop a sudden attack of scruples, she passes herself off as a religious devotee thoroughly acculturated with cultic practices. Such a façade lends her some semblance of credibility (or so she thinks) so as to ease the mind of the young lad who might need to rationalize his sexual (mis)conduct. Religion often justifies some of the most unethical and immoral conduct. But we need not suddenly take her at her word just because her deceptive lips drip religious jargon. Rather, we see through her façade for the duplicitous and deceitful character that she is.

---

53. See Murphy, *Proverbs*, p. 43.

54. Or possibly a modal meaning, 'I am going to fulfill my vow' (Clifford, *Proverbs*, p. 88). Payment of a vow to the temple, argues Karel van der Toorn ('Female Prostitution in Payment of Vows in Ancient Israel', *JBL* 108 [1989], pp. 193–205 [198]), would offer strong motivation for this woman to dress as a harlot and sell herself.

55. The communal meal would not exhaust her cultic obligations. Rather, 'therefore' (v. 15) suggests that sexual intercourse 'constitutes the consummation of her cultic devotions' (McKane, *Proverbs*, p. 337; see also Scott, *Proverbs. Ecclesiastes*, p. 65).

56. Murphy, *Proverbs*, p. 44.

The אשה זרה speaks in the manner that a true spouse might to her husband. In Song 3.1–4 the lover seeks her beloved upon their bed and continues her search through the city streets until she finds him. Similarly, the אשה זרה says to her young paramour lacking in common sense, 'Therefore I came out to meet you/to seek your face, and I found you' (v. 15). Her word choice to describe her late-night encounter with the young lad echoes that of the poet (לקראת 'to meet', vv. 10, 15) and, along with her intentions, should surely dispel any lingering doubts of such a midnight rendezvous as mere happenstance.

Regardless of how the young lad may have construed these obscure words by the אשה זרה (v. 14), she has not yet slain her sacrifice. Clifford cites three pieces of evidence that metaphorically suggest the young lad himself as her sacrificial offering.[57] The first piece of evidence derives from the paralleled echo of the vow of the אשה זרה to that of Jephthah in Judges 11. Jephthah vowed (נדר) whatever came out (יצא) to meet (לקראת) him on his return home from the battlefield (vv. 30–31). Although lexical and thematic similarities exist between these two scenes, the subject ('what comes out') sacrificed differs. And lest we overlook it, the twice-repeated 'turn' of שלם (v. 14) in this vignette reminds of Solomon (שלמה),[58] most especially his sexual (in)discretions with (the) Other Wom(a)(e)n.

Her language enhances the sexual, yet deathly, attractiveness of her bed to the young lad.

> I have prepared my bed with coverings,
> colored linens from Egypt;
> I have sprinkled my bed with myrrh,
> lign-aloes, and cinnamon (vv. 16–17).

Each of the four items – colored linens, myrrh, lign-aloes and cinnamon – figure prominently as symbols of luxury and se(ns)(x)ual enjoyment. The syntagm חטבות אטון contains two hapax legomena in the Hebrew Bible. Nevertheless, context and comparative philology suggest their probable reference to 'colored linen', a luxury commodity exported by Egypt. Myrrh (מר), a fragrant gum-resin from a south Arabian or African balsam, and lign-aloes (אהלים), a spice from southeast Asian eaglewood, appear together in the Hebrew Bible as scents for clothing (Ps. 45.9) and the bed (Prov. 7.17). Myrrh was also used as incense (Song 3.6), as an ingredient in fragrant perfume sachets (Song 1.13) and, along with cinnamon (קנמון), a superior kind of southeast Asian cassia tree, in the fragrant sacred anointing oil (Exod. 30.23; 35.6). Perhaps more to the point, these aromatic spices signify the aphrodisiacal image of sexual love (Song 4.6, 14).[59]

The ambivalent symbolism of these items, the second piece of evidence for the youth as a sacrificial offering, yields ominous nuances. Linens and spices, capable of referring to death as well as to life, were also used in funerary rites. The New Testament attests to the usage of imported color linen as a burial cloth (Mt. 27.59;

---

57. Clifford, *Proverbs*, pp. 88–90.

58. Watson (*Classical Hebrew Poetry*, p. 239) adopts W.K. Wimsatt's designation 'turn' for wordplays involving the repetition of a root-word, or a kind of polysemy.

59. See O'Connell, 'Proverbs VII 16–17', pp. 237–38; Clifford, *Proverbs*, p. 89.

Mk 15.46) or as a binding (Jn 11.44a; 19.40; 20.5–6) and both myrrh and aloes as ingredients of a burial-spice mixture (Mk 16.1; Jn 19.39). Cognizant that such 'evidence' of burial customs obviously postdates Proverbs, O'Connell proffers the reasonable supposition that some such customs prevailed even during the time of Judah's monarchy.[60] But, claims Burns, O'Connell's observations fall shy of the all-too-obvious conclusion connoted by these ambivalent symbols. The bed (מִשְׁכָּב), not just simply the setting for a carnal tryst, connotes a burial-place (cf. Isa. 57.2; Ezek. 32.25) and graphically symbolizes the young lad's bier upon which he is destined to die.[61] With apt words, the seductress lures the foolish, unsuspecting young lad to her (death)bed-chamber where she has spared no expense in preparation for his burial (vv. 22–23).

The royal implications from the abundant usage of these spices by the אִשָּׁה זָרָה, however, subjacently allude to Solomon. Spices were most often prized and displayed as part of a king's treasury (2 Kgs 20.13), and also served as an appropriate present for a peace offering (Gen. 43.11) or simply to make a good impression. In fact, only kings and the wealthy could afford to purchase them in great quantities so as to use them lavishly (Song 3.6–7; Ps. 45.7–8) or expect them to be burnt at their funerals (Jer. 34.5).

Verbal foreplay quickly ceases as the אִשָּׁה זָרָה beckons the young lad 'inside': 'Come, let us drink our fill (רְוָה) of love (דֹּד) till morning/let us delight ourselves with love (אָהַב)!' (v. 18) Her invitation 'Come!' recalls the identical invitation by the 'criminals' (חַטָּאִים) in their speech (1.11). And the consequences of acquiescing to both invitations yield deadly results. Such purposive language declares her lustful desire in a euphemistic manner. Given the potential sememe 'breast' for דֹּד, the innuendo of the אִשָּׁה זָרָה ('let us drink our fill of love') virtually suggests that the young lad engorge himself on her breasts. Moreover, her erotic words, semiotic apples of gold indeed, rival the father by echoing his injunction to the 'son' to let the breasts (דֹּד) of his 'wife' fill (רְוָה) him. He should allow the love (אָהַב) of his 'wife', not that of the אִשָּׁה זָרָה, to seduce him (5.19–20). By comparison, the love of the אִשָּׁה זָרָה and the true wife differ considerably: the love of the true wife will fill her beloved *at all times* whereas the love of the אִשָּׁה זָרָה fills temporarily, lasting only until the morning.

This all-night stand, however, need not bother the young lad as the אִשָּׁה זָרָה quickly reassures. With the alacrity with which she seized him, she dismisses out of hand the threat of her husband who presently is safely away on a lengthy, business trip (vv. 19–20). That fact, along with her lavish preparation of her home and bed, may suggest the husband's occupation as a spice-merchant. Merchants had to

---

60. O'Connell rationalizes that since 'Jesus was buried in accordance with Jewish burial customs' and that since 'funerary rites in most cultures tend to be conservative', then ancient Israel would have had similar funeral customs. In the burial-account of King Asa of Judah (2 Chron. 16.14), his body was laid upon an open bier covered with various kinds of spices (unspecified by the narrator) and blended perfumes. Even the possible use of cinnamon in burial-spice mixtures, designed to mask the unpleasant odors of death, seems not too improbable. 'Proverbs VII 16–17', p. 238.

61. Burns, 'Proverbs 7,6–27', p. 28.

travel great distances to obtain many spices.[62] But her reference to her husband sounds odd to the ear. Rather than the expected 'my husband', she instead refers to him as 'the man/husband'. Such a phrase of emotional detachment likely betrays a deep-seated contempt or even marital estrangement on the part of the wife as previously hypothesized. That she perhaps does not 'get any' at home contributes to her feeling of alienation and her desperate need for sexual satisfaction.[63] Although the man of the house will eventually return, the אשה זרה knows that, from the amount of money that her husband took with him and from his expected return date, she has nothing to fear. Business will keep him away more than long enough for her to ensnare this youth and to have her way with him.

The husband does not plan to return home from business until the 'full moon' (כסא, v. 20), a rare lexeme that only occurs elsewhere in Ps. 81.3 as a reference to a festival day. Whether כסא denotes the religious festival of Passover or Tabernacles, both celebrated on the fourteenth or fifteenth day of the month (Lev. 23.5–6, 34), that is, at the full moon, remains ambiguous. Therefore, the husband's expected return date may coincide with a feast or the wife may simply use the astronomical marker as a means to date his return. At any rate, the danger of spending the night with her seems ever so remote if the 'new moon', suggested by the deep darkness of this night of meeting overemphasized via hendiadys, governs this carnal night. Nevertheless, the lengthy statement of her husband's absence and her insistence intended to allay the nervousness of this young lad are a bit over the top. After all, the young lad is only 'being invited to spend a night, not half a month'.[64] Nevertheless, the wife has created an enticing atmosphere in her house, furnished with foreign decor and perfumes, where she can engage in erotic encounters all the while that her husband remains away. The husband is not the only one taking care of business.

On this deep, dark night, the midnight rendezvous between the אשה זרה and her young paramour reaches its climax. Her sexual conquest results from her chief weapon, 'smooth lips', which alludes to both her seductive speech (v. 5; 5.3) and her sexual prowess. The chiastic form of v. 21 ('She led him with her many persuasions/by her smooth talk she seduced him') has at its very core a polysemic pun לקח/ חלק ('to destroy') that indicates the metaphorical death-effect of her 'instruction' upon this young lad who quite literally has no clue of what awaits him. But she

---

62. Some commentators (e.g. McKane, *Proverbs*, p. 338) speculate that the husband, a foreign merchant residing in Israel, travels abroad purchasing foreign luxuries. Whybray, however, quickly rejects such speculation about the husband's ethnicity because it 'depends largely on the erroneous assumption that the woman in this passage is identical with the *'iššah zarah*…' (*Proverbs*, pp. 115–16).

63. Even though her husband's lengthy absence may contribute to her feelings of alienation and drive her 'relentless pursuit of sexual gratification', she does not find any joy or fulfillment in promiscuity. Instead, her deep, disquieting actions as well as her long entreaty bespeak 'an overwrought tone', argues Fox (*Proverbs 1–9*, p. 253), 'that seems driven by a need deeper than physical desire'.

64. Fox (*Proverbs 1–9*, pp. 253, 248) and McKane (*Proverbs*, p. 338) assume the appointed time of the husband's return as the day of the full moon even though the medievals identified it as the day of the new moon. Thus the wife's lengthy statement, which cannot justifiably be construed as a marriage proposal, indicates that her husband will be away for another couple of weeks.

utilizes more than just speech. The verbal lexemes נטה ('to mislead') and נדח ('to seduce') in v. 21 hint at her physical persuasiveness (cf. v. 13).[65] Moreover, the phonemic contiguity of נדח ('to moisten') with נדח indicates such physical persuasiveness as of a sexual nature. By word and touch, the אשה זרה manipulates the young lad who, by now, has become putty in her hands. She moistens him with the wet kisses of her lips and the young lad impulsively (פתאם, v. 22) hurries off after her, much as he came to her house.

The lexemes נטה and נדח, which sometimes refer to the leading of animals such as a donkey (Num. 22.23) or a sheep (Jer. 23.2; 50.17), anticipate the animal imagery that follows. Three similes of comparison basically describe the youth as a dumb animal led to the slaughter: (1) like an ox that comes to the slaughter (v. 22b); (2) [perhaps] like a stag deer pierced by an arrow (vv. 22c, 23a); and (3) like a bird rushing into a snare (v. 23b). The uncertainty of the second simile results from the fact that the sense of the surface level of expression, which quite literally reads 'like a fetter to the discipline of a fool', does not fit the animal imagery. As a result, many scholars choose the well-trod path of textual emendation. But the graphic contiguity of איל ('stag') to אויל ('fool') invites the intuition of a deer or gazelle caught, tied to a stake and ready for killing,[66] while simultaneously preserving intact textual integrity.

With all of these similes (the third piece of evidence for the youth as a sacrificial offering), the ox, the deer, and the bird never sense their impending death. Likewise, the youth remains sadly oblivious to the fact that his life is at [the] stake. Note for instance the apt conclusion bracketing the animal imagery: 'He goes after her suddenly/…but he does not know that it will cost him his life' (vv. 22a, 23c). Clearly, the youth's death follows immediately upon the sexual act. Burns perceptively comments, 'It is as if *la petite mort* of orgasm leads inevitably to extinction… In a cruel reversal of erotic imagery the one who drove his "arrow" into the woman is himself mortally impaled'.[67] But this vignette concerns more than just a 'naive' young lad. Instead, this literary figure parabolically functions to mirror the virility of Solomon. The surface level of the second simile indeed makes sense after all within the whole of Proverbs 1–9 wherein אויל ('fool'), which occurs only once more (1.7), alludes to the mocking satire of Solomon as a fool. If fools (and how much more this 'son') despise discipline, the second simile sets readerly expectations that this royal fool has no clue when he is being punished via the fetters of poetic satire. The sexual (in)discretions of Solomon with (the) Other Wom(a)(e)n prove the demise of this unsuspecting fool upon his funeral bier of a (death)bed.

---

65. Burns, 'Proverbs 7,6–27', p. 28.

66. Clifford (*Proverbs*, pp. 89–90) comments that v. 22 may refer to an ancient method of hunting. A hunter would chase a deer or gazelle through a gradually narrowing stone fence into an enclosure, called a kite, where it could easily be slaughtered.

67. Similar links between sex and death occur randomly throughout ancient Near Eastern literature (e.g. 'The Tale of Aqhat' and 'Inanna's Descent to the Nether World'). See Burns, 'Proverbs 7,6–27', pp. 29, 33.

The transition 'and now' (v. 24) moves the reader's (and poet's) thoughts from the vignette of vv. 6–23 to the perorations of vv. 24–27. Verse 24, which recalls the earlier discourse of vv. 1–5, virtually mimics Prov. 5.7, though shifting away from its negative tone to a more positive exhortation.

> And now, children, listen to me,
> do not turn away from my words.
> …
> And now, children, listen to me,
> pay attention to my words.

Again, the poet enjoins 'sons/children' (cf. 4.1) if only to bestow upon the story a universal applicability for others not immediately addressed. Yet the singular form in subsequent verses particularly envisions the 'son', inveighed all along within this poetic material, as the addressee. Repeated exhortations for the 'son' to listen closely have not lost their effect, least of all upon the reader. These continual pleas to 'listen' and to 'pay attention', along with other textual signs, imply a prideful unwillingness on the part of the 'son' to accept advice more so than a lack of mental discipline with which to concentrate. After all, why should the 'son' embrace the instructional discipline of the 'father' when this royal fool is already 'wise'?

The poet engages in a bit of overkill if only for the sake of getting an important point across just in case the 'son' overlooks or lacks the perceptibility to intuit it from the vignette. The father urges the 'son' to avoid the אשה זרה by not allowing his sexual libido to override his intellect, symbolized as the heart in Hebrew thought. While the 'ways' of the אשה זרה sexually gratify for the moment, they only lead to destruction, a point reinforced with the lexeme שטה ('turn aside', cf. 4.15). The ways or paths of the אשה זרה, the counterpart to the חטאים ('criminals') in the poetic, dark merismus of *a*parental (in)(de)struction, lie in diametrical opposition to those of Wisdom mentioned beforehand (2.8–20; 4.11, 25–27). By embracing the instructional discipline (מוסר, cf. 4.13) of the 'father', the 'son' can circumvent the dark ways of the אשה זרה and subvert his typecast role as the royal fool.

Acting other than as an autocratic parent, the 'father' provides a *point d'appui* ('point of support') in his injunction for the 'son' to avoid the 'ways' of the אשה זרה. Her reputation, which encompasses more than just her sexual escapades, precedes her in that she has lai(n)(d) many a victim upon (t)he(i)r (death)bed; thus the young paramour is not her first victim. Moreover, the polysemous root חלל indicates that her victims lay slain (חלל) through (sexual) defilement (חלל).[68] The poet's attempt to avert the murder of the 'son' recalls an earlier note ('the waywardness of the simple kills [הרג] them/and the complacency of fools destroys

---

68. The echoes of ancient Near Eastern goddesses, who excelled at love and war, within this striking imagery of the אשה זרה as a warrior with a host of slain victims suggest, according to some scholars, a mythical background. McKane (*Proverbs*, p. 341) detects an allusion to the Canaanite god Mot ('Death') who opens his mouth and swallows up his victims. Apart from other proffered myths (e.g. the Sumerian goddess Inanna, the Babylonian goddess Ishtar and the Ugaritic goddess Anat), Burns ('Proverbs 7,6–27', pp. 20–36) explores an echo of the Phoenician goddess Astarte. Regardless of any possible mythical background, the situation in Prov. 7 does not exactly fit any known myth.

them', 1.32). Yet whether the אשה זרה deliberately sets out to destroy those whom she seduces remains decidedly indeterminable. Nevertheless, she has gone too far toward her own destruction to turn back, and all those whom she beds, she inevitably drags down with her. The hyperbolic imagery of v. 26, which should certainly not be taken literally, strongly emphasizes 'the dire consequences of consorting with an adulteress'.[69]

The story ends in tragedy deep in the land of the dead with 'the ways of Sheol are her house/descending to the chambers of death' (v. 27) echoing 2.18 and 5.5. 'The ways of Sheol' and 'the (bridal)chambers of death' converge at the (palace)-house of the אשה זרה. As a gateway to death, her house becomes the entrance to the descent into the underworld. What appears to be a brothel and a place of luxurious ease becomes an access to the chambers of another house, namely the palace of death.[70] According to Fox, 'Sheol is divided into separate provinces or "chambers", sometimes numbered as seven'. Who resides where in Sheol remains unclear, 'but the "depths" of Sheol (Prov. 9.18) is considered the worst'.[71] Perhaps unbeknownst to the אשה זרה, her 'house', the locus of death, metaphorically swallows up its guests within its barren womb. Those whose desire leads them to go along after the אשה זרה take the road to Sheol only to find that they have arrived at the point of no return. We can imagine the father straining all the more at this point for his words to reach the ear of the young lad as he crosses the threshold into the house of the אשה זרה.

Summary

In Proverbs 5 and 7, the poet employs a plethora of signs (e.g. love language, bridal imagery, sexual connotations, a graphic vignette, the silent youth, the imagery of night and darkness, the symbolism of spices and the perfumed bed, similes of comparison of the youth to animals of sacrifice, and the 'house' to Sheol), signifying, at a metaphorical level, a picturesquely erotic conte(x)(s)t highly reminiscent of the film *Fatal Attraction*.[72] Two kinds of love and two ways of life between the אשה זרה and Woman Wisdom vividly contrast with each another as the poet strongly urges the 'son' to avoid the אשה זרה. The right woman is unmistakably the wife in Proverbs 5; and the right woman, the wife, is indeed Woman Wisdom in Proverbs 7.[73] The high irony of this poetic material and its erotic conte(x)(s)t, along with the paradigmatic code אשה זרה, an associative chain of lexemes and other socio-historical data, altogether invite the subjacent allusion within a semiotic subtext to Solomon and his numerous sexual (in)discretions. Solomon's erotic embraces with

---

69. Whybray, *Proverbs*, p. 118.

70. Contrast with Wisdom's palace of life (8.34). Meinhold, *Die Sprüche*, p. 132.

71. The uncircumcised seem to have their own chamber and may be joined by unburied war casualties (cf. Ezek. 31.18; 32.19–32) (Fox, *Proverbs 1–9*, p. 251).

72. Newsom briefly analyzes the intertextuality of this film and Prov. 1–9 giving particular attention to characters, plot and mythic structure. See 'Woman and the Discourse of Patriarchal Wisdom', pp. 157–59.

73. See Clifford, *Proverbs*, p. 84.

(the) Other Wom(a)(e)n yield no lasting gratification, but only result in 'death' inasmuch as his sexual (in)discretions contribute to the *raison d'être* of this satire whereby the sage fells this mighty king with his pen. If Solomon would seek the erotic embrace of Woman Wisdom as his lover, then she could empower him to discern the אשה זרה as (a) Woman (of) Folly. Woman Wisdom, who awaits her climactic appearance, can rescue the 'son' from (t)his fatal attraction if only he were to channel his sexual desire(s) wisely.

Death's encroachment signals the end (of this text). By foreshadowing the rival houses in Proverbs 9, the 'house' of the אשה זרה becomes an entrance code into another level of meaning within the semiotic (under)world of this text. The erotic poetry of Proverbs 5 and 7 anticipates a much deeper struggle between Woman Wisdom and Woman Folly vis-à-vis Solomon emerging only at the linear text manifestation level of Proverbs 9, though subtly immediate all along within this poetic satire of a royal fool.

Chapter 6

BANQUETS, WINE AND WOMEN: AN EROTICISM OF LIFE OR DEATH

The prologues are over... It is time to choose.
(Wallace Stevens)

Introduction

In a touch of poetic irony, the אשה זרה and the 'son' 'fade to black'. No longer in the foreground, the 'son', nevertheless, remains the implicit object of this poetic *torah*. With little expectation whatsoever, Woman Wisdom abruptly emerges into the foreground breaking her long silence with a rather lengthy discourse (8.1–35) as she assumes the role of an active participant in the parental instruction of the 'son' by buttressing the father's caveat against the seductions of the אשה זרה. This immediate juxtaposition of Wisdom with the אשה זרה reveals striking parallels that merit brief consideration. But the deeper conflict, anticipated all along, remains between Wisdom and Woman Folly, a poetic symbol for the אשה זרה, as it reaches crescendo in Proverbs 9 via an erotic conte(x)(s)t of grave consequence. This chapter examines the contrastive banquet scenes of Wisdom and Folly, which, at another metaphorical level, dramatizes an ominous choice before the 'son' by allegorizing the two alternative paths of life and death, set off only by a brief interlude. Yet prior to an analysis of Wisdom's banquet invitation (vv. 1–6), the brief interlude (vv. 7–12) and Folly's banquet (counter)invitation (vv. 13–18), a prelude briefly summarizes those (dis)similarities between Wisdom and the אשה זרה.

Prelude

The similarities between Woman Wisdom and the Other Woman are strong. Both women target the young, naive male population (פת(א)י׳ם, 1.22; 8.5). Both principally, but not exclusively, seek to influence their target audience through seductive speech. Both frequent public venues (e.g. the streets, market squares and city gates) where business and commercial enterprises take place on a daily basis (1.20–21; 7.8–12; 8.2–3). Both can be grasped and embraced (3.18; 4.8; 5.20), and both also have houses in which they prepare for the entertainment of their guests (7.6–20; 8.34). With so many similarities, how does the 'son' see through them in order to discern between these two women and make a wise choice?

A close reading of the poetic material in this literary corpus, however, detects noticeable differences in spite of the similarities. The speech of Wisdom presents herself as trustworthy and credible in that honest words drip from her lips (8.6–8). Conversely, the Other Woman appears totally unreliable and incredulous in that deceptive words drip from her smooth lips (5.3–4; 7.21). Although both frequent public venues, Wisdom does so in broad, open daylight whereas the אשׁה זרה prefers the dark cover of night. The embrace of Wisdom simultaneously embraces and enhances life while the embrace of the Other Woman simultaneously embraces and enhances death as her 'house' leads to Sheol (3.16, 18, 22; 8.34–5; cf. 2.19; 5.5–6; 7.23, 27). These parallels and the immediacy of the irresistible invitation of the אשׁה זרה would otherwise render the claims of Wisdom suspect; therefore, she appeals to (her) antiquity to justify the veracity of her claims (8.22–31).

The Banquet of Woman Wisdom

The immediate juxtaposition of Wisdom with the אשׁה זרה foreshadows the contrast between her and Folly in the climactic poem of Proverbs 9. The depiction of Folly with terms identical to those of the אשׁה זרה – for example, loudness (המיה), ignorance and Sheol (2.18; 5.5; 7.27; 9.18) – bespeaks Folly as a symbol for the latter.[1] Although Wisdom and her rival have made appeals before, they never occur in direct opposition until Proverbs 9.

Verse 1 has long perplexed its readers, 'Wisdom has built her house/she has hewn out her seven pillars'. When did Wisdom build a house? And what are the 'seven pillars' or 'columns'? Jonas Greenfield has described, and not too unfairly, the numerous theories about the 'seven columns' by interpreters.

> The seven pillars of Wisdom have been variously interpreted: the seven firmaments or heavens, the seven planets, the seven regions or climates, the seven days of creation or the seven books of the law, the seven gifts of the holy ghost, the seven eras of the church, the seven sacraments, the seven liberal arts, and even the first seven chapters of the Book of Proverbs.[2]

The more relevant theories may easily be divided into three interpretative categories as being cosmological, literal, cultic or literary in nature.[3]

---

1. This final pairing of these allegorical women would seem to point in this direction. Carol Newsom, 'Woman and the Discourse of Patriarchal Wisdom', p. 155. Fox (*Proverbs 1–9*, p. 262) diagrams the antitheses as:

(1) the Strange Woman	versus	one's own wife
↓		↓
(2) Personified Folly	versus	personified Wisdom

Thus the אשׁה זרה serves as 'a foil for presenting the charms of Wisdom'. Murphy, 'Wisdom and Eros', p. 603.

2. Greenfield wastes no time in proffering his own theory: the seven pillars refer to the seven pre-Flood sages (*apkallus*) of Mesopotamian lore who established seven ancient cities. 'The Seven Pillars of Wisdom (Prov. 9.1) – A Mistranslation', *JQR* 76 (1985), pp. 13–20. Murphy (*Proverbs*, p. 58) aptly remarks that discussion of these numerous theories is 'like walking through a cemetery; one should leave them all in peace'.

3. The cosmological interpretation (the most ancient), views the seven pillars as upholding the

These multivalent interpretations attest to the textual polysemy of v. 1. While adjudication between these interpretations is unnecessary, textual signs do, nonetheless, figure significantly in the (il)legitimacy of an interpretation and its (im)probability. Even though the textual signs of Proverbs 1–9 admit the plausibility of the cosmological theory, they render the literal and cultic theories as less than convincing. Skehan's theory (which unfortunately goes too far in its detail with the architectural analogy) of Proverbs 1–9 as Wisdom's house has much to commend.[4] But the majority of these theories tend to assume too much literalness as they overlook the poetic quality of this text. Why should we feel compelled to regard Wisdom's 'house' and her 'seven pillars' as anything more than poetic imagery much like that of the depiction of personified Wisdom as a public speaker or as a wife?

world (cf. Ps. 75.3[4]; Job 9.6; 26.11). The force of this interpretation hinges upon the translation of the ambiguous, polysemic lexeme אמון ('artisan', Prov. 8.30), thereby ascribing to Wisdom an active role in creation. The Midrash later connected these pillars with the seven heavens. In recent times, Scott has regarded Wisdom's 'house' as the 'inhabitable world' of Prov. 8.31, with Wisdom, its builder and resident, as 'the constructive power of reason in Yahweh's creation' (*Proverbs*, p. 76).

The literal interpretation assumes dwelling-houses with seven pillars extant in Palestine during the Israelite period. Although some historians (à la Lang, *Wisdom and the Book of Proverbs*, pp. 90–93, and Gösta Ahlström, 'The House of Wisdom', *SEÅ* 44 [1979], pp. 74–76) have identified multiple-pillared houses, even seven-pillared ones, the evidence remains inconclusive. The norm was the four-pillared house. 'To build a house' has strong overtones of stability and permanence, both byproducts of wealth and social status. The similar echo in Prov. 14.1 ('Wisdom has built her house/ but Folly tears it down with her own hands') assures that Wisdom, in contrast to Folly, offers a stable, lasting abode. Thus 'seven pillars' is metonymy for a grand mansion befitting Wisdom's exalted status. See Clifford, *Proverbs*, p. 106, and Whybray, *Proverbs*, pp. 143–44.

The cultic interpretation builds upon the aforementioned literal theory in that its basis assumes the evidence of seven-pillared temple structures attested from the third millennium to the Hellenistic period in parts of the ancient Near East. Like pillars supporting the temple of Solomon (1 Kgs 7.2–6, 15; 2 Kgs 11.14), the 'seven pillars' support the house of Wisdom, a temple. Wisdom, a substitute for a foreign goddess (perhaps the 'Queen of Heaven') from an alien religious tradition, prepares for and extends an invitation to a cultic meal in the temple, not private residence. See Leo G. Perdue, *Wisdom and Creation: The Theology of Wisdom Literature* (Nashville: Abingdon Press, 1994), pp. 88, 94–97; also McKane, *Proverbs*, p. 363.

The literary interpretation rests on an architectural analogy that regards Wisdom's 'house' as none other than the literary edifice of Prov. 1–9 itself. The 'seven pillars' are the seven poems of uniform length extending through chs. 2–7 inclusive, while chs. 1 and 8–9 form a framework to the whole. More specifically, Prov. 1–9 forms the front elevation of the Porch and Annex to the temple structure of the book of Proverbs analogous to Solomon's Temple. See Patrick Skehan, 'The Seven Columns of Wisdom's House in Proverbs 1–9' and 'Wisdom's House', in *Studies in Israelite Poetry and Wisdom* (Washington, DC: Catholic Biblical Association, 1971), pp. 9–14 and 27–45, respectively.

4. Skehan's intuitive, and yet overly ambitious, theory has gained few adherents. Whybray (*Book of Proverbs*, p. 63) attributes this fact to the unclarity of Skehan's hypothesis – i.e. how much is metaphor and how much is literal? But what poetically sensitive reader would construe Prov. 9.1 as other than purely metaphorical? Even Camp admits skepticism (which, she wonders, might outweigh her fascination with the possibility that Skehan could be right) about some of the more admittedly stretched details of Skehan's argument bordering on esotericism ('Reading Solomon as a Woman', in *Wise, Strange and Holy: The Strange Woman and the Making of the Bible* [JSOTSup, 320; GCT, 9; Sheffield: Sheffield Academic Press, 2000], pp. 182–83 n. 28).

Therefore, this analysis construes the poet's depiction of Wisdom's house, like Folly's, as purely figurative.[5]

Immediately following the construction of her palatial house, Wisdom prepares an enormous feast to celebrate the dedication of her house (v. 2). Wisdom's house-dedication echoes that of Solomon who invited the Israelites to an enormous feast to celebrate the dedication of the house of Yahweh, albeit some eleven months after its completion (1 Kgs 8). Wisdom prepares a lavish banquet with meat and wine. Meat, generally reserved for special occasions, was considered a luxury, hence the slaughtering of an animal for keeping open house. The alliterative טבח ('to slaughter') puns זבח ('to sacrifice'), which the אשה זרה held out as an inducement to the young lad (7.14). While the lexeme טבח always refers to a secular slaughter, it 'may include the act of cooking' (cf. 1 Sam. 9.23–24).[6] Its earlier reference to the young lad via simile (7.22) indicates that the meal Wisdom prepares is not a cultic meal. As part of the preparations, Wisdom mixes her wine and, as was customary of a host/hostess, cuts the strong, thick wine with water. Moreover, nothing within this context would preclude the possibility of Wisdom mixing her wine with spices to provide that festal touch (Song 8.2).

Eager to summon guests, Wisdom extends her invitation from the highly visible city-heights (cf. 8.2; 1.21). But does Wisdom extend the invitation or do her maids? The Masoretic text suggests the former with the singular verbs תקרא ('she calls', v. 3) and אמרה ('she says', v. 4). Thus no real incoherence exists. Messages were formulated as the sender's, not the messenger's, words. Although the maid-servants may convey the message, it unequivocally remains that of Wisdom. At any rate, the maidservants issue Wisdom's invitation in the upper parts of the city, the site of palaces, and presumably even at the city-gates (cf. 8.3).[7]

Previously, Wisdom addressed all humankind (8.4), including the naive (פתאים) and foolish (כסילים, 8.5). Now she directs her invitation solely to the naive (פתי) and those lacking common sense (חסד לב, 9.4). But this puzzling question teases: If Wisdom targets the פתי with her invitation, then why would she send messengers to those areas of the city where official heads of state conduct political, legislative and judicial affairs? In the first (and only) occurrence of the singular פתי in this climax, the subjacent satire of Proverbs 1–9 peers forth for a brief moment in this code lexeme for Solomon.[8] In addition, the syntagm חסד לב recalls the young lad, a literary mirror of Solomon, in the vignette of Proverbs 7. That Wisdom issues her invitation throughout the politico-administrative realm does not seem odd, after all, for there it may reach the (deaf?) ears of this naive 'son'. Wisdom, 'the wife of his youth', embarks upon a mission to reclaim her lover from his fatal attraction.

Wisdom offers her bread and mixed wine as an inducement to this naive 'son' (v. 5). This banquet motif echoes a similar scene found elsewhere in Isa. 55.1–2.

---

5. See also Fox, *Proverbs 1–9*, p. 297.

6. Fox, *Proverbs 1–9*, p. 298.

7. Clifford, *Proverbs*, p. 106.

8. In the following verse, the message reverts back to the plural form (פתאים) with its imperatives.

Ho, all who are thirsty,
come to the waters;
and all who have no money,
come, buy and eat!
Come, buy wine and milk,
…
Why pay for that which is not bread,
and your labor for that which does not satisfy?
Listen carefully to me, and eat what is good;
and take great delight in your rich food.

The Isaianic poet explains this metaphorical invitation to eat and drink gratis as listening to the prophetic instruction (vv. 3–5).[9] Moreover, the echoed sapiential tone ('incline your ear/…listen, and you shall live', v. 3) within this intertext suggests that the 'fear of Yahweh' (i.e. Wisdom) provides all the sustenance that this naive 'son' could ever hope to need. The motif of eating and drinking in this banquet scene has an erotic quality. Thus at another metaphoric level, Wisdom invites the 'son' to an erotic repast, the overtones of which receive attention later.

The verbal parallelism of לחם ('to eat') and שתה ('to drink'), which occurs only twice in the Hebrew Bible (Prov. 4.17; 9.5), borrows from the Ugaritic fixed pair *lhm* ('to eat')//*sty* ('to drink').[10] In the Ugaritic myth of Baal-Anat with this banquet motif,[11] the storm-god Baal invites the gods to his newly built palace for a banquet ('My house have I built of silver/my palace, indeed, of gold').[12] Baal prepares for the feast by slaying oxen and other animals ('He slaughters both meat [and] small cattle/fells bulls [together with] fatlings/rams (and) one-year-old calves/lambs…kids'). After the brothers have been summoned, the wine flows freely at the banquet sating the gods ('So eat the gods and drink'). Baal's house symbolizes his authority since he no longer needs to reside at El's palace. In like manner, the house of Wisdom symbolizes her authority. And if the 'son' comes to her banquet, he must acknowledge her authority and rejoice in her company. But how does he acknowledge the authority of Wisdom?

Wisdom places a stipulation upon those guests who would accept her invitation: 'Abandon naiveté and live!' (v. 6) When perhaps no one else might, Wisdom holds out hope that the seemingly unpromising פתי can abandon naiveté (פתאים). In the intertext Isaiah 55 where the poet urges to stop seeking food that does not satisfy for food that does satisfy, vv. 6–7 illumine Wisdom's demand with even greater clarity: 'Seek Yahweh while he may be found… Let the wicked abandon his way, the evildoer his thoughts'. The demand of Wisdom implies less the absence of a quality not yet gained and more the deliberate embrace of a character flaw by the

---

9. Contrast with the menu of the wicked who eat the bread of wickedness and drink the wine of violence (Prov. 4.17).

10. Note the more common Hebrew word pair אכל ('to eat')//שתה ('to drink'). Clifford, *Proverbs*, p. 104 n. 3.

11. For a general overview of the banquet motif, see Murray Lichtenstein, 'The Banquet Motifs in Keret and in Proverbs 9', *JANESCU* 1 (1968), pp. 19–31.

12. All quotations come from 'Poems about Baal and Anath', in *ANET*, p. 134.

פֶּתִי.[13] Wisdom had earlier scolded the 'simple' (פֶּתִים) for loving naiveté (פֶּתִי, 1.22). Her demand resonates with a promise in the prologue – 'to give shrewdness to the naive' (פְּתָאִים, 1.4). Wisdom's stipulation responds to the question of how Solomon acknowledges the authority of Wisdom. Solomon must abandon his 'wisdom', considered naiveté, in order to partake of the only food that gratifies always. The forbidden pursuit of the economic food of wealth unjustly gained and the erotic food of sexual (in)discretions yield only temporary satisfaction. But Wisdom sustains the soul. When a man fears Yahweh, counsels Ben Sira, Wisdom 'will feed him with the bread of insight (לֶחֶם שֵׂכֶל)/and give him the water of understanding (מֵי תְבוּנָה) to drink' (Sir. 15.3).

The imperative 'live' sounds a sense of urgency for, as Wisdom previously fore-warned, 'the waywardness of the simple (פְּתָיִם) kills them' (1.32). In order to live, the 'son' must abandon naiveté. To live means to feast on the rich fares of Wisdom that continually nourish. To live means to avoid death by 'enjoying' Wisdom. To live means to take the path of Wisdom, the straight road leading to understanding, not naiveté. The verbal lexeme אָשַׁר has, in addition to the sememe 'to go straight', the narcotized sememe 'to pronounce happy, blessed'. Embracing Wisdom embraces happiness (אָשַׁר, 3.18) while simultaneously eschewing the path of evildoers or the path of naiveté. Only Wisdom, and neither international fame, nor immense wealth, nor sexual (in)discretions nor a pseudo-wisdom, can provide lifelong happiness.

Interlude

Tone, and ostensibly, subject matter shift abruptly in v. 7 as pithy maxims of an overtly didactic nature eclipse poetic metaphors. Neither the vocabulary nor the themes of vv. 7–12 broach, even indirectly, Wisdom's invitation. As a result, most scholars regard vv. 7–12 as an interpolation,[14] thus neglecting their poetic function. So what poetic function does this interlude have in its intercalation with the allegorical contrast of Wisdom and Folly? To this question the subsequent analysis now turns.

Unexpectedly, the poet advises, 'Whoever instructs a scoffer incurs shame/and whoever reproves the wicked gets abuse'. The recurrence of לֵץ ('scoffer', 'mocker') forms a ripple-like effect in the waters of Proverbs 1–9. Initially, this paradigmatic ripple grammatically paralleled פֶּתִי and כְּסִיל (1.22). Later, the poet contrasted לֵץ with עָנִי ('humble', 3.34). Thus, לֵץ insinuates Solomon as a scoffer due to its para-digmatic relation to the code פֶּתִי. The grammatical parallel לֵץ//רָשָׁע ('wicked'), echoed elsewhere in Ps. 1.1, reveals the לֵץ as no better than the רָשָׁע. Unjust socio-

---

13. Fox (*Proverbs 1–9*, p. 299) comments that 'the view of callowness as a discardable impedi-ment…perceives wisdom as a natural condition that one may reach only by first shucking off psychological encumbrances'.

14. On the originality of these verses, see Whybray (*Composition*, pp. 43–48) and also McKane (*Proverbs*, p. 360) who believes that these verses were added to elaborate upon the role of Wisdom as a teacher. Perhaps on a more positive note, Meinhold (*Die Sprüche*, pp. 45, 150) maintains that these verses play an important role in the composition of both chs. 1–9 and the redaction of the entire book of Proverbs in that they serve as a transitional passage (*Zwischenstück*).

economic policies and sexual (in)discretions by Solomon certainly construe him as
רשע. While perhaps well-intentioned, correction of the ל ץ can only meet with harsh
rejection (and contumely) at that. Even the sounds in colon A reinforce this sense
as both consonance (*l-q*) and assonance (*o-e-e-o*) reverse (*q-l* and *e-o-o-e* respectively). Phonetic reversal mimics the mocker whose relative incorrigibility only
twists sage advice backwards. Fox comments, 'Acceptance of criticism requires the
wisdom of humility, meaning a recognition of one's own limitations'.[15] But can the
'wise' Solomon, whose 'wisdom' surpasses that of all throughout the ancient Near
East, recognize his own limitations and accept the poet's sage instruction?

If the correction of the scoffer only heaps up insults, how much more then the
reproof of a wicked person! The ambiguity in v. 7b revolves around the lexeme
מום ('blemish', 'defect'). Moralistic interpretations regard this lexeme, on the one
hand, as having a connotation of the moral defect of the רשע somehow transferred
to the reprover. On the other hand, מום may connote the defect of the reprover himself. Neither of these moralistic readings, however, seems probable.[16] The parallelism of מום//קלון ('shame') indicates the reprover himself as the object of shame.
But in what sense does shame befall the reprover? A consideration of the other
occurrences of this lexeme in Hebrew literature will aid in its disambiguation. In
eighteen of twenty occurrences, מום denotes a physical blemish or injury, which in
Lev. 24.19–20 appears to be the resultant damage inflicted by another.[17] Therefore,
the abuse incurred by the one reproving a רשע would certainly include, but is not
limited to, verbal insults. Whereas the offenses of the ל ץ seem to lie more in words,
the reproof of the רשע may further provoke physical assault. The intensification of
colon A in colon B poetically admits of the social ignominy of reproving a wicked
person being escalated by physical violence. Whoever would correct a scoffer might
think twice, and that goes for the poet as well. Even the poet risks social ignominy
with his chastising satire of the 'son'. Were such reproof to criticize Solomon
openly as a royal fool, the poet would definitely incur the king's anger to his own
shame for no one provokes the king to anger without suffering serious repercus-
sions (cf. Prov. 20.2).

Verse 8 restates v. 7 in the form of an admonition, but with an explicit reason.
The poet commands: 'Do not reprove a scoffer, or he will hate you/reprove the wise
person and he will love you'. Any attempt to reprove the scoffer will surely result
in the reprover as an enemy. The scoffer considers himself so 'wise' in his own
eyes and above reproach that he needs no correction, and so he promptly rejects it.
Conversely, the wise, apparently docile in outward demeanor, demonstrate wisdom
by accepting sage advice as readily as they dispense it. Wise people appreciate the
disciplinary nature of reproof, which might safeguard against their future shame.
They hold in high regard those who care enough to confront and to correct them,
considering such individuals as friends.

15. Fox, *Proverbs 1–9*, p. 307.
16. See further Whybray, *Proverbs*, pp. 145–46; Murphy, *Proverbs*, p. 59.
17. Chastising a רשע has its consequences. Here, we should understand מום as a physical
wound, such as a broken tooth. When מום refers to moral blemish, however, it means *guilt* (Fox,
Proverbs 1–9, p. 307).

In vv. 7–9 catchwords link the pithy maxims of this short collection to form a distinct chain: v. 7 – לץ ('scoffer'), הוכיח ('reprove'), רשע ('wicked'); v. 8 – לץ, חכם ,הוכיח ('wise'); v. 9 – חכם andצדיק ('righteous'). The transition to v. 9, an expansion of v. 8, is, at the same time, a transition to a new focal subject, the wise. Verse 9, which echoes Prov. 1.5 ('Let the wise person listen and gain instruction…'), virtually affirms the sage as 'always a student, ever eager to learn. The wise pursue wisdom and are always open to receiving it as a gift…'[18] The wise remain wise simply because they accept constructive criticism. Although the verb 'give' lacks a direct object in the Hebrew, we may nonetheless infer תוכחת ('reproof') or מוסר ('discipline') from v. 8 as its direct object. The poet draws the following signifi-cant, contrastive parallels within this short collection: צדיק//חכם::רשע//לץ. The grammatical parallelצדיק//חכם, a peculiarity to Proverbs, equates the wise and the righteous or wisdom and justice. Only the response of either acceptance or rejec-tion of discipline and reproof marks the difference in identity between the 'wicked' and the 'righteous'. If Solomon accepts poetic censure and embraces Wisdom, then he will subvert his typecast role as a fool.

Acceptance of instruction signals the 'beginning of wisdom' (v. 10). While the vocabulary of v. 10 echoes that of 1.7 in the prologue, colon A of v. 10 transposes the syntax withיראת יהוה ('fear of Yahweh') now in the predicate position. How-ever one prefers the syntactical position, the sense remains the same. The poet sounds a strong affirmation about the value of wisdom that offsets any perceived note of futility voiced back in v. 7. Verse 10, itself a chain of syntagmatic con-structs, forms a chiastic structure. At the center of this verse lies the synonymous parallelism 'fear of Yahweh'//'knowledge of the Holy One'.[19]

> The beginning of wisdom
> [is] the fear of Yahweh;
> knowledge of the Holy One
> [is the beginning of] understanding.

The parallelism of the outer frame works on the basis ofבינה ('understanding') as an ellipsis ofתחלת בינה ('the beginning of understanding').[20] This chiastic paral-lelism underscores at its heart a particular disposition (not just cognitive knowledge about Yahweh) of fulfilling one's duty to the deity requisite to illumination.[21] To embark upon the path of wisdom necessitates the possession of an ability to listen, itself a precondition for education, and an openness to reproof designed to (re)ori-ent to the 'fear of Yahweh'. Had Solomon assumed his divinely proscribed role as monarch and evinced a life of Torah devotion all along, he could have spared him-self this satiric reproof. But if Solomon reorients himself to the 'fear of Yahweh', then he will truly be the wise and righteous king full of the wisdom of Yahweh.

18. Clifford, *Proverbs*, p. 106.

19. The pluralקדשׁים ('Holy One') parallels God elsewhere in Prov. 2.7 and Hos. 12.1. This lexeme is probably an epithet for God, hence its usual explanation as an honorific plural à la the 'plural of majesty' (Whybray, *Proverbs*, p. 146).

20. Fox, *Proverbs 1–9*, p. 308.

21. On the discussion of the sign 'fear of Yahweh' (יראת יהוה) and its significations, refer back to Chapter 3.

The stakes grow higher as now acceptance or rejection no longer remains an inconsequential choice, but becomes quite literally a matter of life or death (v. 11). If the beginning of wisdom is the 'fear of Yahweh', then the beginning of wisdom also assumes the good, common sense to take advantage of a good offer when it presents itself. The enigmatic 'by me' in the first colon of v. 11 puzzles: Does this first person pronoun refer to the poet himself or to personified Wisdom? The ambiguity of the immediate context supports both possibilities contra the contention by some that the immediate context clearly favors Wisdom.[22] In fact, the speaker (3.2; 4.10), like Wisdom (3.16, 18; 8.35), holds out the promise of life to the 'son'. As a consequence, the reader may justifiably intuit within this ambiguous sign the subjacent interpretants of Wisdom and Yahweh, who, as 'mother' and 'father', the collective merismus of parental instruction, alone can extend human life. The inducement of life echoes earlier inducements due to the confluence of lexemes from Prov. 3.2 and 4.10.[23] Moreover, the echo of 1 Kgs 3.14 calls to mind the subjacent allusion to Solomon. Who else but Solomon received the promise of long life if he would but follow 'the ways of Yahweh', a metonym for Torah devotion – that is, יראת יהוה? Embracing Wisdom reaps the salutary benefit of life, and long life at that.

As abruptly as the interlude began, so it ends, but with parting sage advice: 'If you are wise, you are wise to yourself/but if you scoff, you alone shall bear it' (v. 12). Although seemingly gratuitous, v. 12 harks back to v. 7 yet shifting the focus from the effect upon others to the effect upon the doer. Neither the benefits conferred by wisdom nor the social ignominy of the scoffer can transfer to others. The effects remain solely with the wise person and the fool, a point emphasized by the lexemes 'for yourself' and 'you alone'. But such a claim, as some criticize, disavows the potential effect of Proverbs 1–9 to impart wisdom to others. In fact, Fox goes so far as to argue that the conditional nature of 9.12a does not mean that wisdom benefits *only* its possessor; otherwise, it would have 'you alone' as in v. 12b.[24] But Fox mistakenly assumes this semantic distinction on the basis of grammatical differences within these semantically contrastive, parallel colons. Parallelism, either grammatical or semantic, is a feature of equivalence primarily and rarely, if ever, a feature of grammatical identicalness.[25] Moreover, Fox's counterargument implies that even those not possessing wisdom could enjoy its benefits. But could a fool honestly reap the benefits of wisdom without possessing wisdom? Only the wise can enjoy the fruits of wisdom, and that not because wisdom is intrinsic to an

---

22. This position hinges on the placement of v. 11, which proponents like Fox believe to have followed v. 6 originally. Anticipating the possibility that v. 11 did not originally follow v. 6, Fox (*Proverbs 1–9*, p. 299) then hypothesizes that v. 11 must have been a fragment of a lost speech by Wisdom.

23. For instance, ירבו ('to be numerous', 4.10b) and ארך ימים ('to lengthen days', 3.2a) converge in 9.11a while יוסיפו ('to add', 3.2b) and שנת חיים ('years of life', 3.2a) combine in 9.11b. Fox, *Proverbs 1–9*, p. 299–300.

24. Fox, *Proverbs 1–9*, p. 317.

25. For further discussion, see Berlin, *Dynamics of Biblical Parallelism*, pp. 31–32, 88–90, 96.

individual but rather simply because said individuals pursue wisdom.[26] Likewise, the 'son', too, can reap the benefit of long life (v. 11) as promised, but only if he pursues Wisdom. And if Solomon should thumb his nose at the poetic *torah* of Proverbs 1–9, then his 'wisdom' renders him wise only in his own eyes.

From the above semiotic analysis, the accumulation of textual signs reveals the poetic function of this interlude as a reflection of the decision facing Solomon (Wisdom or Folly? Life or Death?) within the dramatically contrasted allegory of these banquet scenes.[27] Such discernment, however, requires an ability to read between the lines and discern lexemes such as discipline (מוסר), reproof (יכח, vv. 7–8), יראת יהוה (v. 10) and other linguistic echoes. Who else but the 'son' comes to mind as the poet's chastising satire has had as its goal all along the reorientation of Solomon to his divinely appointed duty to Torah? Solomon's unjust socio-economic policies and sexual (in)discretions certainly do not make him wise, much less righteous. But will the internationally renowned 'wisdom' of Solomon enable discernment of his limitations so that he pursues Wisdom, accepts sage advice and reaps the beneficent promise of life? Or will his inimitable 'wisdom' disable discernment so that he pursues Folly, spurns wise critique and reaps death? The textual signs of this satire, unfortunately, admit of no unequivocal denouement that might move beyond the impasse of its open-ended nature. Nevertheless, textual significations do not dissuade expectations that this royal fool will fail to see the tragedy of his errors and pursue Wisdom.

The Banquet of Woman Folly

With the interlude now over, the poetic contrast of allegorical figures resumes by spotlighting Woman Folly. While the hapax legomenon אשת כסילות quite literally reads 'foolish woman', context dictates its connotation as the personification or embodiment of foolishness. As such, Woman Folly assumes the role of the deliberate antithesis to Woman Wisdom. This antithesis hinges in part on the characterization of Folly as loud, naive and ignorant (v. 13).

First, the character trait of loudness or boisterousness (המיה) harks back to that of the אשה זרה (7.11), who Folly clearly symbolizes. While the same descriptor applies as well to Wisdom who also cries aloud in the town square, the proclamations of Wisdom appear more dignified and lucid.

Second, the personal trait of naiveté (פתיות) emphasizes Folly's gullible nature within this portrait whereas earlier portraits emphasized her deceit. In addition to 'simple' or 'naive', the lexeme פתה also bears the often-narcotized sememes 'persuasive' or 'seductive'. How ironic that Folly should be as gullible as her 'guests', the פתאים! And yet, as noticed in the previous chapter, her persuasive appeal,

---

26. Contrast with the psychological perspective advocated by McKane: 'Wisdom is an inalienable possession. It is part of the man who has it; it makes him what he is and no man can take it from him' (*Proverbs*, p. 369).

27. While the two banquet scenes (vv. 1–6, 13–18) indeed provide clues to the interpretation of their symbolism, the interlude, not the banquet scenes contra Meinhold (*Die Sprüche*, p. 151), makes explicit what is only implicit there.

which stems from her seductive wiles, only convinces those of her own kind within her sphere of influence.

Third, in spite of her self-deluded shrewdness, Folly is ignorant, a faint echo of Prov. 5.6. In addition to her ignorance, the lexeme ידע may also connote 'concern' or 'care' (cf. Gen. 39.6; Job 9.21), hence evoking a dual signification. Folly lacks both knowledge and a concern or care for anyone (except herself of course).

Despite all Folly's mimicries of Wisdom, what she does not mimic stands conspicuously unstated above all else. Folly, unlike Wisdom, does not construct her house. Such an activity presumes knowledge and would undoubtedly controvert Folly's predilection for destruction (cf. Prov. 14.1). Moreover, the energy Wisdom invests in the preparation of her banquet starkly contrasts with the indolence of Folly who invests no energy whatsoever in the preparation of her banquet. Like Wisdom, Folly, too, seeks a public venue wherein to invite her guests. Both women often appear in many of the same places, and perhaps, at times, even in close proximity to one another. For example, Folly and Wisdom both position themselves at the city-heights (מרמי קרת, vv. 3, 14).

Although Folly mimics Wisdom, their strategies toward their target audience differ. Wisdom dispatches messengers to invite her guests whereas Folly opts to sit on her 'throne' (כסא, v. 14), an allusion to the monarch, at the city's apex near 'the entrance of her house' (a sexual allusion) summoning passersby. While Folly's strategy may reflect indolence, it may also indicate that she has evaluated her target audience better, and thus tailored her approach accordingly. After all, would not Folly's direct, informal approach appeal more to the unsophisticated rather than Wisdom's formal, indirect approach, which would naturally appeal to the refined tastes of the sophisticate? As a result, the targeted audience (פתי a.k.a. the 'son') for both Wisdom and Folly as well as the implications from Wisdom's strategy to gear her message to the פתי in the palace-complex only reiterates the allusion to Solomon.

High atop the city overlooking the throngs of people, Folly sits perched scouring the passersby for those special guests to invite to her banquet. She certainly need not concern herself with ensnaring the wicked, for they require no further enticement. Instead, Folly locks her sights on those presumably honest individuals 'going straight on their way' (v. 15), an idiomatic expression which, according to Fox, always connotes 'moral virtue'.[28] Folly shrewdly preys upon the פתי knowing that their naiveté cannot thwart her seductive appeal, which would certainly tarnish any moral virtue in their character. The calculating designs by Folly belie, or so it would seem, the poet's characterization of her as naive. Nevertheless, the naiveté of the פתי ushers in their own demise since their very nature precludes an ability to discern the deceptive invitation by Folly as a ruse.

Folly's mimicry of Wisdom persists as she parrots the opening words of Wisdom's invitation ('Whoever is simple, let him turn aside here!' vv. 4a, 16a). The echo of a similar banquet scene in 'The Tale of Aqhat' illumines the invitation by Folly and, by implication, Wisdom. In this tale, the goddess Anat plays hostess in a

---

28. Fox, *Proverbs 1–9*, p. 301.

banquet scene of the gods to which she invites the young man Aqhat: 'Eat of food, ho!/Drink of the liquor of wine, ho!'[29] Her erotic designs on him soon surface as she asks him for his 'bow' (a sexual reference) in exchange for silver and gold ('Ask silver and I will give it to you/Gold, and I will bestow it on you/Only give your bow to Anat'). When Aqhat refuses, she raises the bid to eternal life with the gods.

> Ask for life and I will give it to you,
> Not-dying and I will grant it to you.
> I will cause you to count years with Baal,
> With the sons of El you will count months.

Aqhat also spurns this offer discerning its deceptiveness since Anat lacks the power to grant eternal life to mortals. Despite the lustful desire of Anat for Aqhat, she responds to her rebuffed advances by plotting the death of Aqhat. Anat, however, must somehow entrance Aqhat who eventually decides to meet up with her on a hunting trip. But Aqhat remains completely oblivious to the fact that he has become the targeted prey of a hunt that will culminate in his death. Although Wisdom's invitation draws upon similar linguistic conventions in Anat's deceitful invitation, Folly's invitation mostly parallels that of Anat in nature and denouement.

Regardless of identical invitations, an artful difference exists in Folly's parody of Wisdom's banquet. While Wisdom offers bread and wine, Folly proffers 'stolen water' and 'secret bread' (v. 17). No wonder that Folly invests no energy in making preparations for her banquet; all her fares are stolen. The chiastic arrangement of food and drink in these two banquet scenes punctuates the inversion of values: v. 5 – bread (לחם) and wine (יין)//v. 17 – water (מים) and bread (לחם).[30] Moreover, the assonance of *a-i* with מים//יין and the phonemic contiguity of גנב ('stolen') with ענב ('grapes') reinforce the parallelism. Semiotically, therefore, the signs do not unequivocally exclude wine from the fête of Folly.[31]

The emphasis of wine and 'water' signifies the inverted value of a bacchanalian feast of sorts. Eating and drinking at feasts often degenerated into inebriation and sexual license. Thus 'eating' often functions as a metaphor for sexual intercourse and when it does not, certainly occurs as a corollary motif in erotic contexts. The erotic imagery of 'water', which can also allude to sexual intercourse, harks back to the poet's previous metaphoric admonition to the 'son' against adultery – 'Drink water from your own cistern' (5.15). Even the lexeme 'secret' evokes the clandestine nature of the rendezvous between the young lad and the אשה זרה back in Proverbs 7. Folly does not propose marriage; rather, she advocates the theft of sexuality belonging to the household of another. By insinuating that legitimate pleasure of sex with one's own is somehow deficient, Folly demurs the notion that

29. All quotations from this Ugaritic tale derive from the partially broken text of the first tablet. See Richard J. Clifford, 'Proverbs IX: A Suggested Ugaritic Parallel', *VT* 35 (1975), pp. 300, 302–303.

30. Yee, '"I Have Perfumed My Bed with Myrrh"', p. 124.

31. This imagery has an earlier antecedent with the metaphor of the bread and wine of the wicked (4.17).

imbibing foreign waters does not gratify. Folly makes promises that she knows she will never keep.

Upon closer examination, Folly never really does offer a menu. Instead, her innuendo tantalizingly promises a clandestine pleasure while simultaneously deceiving. Her 'slippery words' and 'smooth talk', cautioned against all along, finally assume a tangible character. But Folly never actually tells a falsehood; rather, she lures through craftily told truths. After all, illicit pleasures do sexually gratify, hence making them all the more desirable. The allure of Folly, however, cannot be confined to sex. Her invitation applies to every type of illicit gratification. Stolen, clandestine pleasures titillate

> because they give a feeling of surplus of possession, of having more than is one's due. There is also a special sense of power to be had from defying authority and transgressing boundaries, and in that way furtively imposing one's will on a corner of the moral economy.[32]

Who else but Solomon in this satire has transgressed divinely circumscribed boundaries with an insatiable surplus of wealth and women to monopolize every fiber of the Judean economy? Unlike Wisdom who demands that her guests abandon naiveté, Folly trades upon that naiveté in order to exploit the פְּתִי. And herein lies the profound difference between the invitations of Wisdom and Folly. Folly counts on the פְּתִי, who lack discernment, to assume her words as the promise of an erotic repast. As a result, the פְּתִי, like so many of Folly's prior 'dinner' guests, will unfortunately succumb to Folly's deceptively seductive enticement and likewise suffer the same fate.[33] Only the wise can discern the temptingly sweet offer of Folly masking an underlying poison.

As the poem concludes, the פְּתִי reflect another trait in common with Folly, namely ignorance. They have no clue whatsoever concerning the ramifications of accepting Folly's invitation, much less the identity of their fellow dinner guests. Folly has already invited as her esteemed guests the רְפָאִים ('Rephaim', v. 18), a polysemic lexeme, which also connotes 'ghosts' or 'shades'. Such a guest list implies that the פְּתִי, too, are dead, though they remain oblivious to their condition. The banquet and guests of Folly echo a similar mythological motif in a Ugaritic text where the high god El invites the 'shades' (*rpum*) to a feast at his palace.

> Come to my banquet.
> Set off to my house, O shades.
> Into my house I bid you,
> I beckon you into my palace.[34]

---

32. Fox, *Proverbs 1–9*, p. 302.

33. Contrary to the presumed epic type-scene of rebuffed seduction, Fox (*Proverbs 1–9*, p. 304) observes that the narrator, not Wisdom as maintained by Richard J. Clifford ('Woman Wisdom in the Book of Proverbs', in Georg Braulik, Walter Groß and Sean McEvenue (eds.), *Biblische Theologie und gesellschaftlicher Wandel für Norbert Lohfink* [Basel: Herder, 1993], pp. 69–70), unmasks Folly's deceptive offer and exposes the danger of her solicitations.

34. As quoted by Fox, *Proverbs 1–9*, p. 303.

Ugaritic literature regards the 'Rephaim' or 'shades' as ancient dead heroes whereas the 'shades' in Hebrew literature include all the dead, not just the Rephaim. The Rephaim inhabit the underworld, nay the deepest parts of the netherworld (עמקי שאול, 'depths of Sheol'). Folly's banquet, by contrast, is no lively feast in the palace of the high god; rather, her feast is 'a spectral, pallid affair, held in the underworld'.[35] But if the Rephaim, once mighty warriors, now dine at Folly's banquet, how can the פתי possibly withstand her seductive invitation?

The poet mocks the deceitful offer of Folly while proffering a *caveat emptor* to the 'son'. The veiled promise by Folly of an erotic encounter only deceptively 'shade(s)' the existence of the 'son'. As noted in the previous chapter, 'house' plays upon the erotic trope. The *chat(te)(eaux)* of Folly, which leads to death, is itself the netherworld (cf. 2.18; 7.27). While the פתי feast upon the succulent victuals of Folly's *jardin secret* ('secret garden') at this bacchanalian banquet, ghostly dinner guests, 'shades' of once fully animated mortals, reflect to the פתי their own (sh)(f)ading mortality. In contrast to the banquet meal of Wisdom that sustains, the erotic bacchanal of Folly malnourishes, hastening death with every delectable morsel. The 'son' faces a decision: an erotic repast with Wisdom or an erotic bacchanal with Folly? Both are savory and gratify, but only one is life giving, the other toxic.

The banquet motif does not circumscribe metaphoric significations to that of erotic repasts alone. Instead, a fundamental, root trope of life-paths,[36] as discerned by most readers, undergirds the food metaphor as well as others. Various paradigmatic lexemes (e.g. דרך//נתיבה//ארח, 'way'/'path') throughout Proverbs 1–9 have emphasized the life-paths trope. Now, the allegory of personified Wisdom and Folly along with the interlude buttresses this emphasis by signifying two paths of fatal importance. The allegory of Wisdom and Folly poses a choice to the 'son' between two life-paths: the way of wisdom or the way of foolishness. The way of wisdom is the way *of* and *to* life; the way of folly is the way *of* and *to* death. Whosoever invitation the 'son' accepts, his RSVP will certainly reflect his discernment, or lack thereof, of the poet's caveat (with)in this poetic *torah*.

Summary

Death's knell resounds a dark note throughout Proverbs 1–9. A foreboding shadow looms above the 'son' who must now choose which dinner party to attend – Woman Wisdom or Woman Folly? Decisions, decisions, and the fact that both women allure the 'son' with seductive speech and enticing inducements to their respective festal banquets, which, at one metaphoric level, signifies an erotic repast, does not

---

35. Fox, *Proverbs 1–9*, p. 303.

36. For Fox (*Proverbs 1–9*, p. 128), 'BEHAVIOR IS A PATH' is the *ground metaphor*, or, as Norman Habel ('The Symbolism of Wisdom in Proverbs 1–9', *Int* 26 [1972], p. 133) designates it, the 'nuclear symbol' that unifies the teachings of Prov. 1–9. Similarly, Raymond C. Van Leeuwen ('Liminality and Worldview in Proverbs 1–9', *Semeia* 50 [1990], pp. 111–44) proposes two co-ordinated ground metaphors: the two roads and the two women, both based on the even more fundamental metaphor of boundaries or limits.

help matters none. Naturally, such eroticism would naturally appeal to the wantonness of a naive fool whose numerous sexual (in)discretions, in part, elicited this satire of a 'wise' king.

But this dramatically erotic conte(s)(x)t between Wisdom and Folly poses an even graver, ominous choice before the 'son' by allegorizing two alternative life-paths. 'Two roads diverged in a wood' and now the decision before the 'son', in effect, becomes one of life or death. Life-paths have consequences. Once on a path, that path becomes a natural course of life for an individual, and thus typecasts said person. Navigating a straight path to life demands a map of instruction (תורה) and discipline (מוסר). Abiding by the *torah* of Wisdom designates such disposition and behavior as righteous/wise contra the antithetic epithet wicked/foolish. Whichever path the 'son' takes will hinge on either his acceptance or rejection of the reproof of this poetic *torah*, as the interlude subjacently implies. But of the two paths that diverge in this 'wood', only 'the one less traveled by' will have 'made all the difference'.[37]

Although Folly gets the last word in Proverbs 9, a poetic abstract of Proverbs 1–9, her rhetoric by no means nullifies the veracity of Wisdom's claims. Despite Wisdom's promise of life, textual signs elicit the anticipatory interpretant that death will ultimately stake its claim upon the 'son' as ending the beginning brings no denouement to this irresolute satire. While Wisdom wins the ideological battle, Folly will win the war for the royal fool Solomon, 'son' of Yahweh.

37. Robert Frost, *Complete Poems of Robert Frost* (New York: Holt, Rinehart and Winston, 1961), p. 131.

Chapter 7

EPILOGUE: BEGINNING THE ENDING, ENDING THE BEGINNING

In my beginning is my end… In my end is my beginning.
(T.S. Eliot)

'Epilogue', rather than 'conclusion', seems a more appropriate designation to end this study, which, among many things, has a prologue. The word 'conclusion' generally connotes that which is final and determinate. But any concept of finality remains as ephemeral as the reading experience to which it belongs. For were I, or any other reader for that matter, to (re)read this same poetry or any other literature, new significations would surface. These new significations would undoubtedly elicit fresh interpretants that nuance existing insights. Then again, new significations might reconfigure a reading experience with altogether different observations that rewrite Proverbs 1–9 into a text other than satire. This study, however, has tendered nothing of a conclusive nature. Instead, by adopting a 'postmodernist' semiotic approach, this study has proffered an oft-neglected reading of Hebrew poetry as poetry in its modest proposal that Proverbs 1–9 may be read as a satire on Solomon even though said material may not actually be satire in its formal sense.

Beginning the ending returns the reader, in a sense, to the beginning, which, in turn, anticipates its ending. Ending coalesces with beginning to form a type of literary circularity. Marianna Torgovnick states, 'When the ending of a novel clearly recalls the beginning in language, in situation, in the grouping of characters, or in several of these ways, circularity may be said to control the ending'.[1] Closure occurs in Proverbs 1–9 with the thematic 'frame' (a common technique in narrative closural patterns) or the primacy sign יְרַאת יהוה ('fear of Yahweh') and the conceptual climax of personified Wisdom and Folly,[2] to which the poetic material was moving all along. Such closure, however, is incomplete in that this poetic material suspends any denouement to its plot hinted at in the beginning, even though it does come to an end.[3] The open-ended nature of satire, an inadvertent formal failure, undoubtedly engenders, if not accounts for, the lack of denouement to a satirical reading of Proverbs 1–9. Hints, echoes and allusions, among other semiotic phe-

---

1. *Closure in the Novel* (Princeton, NJ: Princeton University Press, 1981), p. 13.
2. According to Barbara H. Smith, other elements, formal (e.g. form, meter and rhyme) and thematic (e.g. repetition, allusion and temporal sequence), may also bring about poetic closure. *Poetic Closure: A Study of How Poems End* (Chicago: University of Chicago Press, 1968), pp. 38–195.
3. The lack of resolution in an ending does not determine its appropriateness. Rather, the proper relationship of an ending to the beginning and to the middle of the narrative's plot determines its appropriateness. Torgovnick, *Closure in the Novel*, pp. 6, 13.

nomena, predominate as they guide the reader's intuitive moves toward the interpretative closure of this satire.

Such literary phenomena, however, do not influence the interpretative moves of various historical- and literary-critical readings of Proverbs 1–9 that have approached this 'orphan' as if it were a mirror. For historical critics, Proverbs 1–9 becomes something like a one-way mirror through which they look behind to catch a glimpse of a distant and ancient epoch. Through the looking glass, source critics, for instance, identify literary sources, whether Egyptian, Mesopotamian or Ugaritic, that directly influenced Israelite wisdom literature.[4] Form critics establish genre and the social background (e.g. royal court, scribal school or family/clan) of Proverbs 1–9,[5] though with no consensus on the latter. And redaction critics trace and reconstruct the compilation stages of Proverbs 1–9 through what resembles a sort of textual cut-and-paste activity.[6]

Similarly, certain literary-critical approaches, namely those with a distinctively feminist slant, have approached Proverbs 1–9 as a conventional mirror reflecting the misogynist nature of a text produced within a patriarchal culture. But the mirror also reflects the ideological biases and presuppositions of these critics.[7] Nevertheless, conclusions by both interpretative approaches seem illusory. Mirrors, by their very nature, are devices of illusion. Unfortunately, the agendas of both interpretative approaches obscured from vision the rich mosaic of textual signs within Proverbs 1–9.

Semiotics concerns itself with these textual signs. The reader contributes to the production of meaning via a broad repertoire of competences (linguistic and literary) and inferential walks (or intertextuality), but not in a way that violates the textual signs. Instead, the repertoire serves as an invaluable means whereby the reader interprets the sign-function abductionally. The semiotic intuition senses and probes connections between signs. Feelings of resemblance usher in the notion that somehow everything might be mysteriously related to everything else. 'To some degree everything is connected to everything else', claims Eco. 'There are always connections; you have only to want to find them'.[8] Exploring connections between sign-

---

4. For example, Whybray, *Wisdom in Proverbs*; McKane, *Proverbs*; and Albright, 'Canaanite-Phoenician Sources', pp. 1–15.

5. On the issue of genre and Prov. 1–9, see Kayatz, *Studien zu Proverbien 1–9*, and Lang, *Die Weisheitliche Lehrrede*. As for the social background of this collection, consult von Rad, *Wisdom in Israel*; Fox, 'Social Location, pp. 227–39, and Crenshaw, 'Education', pp. 601–15.

6. Whybray, *Composition*, and Fox, 'Aspects', pp. 55–69.

7. Note the following statement betraying the feminist bias: 'While patriarchy teaches us to expect a Strange Woman, it also leaves us surprised to find her countered by a Wise Woman, rather than a Wise Man'. Although the wise words of the book of Proverbs belong to Solomon, a man, that does not pose a problem for this conclusion. Given the relationship of Wisdom, personified in Solomon, and Woman, the form of wisdom's personification in Proverbs, which is ascribed to Solomon, Camp engages in an exercise of crossed gender through the triple lens of Woman, Wisdom and Strangeness that intimates 'Solomon is a woman' (Camp, 'Reading Solomon as a Woman', in *Wise, Strange and Holy*, pp. 178, 144–46).

8. Umberto Eco, *Foucault's Pendulum* (trans. William Weaver; New York: Ballantine, 1990), pp. 225, 618.

functions invariably entails the metaphor of play. Imagining suggestive possibilities beyond the surface level of expression empowers the ability to intuit, indeed actualize, *what is not said*.

> Any fact becomes important when it's connected to another. The connection changes the perspective; it leads you to think that every detail of the world, every voice, every word written or spoken has more than its literal meaning, that it tells us of a Secret. The rule is simple: Suspect, only suspect.[9]

By suspecting possible connections between sign-functions, semiotics actualizes the potential, poetic function of Proverbs 1–9 as satire.

No connection between sign-functions appears more self-evident than in the phonetic anagram משלי שלמה ('proverbs of Solomon', 1.1). From the outset, the prologue forces a connection between these signs prompting the consideration of an alternative perspective. In contrast to the traditional denotative marker of a literary collection by Solomon, this sign-function yields the provocative interpretant of a satire on Solomon. Another interpretant, the reign of Solomon, evokes yet another interpretant (an instance of (un)limited semiosis) of such a reign as an illusion of peace. Poetic sarcasm mocks Solomon as the impostor king of Israel to affirm God as the true king of Israel. Solomon's monarchy only evinces a mock-reign of peace giving the illusion of harmony and stability.

At the subjacent level of the prologue, the poet criticizes Solomon on two grounds made more explicit through inferential walks in the Deuteronomistic literature. First, Solomon's lack of discernment demonstrates itself in an impolitic ability to rule with righteousness, justice and equity, thus resulting in the dissolution of the 'United Monarchy'. Second, Solomon's numerous sexual (in)discretions with the נשים נכריות ('foreign women') render him no better than a naive and foolish youth. Implicit within these two critiques lies the fundamental flaw of Solomon to embrace his divinely proscribed task of Torah meditation. Such a flaw deprives him of the 'fear of Yahweh' that would cultivate wisdom. But the 'wise' man turned royal fool gets a second chance to learn the 'fear of Yahweh' and embrace Wisdom. The indirect language and disjunctive syntax of the prologue reflects its cryptic nature reminiscent of a coded message requiring decoding. It cues a reading of the poetic material to follow. If wise, the reader, too, will not discriminate, but rather ponder over data dispersed in various places and gathered again, concealed in one place and disclosed in another.[10]

Two poems in Proverbs 1 and 3 (1.8–19; 3.1–12) pick up on the first point of critique against Solomon with the aim of discerning the true nature of his 'wisdom'. In the first poem mythico-religious symbolism corroborates the semiotic intuition of the 'son' as Solomon. Both father and mother (Yahweh and Wisdom?), a parental merismus, advise their 'son' with correction (מוסר) and instruction (תורה), the proper symbol of wealth befitting the anointed of Yahweh, in order to

---

9.   Eco, *Foucault's Pendulum*, pp. 377–78.

10.   This revised epigraph taken from *Foucault's Pendulum* (p. vii) is apropos for reading the book of Proverbs even though the epigraph originally used 'meaning' rather than 'data' as the object of musing.

modify improper behavior dramatized by the scenario of a group of criminals persuading the 'son' to join in a violent plot to murder innocent victims. But various historical and intertextual data reveal this poem as an extended metaphor for socioeconomic injustice. An inferential walk through the woods of 1 Kings 1–11 provides the concrete details to illumine the socio-economic injustice pervasive in Solomon's reign. Driven by greed, the Solomonic administration implemented, as a means of domestic policy, legislation to despoliate innocent citizens of their material wealth for its own revenue. And what better way to bleed the innocent dry than through the politico-religious sanction of idolatry. This exploitative means of accumulating wealth at the expense of Yahweh's people, however, only profits death as such nefarious policies recoil upon Solomon and his advisors, portending the demise of the monarch(y).

While Solomon may have acted in a manner characteristic of royal ideology in the ancient Near Eastern world, the second poem's instruction, nevertheless, attempts to (re)orient Solomon to Torah ideology. Orientation to Torah instills trust in Yahweh (not political advisors) that does not exploit the royal subjects for personal self-aggrandizement. By internalizing Torah, the 'son' externally demonstrates behavioral traits such as fidelity and kindness (חסד ואמת). In pragmatic terms, he sacrifices by redistributing the wealth extracted from the citizens for the benefit of all within the kingdom instead of amassing and hoarding wealth. But Solomon has foolishly abandoned the Torah, thus incurring the reproof of Yahweh who, like a father, still loves (t)his 'son'. Were Solomon to fear Yahweh through Torah devotion, he would concurrently embrace Wisdom and her concomitant gifts (i.e. invaluable riches, peace and long life) and be restored to a proper relationship with the 'father'. The path to Wisdom lies not only within the narrative Torah of Genesis-Deuteronomy, but also within the poetic *torah* of Proverbs 1–9. Only תורה can empower Solomon to discern between good and evil, and to rule with righteousness, justice and equity.

The poems in Proverbs 5 and 7 take up the second point of critique against Solomon, that is, his numerous sexual (in)discretions. Love language, bridal imagery and various sexual connotations throughout Proverbs 5 portray an erotic conte(x)(s)t between rival lovers – the אשה זרה and the wife – for the affections of the 'son'. Solomon has behaved foolishly by betraying the wife of his youth, Wisdom, to pursue a sexual liaison with (an)Other Wom(a)(e)n. The 'father' attempts to reconcile the 'son' with his daughter Wisdom by advising against embraces with (the) Other Wom(a)(e)n whose 'lips' seduce. Her 'lips' open up to a dysfunctional womb that breeds barrenness and death, unlike most women whose womb reproduces life. Sexual relations with (an) Other Wom(a)(e)n result in a state of depletion: a loss of vigor, life, wealth and the fruit of hard-earned labor. Those who enter her 'house' find themselves, in the end, in the clutches of death. If the 'son' does not channel his sexual drives appropriately, he will, in a brief, but lucid, moment, rue his fate. Even the 'wise' Solomon admits of his own folly. Only erotic embraces with his wife Wisdom can squelch the fatal attraction for (an) Other Wom(a)(e)n.

Paternal efforts to reconcile the 'son' with Wisdom (re)emphasize the consequences of fatal attraction by means of a vignette of a late-night sexual rendezvous between a young lad and the אשׁה זרה at her house in Proverbs 7. After extensive preparations, the Other Woman entices the youth with sexual innuendoes (e.g. engorging himself on her breasts), but only the young lad remains in the dark about his fate if he acts upon her seductions. Animal similes and ambivalent signs metaphorically signify the young lad as a sacrificial offering laid upon his funeral bier of a bed, not simply a setting for a carnal tryst. But the youth is not her first victim, since her 'house' has long been the entrance to the descent into the underworld. This vignette, however, also has a parabolic dimension. The literary figure of the young lad mirrors Solomon whose numerous sexual (in)discretions eventually led to his (death)bed. Only a fool would not embrace Wisdom as an intimate companion and lover. After all, her love fulfills at all times whereas the love of (an) Other Wom(a)(e)n only fulfills temporarily. Wisdom can protect against the seductive charms of the אשׁה זרה, but the 'son' must declare his love for her. Silent passivity will no longer suffice since Solomon's lack of devotion to his wife Wisdom contributed, in part, to his seduction by (an) Other Wom(a)(e)n.

Proverbs 1–9 climaxes with an allegorical contrast between personified Woman Wisdom and Woman Folly in Proverbs 9. Both figures entice the 'son' to a festal banquet, which, at one metaphorical level, signifies an erotic repast. The economic food of wealth unjustly gained and the erotic food of numerous sexual (in)discretions, both forbidden pursuits, reap only temporary gratification for the 'son'. Only the embrace of Wisdom, however, can reap the salutary benefit of long life. Equally as important, this allegory also signifies, at another metaphorical level, the trope of life-paths: the way of Wisdom becomes the way *of* and *to* life; the way of Folly becomes the way *of* and *to* death. Ultimately, this allegory, much like Proverbs 1–9 all along, confronts the 'son' with a decision – life or death? If Solomon accepts the poetic censure designed to reorient him to the Torah, then he will truly demonstrate himself to be the wise and righteous king. By doing so, the 'wise' king subverts poetic satire and no longer assumes his typecasted role as a royal fool. From a semiotic perspective, Proverbs 1–9 may be said to function as a poetic parallel to its narrative complement 1 Kings 1–11 vis-à-vis the story of Solomon in a manner analogous to Judges 5 as a poetic complement to Judges 4.

The highly poetic allegory of personified Wisdom and Folly ends Proverbs 1–9, but it certainly does not conclude, at least in the traditional sense of that word, this collection as its loose ends thwart our predilection for a complete and tidy closure. An erotic conte(s)(x)t between Wisdom and Folly for the affections of the 'son' titillates and tantalizes, yet never satisfies; instead, it remains open-ended, foiling our curiosity for answers to questions never entertained. While the satire of this poetic *torah* offers no denouement, its textual significations, nonetheless, persuade expectations that Solomon did not choose wisely. Even the name שׁלמה (Solomon) offers no promising hope given its phonemic contiguity to שׁלמאל (*shlemiel*, 'fool').[11] Mere coincidence? Perhaps, but that this connection (im)poses itself and

11. The *shlemiel*, who dates back as early as biblical times, gradually, through medieval and Renaissance Jewish literature, became the stock figure and object of humor in Jewish folk tales. In such stories, 'a person was a shlemiel by virtue of what he did, not by what he thought'. Josephine Z. Kopf, 'Meyer Wolfsheim and Robert Cohn: A Study of a Jewish Type and Stereotype', *TJOJT* 10

cannot easily be dismissed only re-emphasizes such expectations. The semiotic insight from this connection reiterates the signifying potential, albeit with a slight nuance, of the initial sign-function מָשָׁל יְשָׁלְמֹה as 'satire of a fool'. Ending indeed returns to (the) beginning, as T.S. Eliot mused:

> What we call the beginning is often the end
> And to make an end is to make a beginning.
> …
> We shall not cease from exploration
> And the end of all our exploring
> Will be to arrive where we started
> And know the place for the first time.[12]

A riddle to end, a riddle that begins: When is a wise king a royal fool?

(1969), pp. 93–104 (95), 99–100; see also Sanford Pinsker, 'The Schlemiel in Yiddish and American Literature', *CJF* 25 (1966–67), pp. 191–95.

12.   T.S. Eliot, 'Four Quartets. Little Gidding, V', in *Collected Poems. 1909–1962* (New York: Harcourt Brace and Co., 1991), pp. 207–208.

BIBLIOGRAPHY

Ahlström, Gösta, 'The House of Wisdom', *SEÅ* 44 (1979), pp. 74–76.

Aichele, George, *Sign, Text, Scripture: Semiotics and the Bible* (Interventions, 1; Sheffield: Sheffield Academic Press, 1997).

Albright, William F., 'Some Canaanite-Phoenician Sources of Hebrew Wisdom', in Noth and Thomas (eds.), *Wisdom in Israel and in the Ancient Near East*, pp. 1–15.

Aletti, Jean-Noël, 'Séduction et parole en Proverbes I-IX', *VT* 27 (1977), pp. 129–44.

Alter, Robert, *The Art of Biblical Poetry* (New York: Basic Books, 1985).

Avishur, Yitschak, and Joshua Blau (eds.), *Studies in Bible and the Ancient Near East* (Jerusalem: Rubinstein's, 1978).

Beal, Timothy K., and David M. Gunn (eds.), *Reading Bibles, Writing Bodies: Identity and the Book* (New York: Routledge, 1996).

Berlin, Adele, *The Dynamics of Biblical Parallelism* (Bloomington, IN: Indiana University Press, 1985).

—*Poetics and Interpretation of Biblical Narrative* (BibLit, 9; Sheffield: Almond Press, 1983; repr. Winona Lake, IN: Eisenbrauns, 1994).

Blenkinsopp, Joseph, 'The Social Context of the "Outsider Woman" in Proverbs 1-9', *Bib* 72 (1991), pp. 457–73.

—*Wisdom and Law in the Old Testament: The Ordering of Life in Israel and Early Judaism* (Oxford Bible Series; Oxford: Oxford University Press, 1995).

Braulik, Georg, Walter Groß and Sean McEvenue (eds.), *Biblische Theologie und gesellschaftlicher Wandel für Norbert Lohfink* (Basel: Herder, 1993).

Brenner, Athalya (ed.), 'On the Semantic Field of Humour, Laughter and the Comic in the Old Testament', in Radday and Brenner (eds.), *On Humour and the Comic in the Hebrew Bible*, pp. 39–58.

—'Proverbs 1–9: An F Voice?', in Brenner and van Dijk-Hemmes (eds.), *On Gendering Texts*, pp. 113–30.

—*A Feminist Companion to Wisdom Literature* (FCB, 9; Sheffield: Sheffield Academic Press, 1995).

Brenner, Athalya, and Fokkelien van Dijk-Hemmes (eds.), *On Gendering Texts: Female and Male Voices in the Hebrew Bible* (BibInt, 1; Leiden: E.J. Brill, 1993).

Brenner, Athalya, and Yehuda T. Radday, 'Between Intentionality and Reception: Acknowledgment and Application (A Preview)', in Radday and Brenner (eds.), *On Humour and the Comic in the Hebrew Bible*, pp. 13–19.

Bryce, Glendon, *A Legacy of Wisdom: The Egyptian Contribution to the Wisdom of Israel* (Lewisburg, PA: Bucknell University Press, 1979).

Burns, John Barclay, 'Solomon's Egyptian Horses and Exotic Wives', *Forum* 7 (1991), pp. 29–44.

—'Proverbs 7,6-27: Vignettes from the Cycle of Astarte and Adonis', *SJOT* 9 (1995), pp. 20–36.

Caesar, Michael, *Umberto Eco: Philosophy, Semiotics and the Work of Fiction* (Cambridge: Polity Press, 1999).

Camp, Claudia, *Wisdom and the Feminine in the Book of Proverbs* (BibLit, 11; Sheffield: Almond Press, 1985).

—'Wise and Strange: An Interpretation of the Female Imagery in Proverbs in Light of Trickster Mythology', *Semeia* 42 (1988), pp. 14–36.

—'What's So Strange about the Strange Woman?', in Jobling, Day and Sheppard (eds.), *The Bible and the Politics of Exegesis*, pp. 17–31.

—'Woman Wisdom and the Strange Woman: Where is Power to be Found?', in Beal and Gunn (eds.), *Reading Bibles, Writing Bodies*, pp. 85–115.

—'Reading Solomon as a Woman', in Camp (ed.), *Wise, Strange and Holy*, pp. 144–86.

—*Wise, Strange and Holy: The Strange Woman and the Making of the Bible* (JSOTSup, 320; GCT, 9; Sheffield: Sheffield Academic Press, 2000).

Capozzi, Rocco (ed.), *Reading Eco: An Anthology* (AS; Bloomington, IN: Indiana University Press, 1997).

Ceresko, A.R., 'The Function of *Antanaclasis* in Hebrew Poetry, Especially in the Book of Qoheleth', *CBQ* 44 (1982), pp. 551–69.

Clements, Ronald E. (ed.), *The World of Ancient Israel: Sociological, Anthropological and Political Perspectives* (Cambridge: Cambridge University Press, 1989).

Clifford, Richard J., 'Proverbs IX: A Suggested Ugaritic Parallel', *VT* 35 (1975), pp. 298–306.

—'Woman Wisdom in the Book of Proverbs', in Braulik, Groß and McEvenue (eds.), *Biblische Theologie und gesellschaftlicher Wandel für Norbert Lohfink*, pp. 61–72.

—*Proverbs: A Commentary* (OTL; Louisville, KY: Westminster/John Knox Press, 2nd edn, 1999).

Clifford, Richard J., and John J. Collins (eds.), *Creation in the Biblical Traditions* (CBQMS, 24; Washington, DC: Catholic Biblical Association, 1992).

Clines, David J.A. (ed.), *The Poetical Books: A Sheffield Reader* (Sheffield: Sheffield Academic Press, 1997).

Cobley, Paul, and Litza Jansz, *Introducing Semiotics* (New York: Totem Books, 1997).

Collins, Terence, 'Line-Forms in Hebrew Poetry', *JSS* 23 (1978), pp. 228–44.

Cook, Johann, 'אִשָּׁה זָרָה (Proverbs 1-9 Septuagint): A Metaphor for Foreign Wisdom?', *ZAW* 106 (1994), pp. 458–76.

Cox, Dermot, 'Fear or Conscience? *Yir'at YHWH* in Proverbs 1–9', *StudHier* 3 (1982), pp. 83–90.

Crenshaw, James L., 'Prolegomenon', in Crenshaw (ed.), *Studies in Ancient Israelite Wisdom* (LBS; New York: Ktav, 1976), pp. 1–60.

—'Wisdom and Authority: Sapiential Rhetoric and Its Warrants', in Emerton (ed.), *Congress Volume: Vienna, 1980*, pp. 10–29.

—'Education in Ancient Israel', *JBL* 104 (1985), pp. 601–15.

—'The Sage in Proverbs', in Gammie and Perdue (eds.), *The Sage in Israel and the Ancient Near East*, pp. 205–16.

—*Old Testament Wisdom: An Introduction* (Louisville, KY: Westminster/John Knox Press, rev. edn, 1998).

Cuddon, J.A., *Dictionary of Literary Terms and Literary Theory* (London: Penguin Books, 3rd edn, 1992).

Culler, Jonathan, *Structuralist Poetics: Structuralism, Linguistics, and the Study of Literature* (New York: Cornell University Press, 1975).

—*The Pursuit of Signs: Semiotics, Literature, Deconstruction* (New York: Cornell University Press, 1981).

—'The Semiotics of Poetry: Two Approaches', in DeGeorge (ed.), *Semiotic Themes*, pp. 75–93.

Dahood, Mitchell, 'Honey that Drips: Notes on Proverbs 5, 2-3', *Bib* 54 (1973), pp. 65–66.
—'Poetic Devices in the Book of Proverbs', in Avishur and Blau (eds.), *Studies in Bible and the Ancient Near East*, pp. 7–17.
Day, John, Robert P. Gordon and H.G.M. Williamson (eds.), *Wisdom in Ancient Israel: Essays in Honour of J.A. Emerton* (Cambridge: Cambridge University Press, 1995).
Day, Peggy L. (ed.), *Gender and Difference in Ancient Israel* (Minneapolis: Fortress Press, 1989).
DeGeorge, Richard T. (ed.), *Semiotic Themes* (Lawrence, KS: University of Kansas Publications, 1981).
Delitzsch, Franz, *Biblical Commentary on the Proverbs of Solomon*, I (Grand Rapids: Eerdmans, 1950).
Eco, Umberto, *A Theory of Semiotics* (AS; Bloomington, IN: Indiana University Press, 1976).
—*The Role of the Reader: Explorations in the Semiotics of Texts* (AS; Bloomington, IN: Indiana University Press, 1979).
—*The Name of the Rose* (trans. William Weaver; San Diego, CA: Harcourt Brace & Co., 1983).
—*Semiotics and the Philosophy of Language* (AS; Bloomington, IN: Indiana University Press, 1984).
—*The Open Work* (trans. Anna Cancogni; Cambridge, MA: Harvard University Press, 1989).
—*Foucault's Pendulum* (trans. William Weaver; New York: Ballantine, 1990).
—*The Limits of Interpretation* (AS; Bloomington, IN: Indiana University Press, 1990).
—*Interpretation and Overinterpretation* (ed. Stefan Collini; Cambridge: Cambridge University Press, 1992).
—*Six Walks in the Fictional Woods* (Cambridge, MA: Harvard University Press, 1994).
—'An Author and His Interpreters', in Rocco Capozzi (ed.), *Reading Eco: An Anthology* (AS; Bloomington, IL: Indiana University Press, 1997), pp. 59–70.
Eliot, T.S., *Collected Poems. 1909–1962* (New York: Harcourt, Brace and Co., 1991).
Emerton, John A. (ed.), *Congress Volume: Vienna, 1980 [International Organization for the Study of the Old Testament]* (VTSup, 32; Leiden: E.J. Brill, 1981).
Eslinger, Lyle, *Into the Hands of the Living God* (JSOTSup, 84; Sheffield: Almond Press, 1989).
Feinberg, Leonard, *Introduction to Satire* (Ames, IA: Iowa State University Press, 1967).
Fish, Stanley, *Is There a Text in This Class? The Authority of Interpretive Communities* (Cambridge, MA: Harvard University Press, 1980).
—*Doing What Comes Naturally: Change, Rhetoric, and the Practice of Theory in Literary and Legal Studies* (Durham, NC: Duke University Press, 1989).
Fontaine, Carol V., *Traditional Sayings in the Old Testament: A Contextual Study* (BibLit, 5; Sheffield: Almond Press, 1982).
—'Proverb Performance in the Hebrew Bible', *JSOT* 32 (1985), pp. 87–103.
—'Wisdom in Proverbs', in Perdue, Scott and Wiseman (eds.), *In Search of Wisdom*, pp. 99–114.
Fox, Michael V., 'Aspects of the Religion of the Book of Proverbs', *HUCA* 39 (1968), pp. 55–69.
—'The Social Location of the Book of Proverbs', in Fox *et al.* (eds.), *Texts, Temples, and Traditions*, pp. 227–39.
—*Proverbs 1–9* (AB, 18a; New York: Doubleday, 2000).
Fox, Michael V. *et al.* (eds.), *Texts, Temples, and Traditions: A Tribute to Menahem Haran* (Winona Lake, IN: Eisenbrauns, 1996).
Frankfort, Henri, *Kingship and the Gods: A Study of Ancient Near Eastern Religion as the Integration of Society and Nature* (Chicago: University of Chicago Press, 1948).
Frankfort, Henri *et al.*, *The Intellectual Adventure of Ancient Man: An Essay on Speculative Thought in the Ancient Near East* (Chicago: University of Chicago Press, 1946).

Frost, Robert, *Complete Poems of Robert Frost* (New York: Holt, Rinehart and Winston, 1961).
Frye, Northrop, *Anatomy of Criticism: Four Essays* (Princeton, NJ: Princeton University Press, 1971).
Gammie, John G., and Leo G. Perdue (eds.), *The Sage in Israel and the Ancient Near East* (Winona Lake, IN: Eisenbrauns, 1990).
Gerstenberger, Erhard, 'The Woe-Oracles of the Prophets', *JBL* 81 (1962), pp. 249–63.
Glück, J.J., 'Paronomasia in Biblical Literature', *Sem* 1 (1970), pp. 50–78.
Goldingay, John E., 'Proverbs V and IX', *RB* 84 (1977), pp. 80–93.
Good, Edwin M., *Irony in the Old Testament* (Philadelphia, PA: Westminster Press, 1965).
Gordis, Robert, 'The Social Background of Wisdom Literature', *HUCA* 18 (1943), pp. 77–118.
Greenfield, Jonas, 'The Seven Pillars of Wisdom (Prov. 9.1)—A Mistranslation', *JQR* 76 (1985), pp. 13–20.
Habel, Norman C., 'The Symbolism of Wisdom in Proverbs 1–9', *Int* 26 (1972), pp. 131–57.
Harris, Scott L., *Proverbs 1-9: A Study of Inner-Biblical Interpretation* (SBLDS, 150; Atlanta, GA: Scholars Press, 1995).
Heijerman, Meike, 'Who Would Blame Her? The "Strange" Woman of Proverbs 7', in Brenner (ed.), *A Feminist Companion to Wisdom Literature*, pp. 100–109.
Highet, Gilbert, *The Anatomy of Satire* (Princeton, NJ: Princeton University Press, 1962).
Iser, Wolfgang, *The Act of Reading: A Theory of Aesthetic Response* (Baltimore: The Johns Hopkins University Press, 1978).
Jakobson, Roman, *Language in Literature* (ed. Krystyna Pomorska and Stephen Rudy; Cambridge, MA: Belknap Press, 1987).
Jemielity, Thomas, *Satire and the Hebrew Prophets* (LCBI; Louisville, KY: Westminster/John Knox Press, 1992).
Jensen, H.J., *The Satirist's Art* (Bloomington, IN: Indiana University Press, 1972).
Jobling, David, ' "Forced Labor": Solomon's Golden Age and the Question of Literary Representation', *Semeia* 54 (1991), pp. 57–76.
Jobling, David, Peggy L. Day and Gerald T. Sheppard (eds.), *The Bible and the Politics of Exegesis: Essays in Honor of Norman K. Gottwald on his Sixty-Fifth Birthday* (Cleveland, OH: Pilgrim Press, 1991).
Johnson, Aubrey R., 'מָשָׁל', in Noth and Thomas (eds.), *Wisdom in Israel and in the Ancient Near East*, pp. 162–69.
—*Sacral Kingship in Ancient Israel* (Cardiff: University of Wales Press, 2nd edn, 1967).
Johnson, John, 'An Analysis of Proverbs 1.1-7', *BSac* 144 (1987), pp. 419–32.
Kayatz, Christa, *Studien zu Proverbien 1–9: Eine Form- und Motivgeschichtliche Untersuchung unter Einbeziehung ägyptischen Vergleichmaterials* (WMANT, 22; Neukirchen–Vluyn: Neukirchener Verlag, 1966).
Keel, Othmar, *The Symbolism of the Biblical World: Ancient Near Eastern Iconography and the Book of Psalms* (New York: Crossroad, 1978).
Kennedy, James M., 'The Structural Semantic Analysis of Selected Biblical Hebrew Words for Punishment/Discipline' (PhD dissertation, Drew University, 1986).
—'The Social Background of Early Israel's Rejection of Cultic Images: A Proposal', *BTB* 17 (1987), pp. 138–44.
Knoppers, Gary N., ' "There Was None Like Him": Incomparability in the Books of Kings', *CBQ* 54 (1992), pp. 411–31.
—'The Deuteronomist and the Deuteronomic Law of the King: A Reexamination of a Relationship', *ZAW* 108 (1996), pp. 329–46.
Kopf, Josephine Z., 'Meyer Wolfsheim and Robert Cohn: A Study of a Jewish Type and Stereotype', *TJOJT* 10 (1969), pp. 93–104.

Kugel, James L., *The Idea of Biblical Poetry: Parallelism and Its History* (New Haven, CT: Yale University Press, 1981).

Lang, Bernhard, *Die Weisheitliche Lehrrede. Eine Untersuchung von Sprüche 1-7* (SBS, 54; Stuttgart: KBW Verlag, 1972).

—*Wisdom and the Book of Proverbs: A Hebrew Goddess Redefined* (New York: Pilgrim Press, 1986).

Lasine, Stuart, 'The Ups and Downs of Monarchical Justice: Solomon and Jehoram in an Intertextual World', *JSOT* 59 (1993), pp. 37–53.

—'The King of Desire: Indeterminacy, Audience, and the Solomon Narrative', *Semeia* 71 (1995), pp. 85–118.

Lichtenstein, Murray, 'The Banquet Motifs in Keret and in Proverbs 9', *JANESCU* 1 (1968), pp. 19–31.

Martin, James D., *Proverbs* (OTG; Sheffield: Sheffield Academic Press, 1995).

McCreesh, Thomas P., *Biblical Sound and Sense: Poetic Sound Patterns in Proverbs 10–29* (JSOTSup, 128; Sheffield: JSOT Press, 1991).

McKane, William, *Prophets and Wise Men* (SBT, 44; Naperville, IL: Alec R. Allenson, 1965).

—*Proverbs* (OTL; Philadelphia: Westminster Press, 1970).

Meinhold, Arndt, *Die Sprüche*, I (ZBK, 16; Zürich: Theologischer Verlag, 1991).

Miles, Johnny, 'When Is a Wise Man a Fool? A Semiotic Analysis of Proverbs 1–9 as Satire' (PhD dissertation, Baylor University, 2001).

Moss, Alan, 'Wisdom as Parental Teaching in Proverbs 1-9', *HeyJ* 38 (1997), pp. 426–39.

Murphy, Roland E., 'Assumptions and Problems in Old Testament Wisdom Research', *CBQ* 29 (1967), pp. 102–12.

—'Wisdom and Creation', *JBL* 104 (1985), pp. 3–11.

—'Wisdom's Song: Proverbs 1.20-33', *CBQ* 48 (1986), pp. 456–60.

—'Wisdom and Eros in Proverbs 1–9', *CBQ* 50 (1988), pp. 600–603.

—*The Tree of Life: An Exploration of Biblical Wisdom Literature* (ABRL; New York: Doubleday, 1990).

—*Proverbs* (WBC, 22; Nashville, TN: Thomas Nelson, 1998).

Newsom, Carol A., 'Woman and the Discourse of Patriarchal Wisdom: A Study of Proverbs 1–9', in Day (ed.), *Gender and Difference in Ancient Israel*, pp. 142–60.

Noth, Martin, and D. Winton Thomas (eds.), *Wisdom in Israel and in the Ancient Near East* (VTSup, 3; Leiden: E.J. Brill, 1955).

Nöth, Winfried, *Handbook of Semiotics* (AS; Bloomington, IN: Indiana University Press, 1995).

O'Connell, Robert H., 'Proverbs VII 16-17: A Case of Fatal Deception in a "Woman and the Window" Type-Scene', *VT* 41 (1991), pp. 235–41.

Parker, Kim I., 'Solomon as Philosopher King: The Nexus of Law and Wisdom in 1 Kings 1–11', *JSOT* 53 (1992), pp. 75–91.

Perdue, Leo G., *Wisdom and Creation: The Theology of Wisdom Literature* (Nashville: Abingdon Press, 1994).

Perdue, Leo G., Bernard B. Scott and William J. Wiseman (eds.), *In Search of Wisdom: Essays in Memory of John G. Gammie* (Louisville, KY: Westminster/John Knox Press, 1993).

Perry, Theodore A., *Wisdom Literature and the Structure of Proverbs* (University Park, PA: Pennsylvania State University Press, 1993).

Petrilli, Susan, 'Towards Interpretation Semiotics', in Rocco Capozzi (ed.), *Reading Eco: An Anthology* (AS; Bloomington, IN: Indiana University Press, 1997), pp. 120–36.

Pinsker, Sanford, 'The Schlemiel in Yiddish and American Literature', *CJF* 25 (1966–67), pp. 191–95.

Polk, Timothy K., 'Paradigms, Parables, and *Mĕšālîm*: On Reading the *Māšāl* in Scripture', *CBQ* 45 (1983), pp. 564–83.

Preminger, Alex, and T.V.F. Brogan (eds.), *The New Princeton Encyclopedia of Poetry and Poetics* (Princeton, NJ: Princeton University Press, 1993).

Pritchard, James B. (ed.), *Ancient Near Eastern Texts Relating to the Old Testament* (Princeton, NJ: Princeton University Press, 3rd edn, 1969).

Pyper, Hugh S., 'Judging the Wisdom of Solomon: The Two-Way Effect of Intertextuality', *JSOT* 59 (1993), pp. 25–36.

Rad, Gerhard von, *Wisdom in Israel* (London: SCM Press, 1972).

Radday, Yehuda T., 'Humour in Names', in Radday and Brenner (eds.), *On Humour and the Comic*, pp. 59–97.

—'Between Intentionality and Reception: Acknowledgment and Application (A Preview)', in Radday and Brenner (eds.), *On Humour and the Comic*, pp. 13–19.

Radday, Yehuda T., and Athalya Brenner (eds.), *On Humour and the Comic in the Hebrew Bible* (JSOTSup, 92; Sheffield: Almond Press, 1990).

Renfroe, Fred, 'The Effect of Redaction on the Structure of Proverbs 1.1-6', *ZAW* 101 (1989), pp. 290–93.

Riffaterre, Michael, *Semiotics of Poetry* (AS; Bloomington, IN: Indiana University Press, 1978).

Ruffle, John, 'The Teaching of Amenomope and Its Connection with the Book of Proverbs', *TynBul* 28 (1977), pp. 29–68.

Saydon, P.P., 'Assonance in Hebrew as a Means of Expressing Emphasis', *Bib* 36 (1955), pp. 36–50, 287–304.

Scholes, Robert, *Semiotics and Interpretation* (New Haven, CT: Yale University Press, 1982).

Scott, R.B.Y., 'Solomon and the Beginnings of Wisdom in Israel', in Noth and Thomas (eds.), *Wisdom in Israel and in the Ancient Near East*, pp. 267–79.

—*Proverbs. Ecclesiastes* (AB, 18; Garden City, NY: Doubleday, 1965).

—'The Study of the Wisdom Literature', *Int* 24 (1970), pp. 20–45.

Sebeok, Thomas (ed.), *The Tell-Tale Sign* (Lisse: de Ridder, 1975).

Selden, Raman, Peter Widdowson and Peter Brooker, *A Reader's Guide to Contemporary Literary Theory* (London: Prentice Hall, 4th edn, 1997).

Seybold, Klaus, *Satirische Prophetie. Studien zum Buch Zefanja* (Stuttgart: Katholisches Bibelwerk, 1985).

Skehan, Patrick W., 'The Seven Columns of Wisdom's House in Proverbs 1–9', in *Studies in Israelite Poetry and Wisdom* (Washington, DC: Catholic Biblical Association, 1971), pp. 9–14.

—'Wisdom's House', in *Studies in Israelite Poetry and Wisdom* (Washington, DC: Catholic Biblical Association, 1971), pp. 27–45.

Smith, Barbara H., *Poetic Closure: A Study of How Poems End* (Chicago: University of Chicago Press, 1968).

—*On the Margins of Discourse: The Relation of Literature to Language* (Chicago: University of Chicago Press, 1978).

Stevens, Wallace, *The Collected Poems of Wallace Stevens* (New York: Knopf, 1954; repr. New York: Vintage, 1990).

Story, Cullen I.K., 'The Book of Proverbs and Northwest Semitic Literature', *JBL* 64 (1945), pp. 319–37.

Test, George A., *Satire: Spirit and Art* (Tampa, FL: University of South Florida Press, 1991).

Thompson, John Mark, *Form and Function of Proverbs in Ancient Israel* (SJ, 1; The Hague and Paris: Mouton, 1974).

Tiefenbrun, Susan W., 'The State of Literary Semiotics: 1983', *Semiotica* 51 (1984), pp. 7–44.

Todorov, Tzvetan, 'Literature and Semiotics', in Sebeok (ed.), *The Tell-Tale Sign*, pp. 97–102.

—*Introduction to Poetics* (Brighton: Harvester Press, 1981).

Toorn, Karel van der, 'Female Prostitution in Payment of Vows in Ancient Israel', *JBL* 108 (1989), pp. 193–205.

Torgovnik, Marianna, *Closure in the Novel* (Princeton, NJ: Princeton University Press, 1981).

Toy, Crawford H., *A Critical and Exegetical Commentary on the Book of Proverbs* (ICC; Edinburgh: T. & T. Clark, 1899).

Trible, Phyllis, 'Wisdom Builds a Poem: The Architecture of Proverbs 1.20-33', *JBL* 94 (1975), pp. 509–18.

Twain, Mark, *Adventures of Huckleberry Finn* (New York: Chas. L. Webster & Co., 1885; repr.; Berkeley, CA: University of California Press, 2001).

Van Leeuwen, Raymond C., 'Liminality and Worldview in Proverbs 1-9', *Semeia* 50 (1990), pp. 111–44.

Walsh, Jerome T., 'The Characterization of Solomon in First Kings 1–5', *CBQ* 57 (1995), pp. 471–93.

—*1 Kings* (BerO; Collegeville, MN: Liturgical Press, 1996).

Waltke, Bruce K., 'The Authority of Proverbs: An Exposition of Proverbs 1.2-6', *Presb* 13 (1987), pp. 65–78.

—'Lady Wisdom as Mediatrix: An Exposition of Proverbs 1.20-33', *Presb* 14 (1988), pp. 1–15.

Washington, Harold C., 'The Strange Woman (אשה זרה/נכריה) of Proverbs 1-9 and Post-Exilic Judean Society', in Brenner (ed.), *A Feminist Companion to Wisdom Literature*, pp. 217–42.

Watson, Wilfred G.E., *Classical Hebrew Poetry: A Guide to Its Techniques* (repr.; JSOTSup, 26; Sheffield: Sheffield Academic Press, 1995 [1984]).

Weeks, Stuart, *Early Israelite Wisdom* (OTM; Oxford: Oxford University Press, 1994).

Weisman, Ze'ev, *Political Satire in the Bible* (SemeiaSt, 32; Atlanta, GA: Scholars Press, 1998).

Whybray, R. Norman, *Wisdom in Proverbs: The Concept of Wisdom in Proverbs 1–9* (SBT; Naperville, IL: Alec R. Allenson, 1965).

—'Some Literary Problems in Proverbs I-IX', *VT* 16 (1966), pp. 482–96.

—*The Intellectual Tradition in the Old Testament* (BZAW, 135; Berlin: Walter de Gruyter, 1974).

—'The Social World of the Wisdom Writers', in Clements (ed.), *The World of Ancient Israel*, pp. 227–50.

—*Wealth and Poverty in the Book of Proverbs* (JSOTSup, 99; Sheffield: JSOT Press, 1990).

—*The Composition of the Book of Proverbs* (JSOTSup, 168; Sheffield: JSOT Press, 1994).

—*Proverbs* (NCB; Grand Rapids: Eerdmans, 1994).

—*The Book of Proverbs: A Survey of Modern Study* (HBInt, 1; Leiden: E.J. Brill, 1995).

Williams, James G., 'The Power of Form: A Study of Biblical Proverbs', *Semeia* 17 (1980), pp. 35–58.

—*Those Who Ponder Proverbs: Aphoristic Thinking and Biblical Literature* (BibLit, 2; Sheffield: Almond Press, 1981).

Worcester, David, *The Art of Satire* (New York: Russell & Russell, 1960).

Yee, Gale A., 'An Analysis of Prov. 8.22-31 According to Style and Structure', *ZAW* 94 (1982), pp. 58–66.

—'The Theology of Creation in Proverbs 8.22-31', in Clifford and Collins (eds.), *Creation in the Biblical Traditions*, pp. 85–96.

—' "I Have Perfumed My Bed with Myrrh": The Foreign Woman (*'iššā zārâ*) in Proverbs 1–9', in Brenner (ed.), *A Feminist Companion to Wisdom Literature*, pp. 110–26.

—'The Socio-Literary Production of the "Foreign Woman" in Proverbs', in Brenner (ed.), *A Feminist Companion to Wisdom Literature*, pp. 127–30.

INDEXES

INDEX OF REFERENCES

BIBLE

INDEX OF AUTHORS